An Insider's Guide
to
the Mining Sector

How to make money
from gold and mining shares

An Insider's Guide
to
the Mining Sector

How to make money
from gold and mining shares

by Michael Coulson

HARRIMAN HOUSE LTD

43 Chapel Street
Petersfield
Hampshire
GU32 3DY
GREAT BRITAIN

Tel: +44 (0)1730 233870
Fax: +44 (0)1730 233880
email: enquiries@harriman-house.com
web site: www.harriman-house.com

First published in Great Britain in 2004

Copyright Harriman House Ltd

The right of Michael Coulson to be identified as the author has been asserted
in accordance with the Copyright, Design and Patents Act 1988.

ISBN 1-897-59738-X

British Library Cataloguing in Publication Data
A CIP catalogue record for this book can be obtained from the British Library.

Printed and bound by Ashford Colour Press Ltd, Gosport Hampshire.

This is dedicated to all those people, many of them now friends, who, over the last thirty years, have made participation in the mining 'game' such a memorable and enjoyable experience

Contents

Detailed contents

About the author

Born in 1945 Michael Coulson has been associated with the mining sector for over thirty years, although his university background is in economics where he holds a BSc from the University of London. He first worked as a graduate trainee on the legendary mining desk at James Capel in 1970, for many years the leading mining stockbroker in the City. After that he became a mining salesman at Sterling & Co and also developed the firm's research coverage of the sector. In 1973 he joined Fielding Newson-Smith (later to become NatWest Markets) as a gold mining analyst where he began a long association with the South African gold mining industry. Two years later he became senior mining analyst at L Messel (latterly Lehman Bros) where he started to produce an annual gold review which he published every year until 1991. In 1979 he moved to Panmure Gordon and in 1982 he left and joined Phillips & Drew (UBS) with the task of establishing the firm in the mining market.

After a successful four years there, where two years running he was voted No 2 gold analyst in the Extel Analysts Survey, he moved to Kitcat & Aitken where he set up a highly regarded integrated mining desk. In 1990 the firm's Canadian owners closed the firm and he was briefly with County NatWest. The following year he set up a small mining team at Durlacher, but in 1992 was back in the mainstream at Credit Lyonnais Laing where he was a salesman/analyst on the firm's specialist mining team and established an expertise in African shares. He was then approached by South African bank, Nedcor, to join a start-up broking operation the bank was establishing in London. This operation was closed in 1997 and the following year he joined Paribas to head its Global Mining Team.

He left Paribas in 2000 following the completion of the merger with BNP. Since then he has been doing independent research, mainly on a commissioned basis, primarily for small UK brokers lacking mining expertise. He is currently Chairman of the Association of Mining Analysts and is a non executive director of City Natural Resources High Yield Trust.

He lives in Wandsworth with his wife and, on-and-off, three daughters. He has a lifelong passion for cricket and football and also enjoys a glass or two of wine sitting in his moderately well cultivated garden listening to music from another age!

Acknowledgements

This book is the result of over thirty years of following the mining sector and investing in it, both directly and for others. I have drawn upon a large number of personal experiences in describing the workings of the global mining industry and share market. Having worked at a large number of stock brokers I have observed the sector from many different angles and worked in often quite different environments - experiencing both the often structured world of Phillips & Drew and Paribas and the far more entrepreneurial approach of Kitcat & Aitken and Credit Lyonnais Laing. Unknown to them, colleagues and friends from these days have played a key part in the writing of this book, for truly the mining sector is a global village where, whether it be London or Johannesburg, Toronto or Sydney, we participants and observers cannot help but have an impact on each others actions and attitudes both on and off the 'field'.

I would like to pay particular thanks to two people for their role in this book. My editor Stephen Eckett whose enthusiasm for the project has kept the whole show on the road. With such a wide ranging subject as mining it is easy to get side tracked with a consequent unravelling of the narrative. Stephen's comments and advice have been invaluable in moulding the book into a coherent entity that hopefully readers will find both interesting and helpful, and his nose for data sources has led to the inclusion of more tables and charts than I had thought possible when starting out. In this particular area I would also like to thank my old colleague and friend Charles Kernot, now of Seymour Pierce, who provided invaluable help in locating many of the charts used.

Acknowledgements

Foreword

For those of us who work in and follow the mining industry and believe in its long term future, the decade of the nineties was a frustrating and difficult time. It was a particularly difficult period for gold and for those of us that mine the fascinating metal, and as I know from personal experience when I was Chairman of Harmony Gold, some very awkward decisions had to be taken, particularly in South Africa, to keep the industry afloat. During that period interest in mining withered away, and with it many of the information sources that both investors and industry participants had relied upon to keep them informed over the years. The investment banking and stockbroking business in particular turned its back on mining, concentrating its attention instead on the rampant TMT sector.

The survivors from this cull were very few, a mere handful, but Michael Coulson is one of the most knowledgeable of this surviving group, having covered the mining sector for over thirty years. This book is a tribute to his understanding of what is still one of the most global of all industries, and he provides an invaluable insight into all aspects of mining and mining investment. The age of the internet has paradoxically helped the mining industry by providing it with its own window onto the world even as the traditional information providers and opinion formers were deserting it. But expert comment and interpretation is vital if this information is to be of real value. Michael's book provides us with the sort of practical and historical view that will help investors, in particular, to develop a context in which to assess the information they collect. But as well as being a practical guide the book also captures the fun and exhilaration of the mining industry, emotions that are widely frowned on in these days when bland, mechanical analysis is too often the requirement for the mainstream of the stock market.

Mining is an industry that cannot be ignored and even after years in the investment wilderness always comes back into its own. When that happens investor interest inevitably revives, for once you have caught the mining bug there is probably no known cure. With the help of Michael's book investors will be better placed to navigate their way through the mining market's sometimes dangerous inshore shoals to the open seas where those with both knowledge and experience should find the fishing good. For, once or twice in a century, the opportunity for making great fortunes in mining is presented. I believe now is one of them.

Adam Fleming, March 2004
Chairman, Witwatersrand Consolidated Gold Reserves

Preface

What the book covers

This book covers those subjects that I believe are fundamental to acquiring sufficient knowledge about the mining sector to invest in it with confidence. In doing this I have dipped into a wide number of subjects and tried to extract the points and issues most relevant to successful investing.

The key subjects looked at cover the main mining countries which have listed mining companies, metals both great and small with a separate section for gold, the listed mining companies themselves from the giant diversified groups to the minnows of the exploration sector, the main mining stock markets, and some history (always important in analysing mining markets where lightening often does strike twice) including a view on the Bre-X disaster and the 60s Australian nickel boom.

The book finishes with a section on the main issues relating to dealing, settlement and information sources.

Who the book is for

The book is for anyone interested in mining, and particularly mining as an investment sector. Whilst I think that the book contains material which will be useful to even experienced followers of the mining sector, its main target is those who are interested in mining but perhaps not particularly familiar with the sector, and would like to know more. This means private investors, non specialist institutional investors, generalist stock brokers and financial advisers, and even the media.

Mining has been out of favour for many years which has led to a sharp fall in coverage as attention has shifted to the growth sectors of technology/media/telecommunications. Over the last year or so we have seen quite a sea change again, with interest in mining rising once more. However, for the moment information distribution has lagged behind, with many brokers still unfamiliar with the sector. Investors have therefore had to fall back on their own devices, surfing the net in pursuit of value enhancing information in many cases.

I hope this book will provide useful background for investors, enabling them more accurately to focus their information search and enhance their subsequent investment decisions.

How the book is structured

Whilst the book is compartmentalised to some extent –

- the first part covering mining countries and metals in a general sense,
- the second part companies, how they are valued and where they fit in the overall industry, and
- ending with the subjects of dealing, and information sources

there is some overlap and even repetition which is unavoidable.

The mining industry is large but at the same time compact in that it concentrates on a fairly limited number of influences. Thus the key issues facing a mining company cover

1. the demand and price of metals,
2. the search for these metals and
3. the economics of developing and running a mine.

It is thus difficult to write about and analyse mining without jumping about between these three key elements. The base structure of the book, however, is logical and is intended to lead the reader naturally from the subject of where mining is carried on and the key metals mined, to the main markets where mining shares are traded and the kind of companies that make up the global mining share sector and how it is valued, to the final section on information sources and dealing in mining shares.

One word of warning. Comments and statements about such a fast moving sector as mining can get overtaken by events. It is possible that readers may spot something in the text that they think is incorrect. It may well be that when the book was published that fact/comment was correct but has been overtaken by subsequent events. The most common differences would likely be issues dealing with share prices like market capitalisation; these figures are changing all the time and often the change is significant. Another example would be Ashanti Goldfields which when the book was being written was still an independent company deserving of its own comment as a quoted stock incorporated in an emerging market country. When the book was completed Ashanti's independence was gone and the text had to be amended to take account of that fact.

A note on currencies and metals prices

Most metals are priced in US dollars which is also often the currency of corporate earnings reports even if the reporting company is not a US company. The reader, however, should be aware that particularly where we are looking at historic events other currencies creep into the text. This is deliberate and is often as a result of the way historic information has come to me. The dollars referred to in the text are usually US, but keep an eye out for the Australian and Canadian versions. Sterling is often used in keeping with the UK's position at the centre of international mining, but the euro does not intrude in these pages. As to weights and measurements the book reflects the real world, not the bureaucrats' version, so imperial/American and metric are both used and often in the same breath. Thus a gold mine's reserves are measured in grams per metric ton (tonne) but the gold in those reserves is valued on the basis of troy ounces. Similar examples of mixing measurements can be found with base metals such as copper, nickel and zinc.

Supporting web site

The web site supporting this book can be found at:

www.harriman-house.com/mining

Introduction

Give us the boy

It was a bright morning in early 1971. I had been seconded as part of my graduate training course at London stock brokers James Capel to assist on the mining desk, having expressed an interest in becoming involved in international securities rather than the domestic share market. As the Jesuits say, give us the boy and we will have him for life. My lifetime addiction to mining began that spring day.

As a trainee I was not expected to arrive at the same time as the department, trainees have a way of getting under everyone's feet and their absence is seldom regretted. As I opened the mining department door that morning I was met by a scene of pandemonium. The mining desk stretched across the institutional equities department, and was open on one side to the desks of the UK institutional salesmen. On the other side there was a partition, on which the mining share prices and dealing boards were fixed, separating the mining sales desk from the specialist mining research group who beavered away behind the partition. I looked down the desk at gesticulating arms and waving telephones as the mining sales team urged their clients into action.

At the end of the desk on the left against the window which overlooked the eastern end of London Wall sat Shane Norman, assistant to the Mining Partner, Julian Baring, who was on his right. Latterly Baring was to become the City's leading gold guru, first as a broker and then as a fund manager. Next to him sat Andrew Malim and next to Malim was Peter Bugge. On the other side of the desk was David Dugdale, part time mining dealer later to become managing director of James Capel following its *big bang* takeover by HSBC. Next to him sat Mike Bevan, senior mining dealer, who, that morning, had yet to go down to the Stock Exchange floor, so frenctic was the dealing on the desk. Next to him was Alan Robinson booking the deals. My seat was next to Alan in the corner opposite Shane Norman and Julian Baring. In those very early days of specialist sector coverage in London, James Capel's mining team was a large and formidable entity.

That morning Ashley Down, the Australian Partner, was on the mining desk as well, for what I was witnessing was the announcement of the Agnew nickel find in Western Australia by UK mining groups, Selection Trust and CAST. Agnew turned out to be the last lash in the tail of the Australian mining boom which had started with the discovery of nickel at Kambalda in Western Australia in 1966 and peaked with the Poseidon nickel discovery in 1969. Unfortunately due to then tight Australian exchange controls, Australian investors were frozen out of Agnew, but UK and Continental investors were having a ball that morning.

For a relatively young and certainly impressionable trainee on the first rung of a stock exchange career the Agnew discovery was heady stuff and confirmed the attractions, albeit it in a superficial way, of the mining sector. Overnight the prospects of two mining groups had been potentially transformed by a major minerals discovery. Of course the effect of such a discovery on Selection Trust and CAST, who already had significant sources of mining earnings, would have been less than say its effect on a 'penny' stock like Poseidon, whose earlier nickel discovery had propelled its share price from 6 old pence (2.5p) in 1968 to over £120 in early 1970. However, the excitement of mining with its hope of instant riches was addictive.

Beyond speculation

But if the prospect of instant riches gave the mining sector obvious glamour, I rapidly discovered that it had other attractions, and pitfalls, as well. Attitudes towards investment in industrial equities can change markedly over time, the bulls of the late 60s were followed by the bears of the mid 70s who in due course were followed by the bulls of the late 90s replaced in their turn by the post IT boom bears of the new millennium. Against this background the mining sector can provide some counter cyclical relief, the major boom in South African gold shares in the 70s followed on nicely from the nickel boom and gave some protection from the ravaging of world equity markets in the wake of the 1973 oil price shock. Here the attraction was less in the discovery of new mineral deposits and much more in the prolonged surge of the gold price which transformed the outlook for the gold mining industry and its earnings and dividends.

Whilst the speculative attractions of mining share markets are, therefore, easy to appreciate, the size and importance of the worldwide mining industry should not be ignored either as that gives the sector its underpinning. Although there are still a number of state mining companies the industry is heavily in private hands, and many producers are publicly quoted. The industry itself is widely spread round the world and no continent or island, however small, is without a minerals operation even if it is only a basic small stone quarry.

However mines also are controversial due to their impact on the environment; a deep level mine may be inherently dangerous to work in and an opencast mine may be viewed as an unacceptable scar on the landscape. The degree of disapproval will also vary, with Africa less likely than the western USA to create difficulties for new mine developments.

Mining today

There are those who believe that mining is an old industry with limited attractions, if any at all, for the modern investor. A widespread view as the 21st century dawned, and the TMT boom reached its peak. Indeed mining has often been written off as a sunset industry; it hardly rated a mention in the early 60s as a previous high technology boom unfolded. Yet as we saw above, that decade ended with one of the century's greatest stock market booms, in Australian mining shares.

It is, however, true that mining has struggled with the technological revolution, and metals, as a component of economic growth, have lost ground as the knowledge based economy has overtaken the raw material based economy, particularly in the advanced world. Having said that, the rising economic power of China and India and the still relative poverty of their people suggest that raw materials, the bedrock of both basic industry and social infrastructure, may not have had their day. It is also the case that the real price of metals has tended over the longer term to fall, although this is not a straight line process, as the inflationary 70s showed.

As an investment proposition the mining sector has waxed and waned with regularity. It is interesting to note that institutional portfolio weightings for mining shares in mining countries such as South Africa, Australia and Canada are often below, even well below, their correct weighting in market capitalisation terms. In the UK some general stockbrokers see the sector as difficult to understand, both on a macro and a micro level. The fact that some of the best mining shares are foreign listed and have to be dealt and settled overseas is another check on their enthusiasm. Although dealing in overseas mining stocks did not trouble Julian Baring and the James Capel mining team, or indeed rival mining teams, in the 70s and 80s.

A global business

Whatever reluctance stockbrokers may have in dealing in overseas mining shares, it is important for investors to see mining shares as inhabiting a truly global sector. Much is made today of looking at market sectors on a regional basis rather than just a narrow national one. The phenomenon of Europe-wide sector research and dealing is well established, but the imperatives of national economic trends have an irritating way of reasserting themselves. For mining the global picture is paramount - a gold mining company may have operations in half a dozen countries but the market and price for its product is international, homogenous and largely unaffected by local considerations. Even those other great international leviathans, the oil majors, can find downstream profitability materially affected by local conditions.

Mining then is an industry which requires an international outlook from investors. An open and enquiring mind is essential and in order to make informed judgements about investment possibilities a wide body of knowledge about the world is essential. Many people make the mistake of thinking that the mining sector is difficult because it requires technical knowledge of the industry itself, and unless one is familiar and comfortable with engineering and geological concepts one is bound to flounder. Although it is true that some knowledge of the *mechanics* of mining is needed in reviewing mining investment ideas, understanding of both macro and micro economic trends which drive the demand for, and price of, metals is equally important.

Perhaps one of the most compelling things about mining is that it forces us to open our eyes to the world. It is rewarding to specialise in one country's mining industry as I did with South Africa, and in doing so become familiar with a country that in my youth I had had no contact with and knew very little about. But mining is a global business and to engage successfully with it investors and analysts must acquire a catholic attitude. That is why, certainly in the past, UK mining analysts and investors were held in such high esteem, their global outlook and understanding being in often stark contrast to the parochial attitudes of many of their overseas peers. But if the mining sector's global focus has been educational and rewarding, on a more basic level the sector has been (indeed still is) enormous fun to follow and invest in. I hope this book reflects that and also provides some thoughts as to how this fun can be turned to profit.

1. Industry Background

We start the book with a broad look at the worldwide mining industry, concentrating on those countries who have a substantial private mining sector and have listed mining companies. Since this book is primarily about investing in mining shares I have not included countries such as Russia, China or Indonesia which have large mining industries and developed stock exchanges but little, for the moment, in the way of quoted mining companies. In due course these and other countries will probably develop a listed mining sector, but for the moment the way into these countries is through foreign mining companies most of whom are listed on the main five mining markets described below.

Mining countries

As I have said there is scarcely a country in the world that does not have some semblance of a mining industry, even if it is no more than a chalk quarry or a sand and gravel pit. However, the number of countries with substantial mining industries is far more limited, and not all of those would be considered ideal environments for investors.

From the perspective of the investor familiarity is a good starting point, and that can cover a number of issues including language, legal integrity, environmental constraints, economic policy and political prejudices. If one looked at the portfolios of the bigger specialised mining investment funds one would find that the majority of stocks held came from a very limited number of countries, primarily

- Australia,
- Canada,
- South Africa,
- UK, and
- US.

The question of location

Here we define the *country of origin* as where the mining company has legally incorporated itself. Following the demise of its coal industry the UK is no longer an important mining country, but the world's three largest mining groups (Anglo American, BHP Billiton and Rio Tinto) are all incorporated in the UK.

Part of the reason why the majority of mining stocks came from a very limited number of countries is the historic structure of many mining industries which were formerly owned and run by the state, and have only recently entered the public domain following privatisation in the last ten years or so.

Of course a mine is where you find a mineral deposit, unlike a factory which can be put up in the most beneficial location. This means that many mining companies from, let us call them, the big five countries, operate outside their geographical incorporation. Although Chile is a large producer of copper, few funds would buy a Chilean mining stock direct even if they could. Rather, they are exposed through holdings in major groups such as Antofagasta and Rio Tinto which have substantial operations there. This is repeated in other Latin American countries, in eastern Europe and in the old Soviet Union. Having said that, locally incorporated stocks such as Buenaventura in Peru, Grupo Mexico, CVRD in Brazil, KGHM in Poland and Norilsk in Russia are frequently to be found in foreign portfolios.

Australia

For many older investors Australia, as far as mining is concerned, conjures up the image of free booting entrepreneurs pushing prospects and projects at unsuspecting punters, an image heavily influenced by the nickel boom of 35 years ago. Even in today's heavily regulated markets, the Australian mining industry still creates larger than life characters - Canada has also done well in this regard in recent years.

Australia has a long history of mining and because its economy is relatively small, particularly when compared to its mineral output, it has always been a large exporter of its mineral production. Historically its customer focus used to be the old world of Europe, but over the last thirty years it has increasingly supplied the rapidly growing industries of Japan and the Far East. Although Australia is one of the most stable countries in the world in economic and political terms, operating there, nonetheless, has not always been straightforward and even today investors need to keep their eyes open.

The British connection

Like South Africa, the early days of Australian mining, particularly the great Western Australian gold rush of the late 19th century, were heavily financed by British investors. As Australia did not become a free governing Commonwealth until 1901, and only in 1942 gained full autonomy from the UK in both internal and external affairs, this financial link is not surprising. It also means that there are established conduits between the UK and Australia for share dealing, although it can be argued that these have been allowed to get 'rusty' in recent years. British investors historically are comfortable with Australia, and the so-called Poseidon nickel boom of the late 60s still retains its fascination to this day.

The record of the country in developing its mining industry over the relatively short period from the early 60s to the mid 70s is impressive adding further support for investor interest. In that time Australia discovered and developed a huge bauxite/alumina industry, the world's largest iron ore export industry, a major new nickel province, large oil and natural gas fields, and a number of huge uranium deposits.

The 70s saw a growing independence

The 70s were years of change around the world and in the wake of the Vietnam War a new radicalism arose. In Australia it swept away the cosy relationship with Britain which had existed for decades, and was critically assisted by British entry to the European Common Market. Australia turned instead to its own back door, the Far East, and historically a proud nation it also adopted a more nationalistic approach to its commercial relationship with the rest of the world. This was in part stimulated by the election of a radical Labor Government in 1972.

A number of actions flowed from that political event including restricting foreign ownership of an Australian company's share capital to no more than 40%. Historic relationships like Rio Tinto and CRA, Rio's listed Australian subsidiary where Rio had an 81% stake then, were allowed to continue, although a reduction over the medium term was expected.

The problem of uranium

However, bearing in mind the massive growth in mineral output over the previous decade, a major concern was raised by the attitude of the new Labor Government to the development of Australia's new uranium deposits. The green light had already been given to the Ranger project in the Northern Territories but Pancontinental Mining had discovered an even bigger deposit at Jabiluka nearby. There had been a number of issues regarding the deposit's proximity to a national park and the importance of the area to aborigines due to sacred sites, these problems were eventually ironed out. However, Labor were implacably opposed to nuclear use in the weapons and energy fields, and refused permission for Jabiluka to proceed. Although in due course uranium export restrictions were eased and much work was done over the years on Jabiluka, no uranium was ever commercially produced due to environmental pressure and, eventually, a deteriorating market for the mineral did for the project.

Nationalistic, environmental and ethical issues have been an important part of the Australian mining scene ever since, although Liberal Governments have tended to be more accommodating than Labor over minerals policy. Today foreign ownership is no longer the burning issue that it became 30 years ago and the 40% rule is long gone. Canada's Placer Dome, for example, was able to acquire Aurion Gold in a disputed takeover in 2002 without any government comment or action. On the other hand, the merger between Australia's natural resources giant BHP and Billiton of the UK had to be handled very diplomatically leading to an unusual corporate structure that effectively meant the merged entity was one company with two incorporations - Australia and the UK.

The issue today - aboriginal rights

Perhaps the biggest issue facing investors looking at Australian mining today is aboriginal rights. The official term is *native title*, and it seeks to confront the situation where a company, following a successful exploration programme, wants to develop a mine on a particular lease. Until the question of native title has been dealt with no development can proceed. Aboriginal leaders and their advisers can claim that the ground on which the company seeks a permit to develop a mine has historically been used by Australia's native people (the aborigines). This then requires that they be offered compensation for the loss of their rights, or *in extremis* that permission be refused for a development. It goes without saying that investors need to establish the native title position if they are interested in the prospects of a particular exploration company.

As labour costs in Australia are high this tends to mean that mining operations are capital intensive with consequently small workforces. The highly mechanised iron ore operations in the Pilbara in Western Australia are a case in point. These are huge open pit operations, with massive trucks lifting the ore which is loaded directly or via a beltway onto some of the longest goods trains in the world. These take the ore to port where it is loaded via another beltway directly onto large ore carriers. Similar large scale mines, such as in the coal and bauxite industries, where mining techniques bear more than a passing resemblance to earth removing are typical of the Australian scene.

Although the issues of the environment and aboriginal rights are delicate ones Australia is a huge country, a continent indeed, with a relatively small population which lives mainly around the long coastline and in the central/south eastern corner of the country. This means that a huge empty and accessible interior with high prospectivity for mineral discoveries underpins the mining industry.

Canada

Despite its strong historic links to the UK, it has been the case for many decades that Canada in economic terms has been primarily influenced and dominated by the US. Conversely it is also the case that today Canadian mining groups, particularly in the field of gold mining, have a powerful leading position in US mining, and we will hear more of this later. Canada, due to this US influence, was never a member of the Sterling Area unlike Australia and South Africa. When UK exchange controls were tightened due to the Second World War and its aftermath, capital was still allowed to flow within the Sterling Area, although it was tightly restricted outside including Canada.

The influence of the US

Canada is often thought to be highly sensitive of its proximity to its giant neighbour. It is certainly aware that it is not very high in the thoughts of US citizens. This was demonstrated by a poll commissioned by Toronto's Globe and Mail in the late 80s where well over half the US citizens approached had difficulty either positioning Canada or correctly answering the most simple questions about the country. However, US mining share funds are very much more in tune with what makes Canada tick and have significant stakes in most of the leading Canadian miners, particularly in the gold area. Neither does this seem to worry Canadians unduly, perhaps because they realise the important stakes their companies hold in the US mining industry.

Like Australia there has always been a strong junior mining sector in Canada which provides essential seedcorn capital for exploration. However, Canada is in certain respects a mature minerals province, and its major base metal operations such as nickel and zinc tend to have been established for many decades. Many of its gold mines are also mature but the industry has a strong reputation for finding new ore in traditional gold camps as has happened at Red Lake in Ontario. Neither has the Canadian mining industry lost its ability to find entirely new mineral provinces as has been demonstrated by the discovery of diamonds in the North West Territories in the 90s, setting off a frenzied if relatively short lived stock market boom. The discovery of a brand new nickel province in Labrador in the same decade was an additional demonstration that Canada was not dead ground as far as exploration went, even if many Canadian companies were concentrating their efforts overseas.

The 90s saw success with aggressive financing, but then Bre-X

It was also the case in the 90s that Canadian investment banks and brokers, encouraged by exploration successes in the junior sector like the diamond discoveries, established a reputation for aggressive fund raising on the sector's behalf. How much of this money was actually raised from Canadian investors is open to question, and there are those who claim that most of the mining capital was raised in the US and Europe by the overseas branches of Canadian brokers. Whatever the truth none of this activity did the Canadian mining industry any harm until the Bre-X scandal - which we will cover in detail later in the book - ruined everything. Since Bre-X, Canadian brokers and even the Canadian mining industry have had to struggle hard to persuade investors that the sector has not reverted to wild west status, although latterly they have had some success in re-stimulating overseas interest in Canadian mining companies.

South Africa

Whilst South Africa with its new democratic dispensation is now viewed as a legitimate investment destination for investors, the years of apartheid stretching back to the late 40s saw the country shunned by many funds. Some people went to considerable lengths to express either their disapproval of the regime or their lack of enthusiasm for investment in such an unstable environment. One of the more startling statements was that made by the UK based African mineral explorer, Reunion Mining, who on the cover of its 1991 annual report featured a tracing of the African continent with South Africa completely cut away.

Others were not so squeamish, for the country dominated world production of gold and platinum and controlled the diamond industry. In the inflationary 70s and early 80s these were critical metals and minerals to be exposed to. Today South Africa remains a key player in all these precious metals and minerals, but the most powerful mining group in the country, Anglo American, has re-located to London and over the last 20 years other countries have expanded gold production as South Africa's has halved. There are also new international players in diamonds following the discovery of economic deposits in Canada, and the fall of the Soviet Union which led to changes in the industry there. For platinum there remains no viable alternative in terms of country.

However, the desirability or otherwise of investing in South Africa remains in dispute even though apartheid has been dead for over 10 years. Recently the South African Government has ruled on three particular areas of material interest to the mining industry

- mineral leases,
- black empowerment, and
- mineral royalties.

Mineral leases

The issue of mineral leases caused some controversy as the Government was seeking in effect to nationalise them; its prime aim being to stop companies acquiring freehold leases and then not working them thereby completely anaesthetising any minerals that might lie on the property. Although there were concerns that this added up to backdoor nationalisation of the industry, the Government preferred to see its policy as promoting the concept of *use it or lose it*. In the aftermath of the adoption of the policy a significant number of dormant mineral leases have been re-assigned, often to smaller mining companies, leading to development of new platinum, diamond and gold operations over the last couple of years. The issue of leases in terms of the outside world has been less controversial as most countries with mining industries vest mineral leases in the State, and operate on the basis of granting these leases for exploration and development.

Black empowerment

Black empowerment is a highly sensitive political issue and one which the Government is pushing very hard. The idea is that in order to right the wrongs of the apartheid era previously disadvantaged groups, primarily but not exclusively blacks, must be given assistance so they can participate in the mainstream economy. This policy is not only aimed at the mining industry and indeed now affects decision making in all parts of commercial and public life. The mining companies have in a number of instances been commendably quick to construct black empowerment deals. These usually take the form of either joint ventures with black groups or selling mining assets to black businesses. In the course of this a number of new mining companies have sprung up of which ARMGold, now merged with Harmony Gold, is probably the best known.

However, there are a number of problems associated with these deals. The main one is the question of how they are financed, as many of the interested groups do not have the resources to make straight asset purchases. The most usual route is for the empowerment group to borrow money to make the purchase, using the cash flow from the asset to pay interest and principal. The recent Mining Charter, which refines the principles of empowerment as they relate directly to the industry, lays down percentages and timescales for direct black shareholdings in mining operations, ultimately within ten years companies will need to show 26% ownership of themselves or their operations by so-called black empowerment groups. Unfortunately there has been some confusion over whether companies get a credit towards the required percentage for group assets already sold to empowerment groups. AngloGold was one company with a problem in this area, as it had done a number of empowerment deals by selling assets but had no current disadvantaged shareholding in the group itself or sufficient joint ventures.

Mineral royalties

As far as the issue of mineral royalties goes, again, as with the introduction of State mining leases, nothing unusual was being proposed as the practice is widespread throughout the world, although exceptionally Chile does not charge royalties and Canada's are based on net profits not turnover. Indeed in the past the South African gold mines used to have to pay a lease payment although this was based on a formula linked to profitability and this payment was allowed against income tax. What is now proposed is a straight royalty based on turnover and unrelated to profitability which provisionally is to be set at 3% for gold, 4% for platinum and 8% for diamonds. The industry itself believes the rates are too high and will lead to the closure of marginally profitable mines which are already very sensitive to exchange rate changes.

More recently the threat of private legal action has arisen in the US aimed at major international companies with big South African operations such as Anglo

American who are thought to have benefited from the years of apartheid. This may well have been stimulated by the Truth and Reconciliation Committee's (TRC) announcement in early 2003 that a system of reparations should be put in place to compensate victims of the old regime. Whilst the TRC's action is aimed at any company who is thought to have made money out of apartheid, mining companies are expected to bear the brunt of any costs, although South African government support for the idea has not so far been forthcoming. This situation is at a very early stage of development, and any legal action will undoubtedly drag on for a long time, adding another uncertainty to investing in South African mining shares. Of course it could be said that veterans of the mining scene have always been aware of the risk element in the South African sector and that new problems are probably not unexpected.

USA

No longer a prime mining nation

The US can no longer be viewed as a prime mining nation, certainly as far as output growth is concerned. As one of the earliest countries to embrace the industrial revolution it developed its mineral resources quickly in order to provide its own raw materials to feed plants and factories. Today the country remains a major producer of coal, copper, gold and other metals. However, a combination of very tight environmental legislation and the fact that the most attractive sources of metals have already been exploited means that interesting investment opportunities in the US mining industry are scarce. Neither are the US incorporated mining companies large by the standards of the UK giants, with the exception of Alcoa which is more of an integrated aluminium group than a mining company. Newmont, which was once controlled by long departed UK gold miner Consolidated Gold Fields, is one of the three largest gold mining groups in the world by market capitalisation. The US's only other significant metal company, is copper miner Phelps Dodge.

Increasing ownership and control by foreign companies

A measure of the fall from grace and influence of the US mining industry is the fact that the once mighty lead/zinc group, American Mining and Smelting (AMS), is now owned by Grupo Mexico, and the country's only serious platinum group metals producer, Stillwater, is controlled by Russia's Norilsk. This emphasises the point that if US investors want to benefit from a metals and mining share bull market they are forced to look to overseas markets and stocks. Because of this many overseas mining groups now have their shares listed in New York to facilitate trading by American investors. Nonetheless when one sees US ownership, and therefore influence, in such an important industry as mining at such modest levels, it underlines the shift in the world's largest economy away from heavy industrial manufacturing.

Having said all this there is still, as mentioned above, significant metal output coming from the US but a growing amount of that is under the control of foreign groups like Rio Tinto of the UK. It is also interesting to note the prominence of foreign groups in what once would have been a highly strategic part of the mining industry - gold. Here the Canadians are particularly strong with companies like Barrick, Placer Dome and Kinross having substantial gold mining operations in the US. Investors looking for exposure to the US mining industry will therefore in the main have to look outside the country for shares.

The attraction of the US to investors generally is the robust approach to business of US companies; and the perception that business in the US operates in a much more friendly environment than it does in the heavily regulated European Union or structurally challenged Japan. Whilst there is something to this, certainly as regards sunrise industries such as technology, the picture is less clear as regards the exploitation of minerals. Many states have very strict rules regarding the environment, particularly where pollution may be a particular hazard often as a result of mining companies actions in the past. The collapse of Galactic Resources in 1992 and the serious pollution caused by the bursting of the slimes dam, left the US state of Colorado with a huge clean up bill. In the light of that incident, as well as the growing inheritance of polluted mine sites in the US following operational closure, environmental laws were materially tightened.

United Kingdom

Little mining activity left

One of the most interesting business developments in recent years has been the re-location to and re-incorporation in the UK of a number of very large mining companies. This has meant that the three largest mining companies in the world - Rio Tinto, Anglo American and BHP Billiton - have UK incorporation and they have been joined by Swiss based Xstrata; all are part of the FTSE100 share index. It is important to appreciate, however, that any UK mining operations that these companies have are very small. Indeed mining in the UK is itself confined to speciality minerals such as china clay, sand and gravel and a rapidly contracting (though once powerful) coal mining industry.

The financial attractions of London

Therefore, with little mining activity in the UK the reasons for the presence of these companies in London is primarily financial. The banking system is seen as sophisticated and experienced in financing mining developments. Operating as a

UK company means that the cost of capital can be much lower than in countries like South Africa. The historic links between the City of London and the mining industry mean that there is understanding of the risks and rewards of financing mining companies. When UK exchange controls were swept aside in 1979/80 the equity market was once again able to look to British institutions and private investors to finance mining companies as they did in the 19th century at the height of Empire. There was also a ready built expertise in the stockbroking community, which curiously was developed in the years of exchange controls primarily to service more fortunate investors in countries such as Switzerland which had no controls. How extensive that expertise is today is less clear and we will be considering that issue later. The existence of tax treaties, avoiding punitive double taxation implications for mining companies incorporated in the UK and operating elsewhere, is also helpful.

The revival of the UK mining company sector is also interesting when one remembers the decline that had set in by the 1960s. In the early part of that decade two South African groups, Johannesburg Consolidated and Union Corporation, moved management and control from London to Johannesburg. In the early 70s New Broken Hill, a UK company with Australian base metal interests, also re-incorporated in Australia. Before that in the 50s London based African copper mining companies like Bancroft, Rhokana and Rhodesian Anglo American, which latterly became Minorco, had moved control to the then Northern Rhodesia which gained independence as Zambia in the 60s. In the 70s many of the London based Malaysian tin mining companies also upped sticks for the Far East.

By the 70s the remaining UK mining houses consisted of RTZ (now Rio Tinto), Consolidated Gold Fields (eventually taken over by Hanson and broken up), Selection Trust (taken over by BP as big oil diversified into mining) and Charter Consolidated (Anglo American of South Africa's offshore mining arm now metamorphosed into an ailing engineering conglomerate). Other smaller UK incorporated mining companies included Consolidated African Selection Trust (quickly swallowed up by parent Selection Trust), Lonrho (more an African conglomerate until the non mining interests were split off in the late 90s) and London, Australian and General (a South African based mining group controlled by financier Oliver Jessel).

The 90s saw the rapid recovery of the mining sector

By the early 90s the UK was down to Rio Tinto as its sole major mining group, and the relevance of London as a mining centre had all but disappeared. Since that time a remarkable transformation has occurred that has led to the establishment of three further UK mining groups alongside Rio Tinto, all large enough to be constituents of the FTSE100. In addition, Antofagasta, which had been a small capitalisation South American based railway company, is now a substantial and growing producer of copper in Chile and also a FTSE100 company, and Lonmin (formerly Lonrho) is one of the platinum industry's 'big three'. Some newcomers have not come fully into the UK but incorporated in the UK's offshore islands with a London market listing, West African gold company Randgold Resources, a Jersey company, is a substantial example of that.

The rapid recovery of the London mining sector in recent years is further underlined by the rise in the number of foreign mining companies seeking admission to the Alternative Investment Market (AIM), either to achieve dual listing alongside their home exchange or to re-locate to the UK. Although this trend can be seen as support for London's rising reputation amongst foreign mining companies, the actual price performance of a number of the companies listed has been very poor.

On the whole the UK currently has few problems for investors, although that has not always been the case - as those with memories of the often desperate 70s will know. However, since UK mining companies largely operate overseas the issue of country risk is one that still has to be evaluated. It is, therefore, helpful that the major UK mining groups have at least some geographical spread. Anglo American, with 50% plus of its earnings coming from Africa and South Africa is the most focused, Rio Tinto with its broad spread of interests is the least focused from the country risk angle. The smaller companies are unsurprisingly less broadly spread.

Other countries

The question of country risk

The five countries reviewed above make up the prime targets for investors seeking stock market exposure to the sector. They are familiar to many investors which helps in terms of comfort, and the fact that all information flowing to the market about the quoted companies is in English is additionally helpful. However, there are other countries and markets, as mentioned earlier, where interesting situations can be found; the problem lies in whether the country risk is acceptable. Some might say that, despite the size of its mining industry, South Africa remains, in the post apartheid era, a risky country with the pressure for addressing past injustices, particularly, creating unwelcome financial uncertainty.

The questions that an investor has to ask himself when considering buying shares in Russia's Norilsk or Brazil's CVRD is about the quality of the information available, and how much of it is in a language he can understand, and also whether, as a foreign shareholder, he will be treated fairly. There is also the issue of political risk. Is the business environment stable? Is the tax regime fair and likely to remain so? Is it possible freely to remit dividends and share sale proceeds overseas? Foreign investors must also weigh up the chances of unilateral expropriation, perhaps a minor worry in an age of economic globalisation and interdependence, but real enough for those whose memories go back forty years to when countries like Cuba and Chile did just that.

Some reassurance can be gained from the fact that most of the non mainstream (in market terms) companies that might interest investors have listings in other major markets like London and New York, which makes both dealing and settlement relatively straightforward. This, of course, would not protect foreign investors from any precipitate action which undermined their interests, but since their shares would be held by powerful international custodians that could well act as a disincentive against such action.

The issues of choice

There are obviously pitfalls in investing in any mining country, with the environmental angle being common to all. Australia has to be particularly sensitive about the interests of its indigenous people, even though they comprise only a small minority of the population. In Canada and the US the environmental issue is a major problem and labour costs are also high. Canada in particular is still prospective as a minerals province, and the establishment of substantial diamond mining operations in the last few years is an example of this. Canadian mining companies are also successfully active in other parts of the world, particularly Latin America.

South Africa remains the most problematic country. It has a great mining tradition and much of the expertise associated with that remains in place. Its central importance to the economy is unarguable, but this does give it a high profile, and because of that it is currently in the firing line of both government and political groups seeking to siphon off its cash flow. During the apartheid era most South African mining companies could be counted on to pay out good dividends as a counter to the perceived political risk. These days dividend flows from South African companies, with the possible exception of the fairly full distributions of the platinum companies, are more modest as companies seek to emphasise the growth prospects of retaining earnings for expansion.

The UK plays host to the three largest mining groups in the world and all of them have a reasonable spread of operations both in respect of countries and metals. Conservative investors and, in these days of litigation and the suspension of *caveat emptor*, their advisers also, find this re-assuring but the underlying country risk is only hidden by their UK incorporation not banished.

Farther afield there are opportunities, but perhaps we are living in a particularly benign time for investment in faraway places about which we know little. Worthless share and bond certificates from an earlier age can still be found in many a trunk in many an attic, relating to countries that sank into economic chaos or political despotism but which in recent years have risen again to become the emerging markets of today.

Whilst mining remains a large and important industry for a large number of countries its position as far as total GDP goes is relatively modest. This is not really unexpected as many mining countries are advanced or relatively advanced economies, and their GDP is dominated by services and value added activities which have a final value far in excess of the value of their mineral output, as the figures show below.

Table 1.1 - Mining country GDP and minerals value

	Currency	GDP billion	Minerals value	% of GDP
Australia	$A	759 bn	26 bn	3.4
Brazil	Real	1,321 bn	30.5 bn	2.3
Canada	$C	1,211 bn	19 bn	1.6
Chile	Peso	45,762 bn	2,979 bn	6.5
China	Yuan	10,239 bn	662 bn	6.5
Russia	Rouble	10,863 bn	486 bn	4.5
South Africa	Rand	1,159 bn	71 bn	6.1
United States	$	10,777 bn	27.6 bn	0.3

Source: IMF Statistics, HSBC, UN Statistics (Latin America), African Business, National Data Book (US), Statistics Canada, Natural Resources Canada.

Note: The GDP figures relate to mid 2003 annualised figures from the IMF. The figures for minerals value are drawn from a variety of sources but are not necessarily up-to-date and are subject to revision. However they do enable readers to get some idea of the relative importance of national mining industries within the general economy.

The world of metals

Metals can be split into a number of groups but we are going to divide them into four categories plus gold. Those categories broadly cover

- major industrial metals,
- minor/specialist metals,
- industrial minerals, precious metals minus gold, and
- gold itself.

Although categorising metals could be construed as subjective, mining share investors need to have some basic support for their investment decisions, and knowing which metals provide the most likely stock market returns is a good foundation for such decisions.

The special cases of steel and aluminium

In the mining sector there are two anomalies which need to be defined. Most metals are mined and after processing used in their native state. For example, copper ore is mined and then processed into copper metal which has a number of applications in its own right. Two key metals are not mined in their native state – aluminium and steel; as explained below they are derived from bauxite and iron ore respectively. It is therefore arguable whether stockbrokers' mining analysts should cover the steel and aluminium industries as they are processing industries with more in common with the *metal bashing* side of engineering than with mining.

Relationship between metals and the macro-economy

It is also worth considering, as a broad point, where the various groups of metals fit into the macro picture. Major industrial metals, including the well known base metals, are primarily affected by prospects for economic growth, thus in an economic upturn demand for and the price of the metals will tend to rise. It is extremely unlikely that such metals will do well in price terms if economic conditions are unpromising. There is one possible exception to this rule, price movements at times of high inflation - as we saw in the 70s. Then investors might well look at metals as hedges against inflation, although if inflation leads on to a squeeze by the authorities the ultimate fall in real consumer demand will eventually prick the speculative metal price bubble.

Chart 1.1: Economist Dollar Metals Price Index & CPI (US)

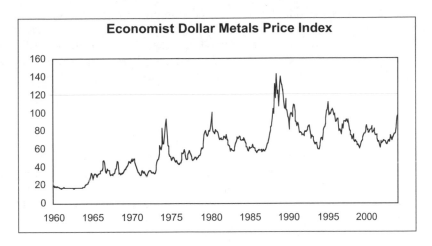

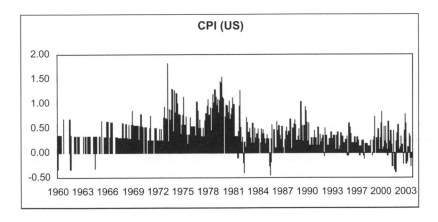

Source: Datastream

Minor metals

Minor and specialist metals are unlikely to be targets for investors in commodities as the markets in such metals are usually very thin and illiquid. Minor metals are therefore influenced primarily by economic growth prospects as are major metals. There is, however, the possibility that a minor metal may have particular application in a fast growing industry which has a momentum quite separate from the mainstream economy, specialist metals used in mobile phones in the late 90s would be an example of this.

Industrial minerals

Industrial minerals are primarily mined as soft crumbly ore and then processed into metals. Whilst economic growth rates have an effect on prospects industrial minerals are often low value bulk commodities where basic demand is relatively inelastic as far as the economic cycle is concerned, and price changes are usually the result of natural shortages or surpluses.

Precious metals

The other area we look at below is the precious metals sector, including gold. Gold is a metal with characteristics which mean that it can perform very well during times of economic weakness if that weakness is accompanied by inflation and/or strains in the financial system. It also does have linkages with the economic cycle, as one of the key areas of consumer demand for gold is jewellery. Other precious metals particularly platinum are influenced by consumption driven economic growth, although platinum is seen as something of a technological metal which does give it some ability to outperform the economic cycle.

Diversification against specialisation

It can be taken as read that mining companies are primarily driven by the demand for and price of the metals they produce. At certain times and in certain conditions, for instance when strong economic growth is driving demand for raw materials, investment in companies with a wide spread of metals may be thought sensible. Some of those may be major industrial metals such as iron ore and copper. Others may be more exotic metals such as tantalum and magnesium for which there is accelerating demand from a low base level, providing the possibility of long term growth. This spread is often seen as prudent, providing some protection against weakness in one metal when others are perhaps performing satisfactorily. In some circumstances market attention is caught by just one metal, and diversified mining groups are ignored as investors seek shares that maximise their exposure to the desired metal; in recent years platinum has been one of those metals.

The nature of cyclicality

Some of the principles that should be applied to investing in mining shares are not exclusive to that sector but can be used across quite a sizeable part of the stock market. What we are particularly talking about here is cyclicality, because demand for metals is driven by the waxing and waning of the economic cycle and that is a key component of metal pricing. Cyclicality, though, could equally be applied to, say, retailing where the personal debt cycle would have a critical influence on people's spending plans and therefore on the turnover and profits of retailers.

The nature of the economic cycle means that even if growth is a long term phenomenon there are periods, fortunately usually short lived, when economies stall or even weaken. The effect on metals of these slowdowns can be severe these days for two reasons.

1. A large component of economic activity derives from the service sector which is a minor consumer of metals and also tends to perform better than manufacturing during an economic downturn.

2. There is a tendency these days in manufacturing to use less metal and of a lighter weight than formerly, motor cars would be a good example of this. Manufacturing growth also tends to be faster in items such as electronic goods where the metals used are less important in terms of the selling price than the value added technology that goes into the goods.

Chart 1.2: Economist Dollar Metals Price Index

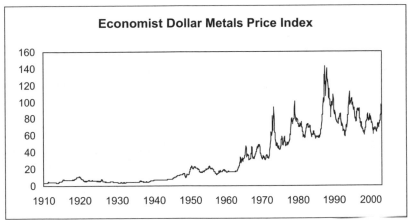

Source: Datastream

Have metals had their day?

From the above it might be thought that metals have had their day and become merely a sideshow to the main event of service industry/high technology powered growth. Certainly during the internet boom between 1998 and 2001, investors would have found little to excite them in the mining sector. But it was midway through 2001 that the gold price finally bottomed and gold shares began a rise that within a year saw some of them achieve price increases of five times and better.

However it could also be argued that infrastructure spending in both private and public sectors, which is heavily skewed towards raw materials, remains a priority for the poorer countries of the world and for some of the larger ones also. Infrastructure development and renewal, with its high consumption of metals and other minerals, will surely continue at a rapid rate for many decades in China, Russia and India. It could also be argued that even advanced economies like the UK are in need of heavy spending on capital investment over the longer term in a number of areas, including transport, health and education, owing to the country's position as the oldest advanced industrial economy. And even the mighty US economy has its infrastructure problems, and the power blackout in the US in 2003 is a dramatic example of the consequences of failing to renew the physical power network.

Privatisation of mineral production

So even though raw materials no longer have a central position in the advanced economies their importance is not to be underestimated. There is also another interesting factor to be borne in mind relating to the steady privatisation of mineral production around the world. When government ownership of mineral production was widespread in the decades immediately after the Second World War there was a tendency for the financial disciplines critical to the health of the private sector to be ignored. This meant that mineral production was often hopelessly uneconomic as the state underwrote any losses, and developed mines and stockpiled metals for strategic reasons irrespective of the economic cost. Those days are long gone and production levels are now kept much closer to demand levels than formerly. This can lead to sudden shortages when economic activity picks up, with a coincident and positive effect on metal prices and on mining shares. This is a little different from the past when overproduction meant that shortages of metals, and thus an increase in their price and a rise in mining share prices, tended to happen much later in the economic cycle.

Major industrial metals

Industrial metals are those used in the broad manufacturing and construction process. The major metals are those that are most widely consumed using measures of both value and volume. Some of these metals are referred to as *base metals* including copper, lead, zinc and tin. We would also include nickel in the group, although nickel is sometimes described as a steel industry metal. Base metal is not a precise term but refers to the better known chemically active metals. Steel, and aluminium are two of the prime major metals and are found in almost every area of manufacturing and construction, although they are not base metals as they are processed from primary raw materials, iron ore and bauxite.

Since the key to profitable mining share selection is picking not only the right moment in the cycle but, at least as equally important, picking the metal with the best growth prospects, an appropriately analytical approach is required for the task. Questions that need to be asked include-

• Which metal has the best fundamentals as far as supply and demand is concerned, i.e. where is an actual or probable deficit in supply to be found?

• Which metal has the best fundamentals regarding growth in consumption?

• Which metal has the best stock market exposure, i.e. where is there likely to be sufficient liquidity due to plenty of stock choice to allow big funds to join the action?

Copper

Copper is one of the most widely followed metals. It is mined in a large number of countries and has important uses particularly in construction/housing and electronics where its key property as a highly efficient conductor of electric current is prized. There is an element of national custom in the uses of copper, although its use in electric cable is universal. Copper for domestic water piping for example is more common in the UK than in many other countries where plastic or steel/iron piping is often preferred, even though it is much easier to work and shape copper piping.

Pricing is always an issue for metal usage. The boom in base metals in the late 60s led to a substantial jump in the copper price. Around that time there was a widespread investment programme in electricity generating capacity and a consequent increase in the building of pylons and laying of electric cables. Although copper cable is arguably the most efficient conductor of electric current, the rapid rise in the metal's price led to a reduction in the use of copper in generating cable by cladding the cable with aluminium, and this kind of cable became the industry standard .

The main diversified mining companies, including Rio Tinto and Anglo American, all operate copper mines and count this as a core part of their businesses. In addition there are a significant number of smaller companies including Antofagasta, Xstrata, Phelps Dodge and Inco who are sizeable producers. After gold there is no other metal whose price movements have such an impact on the mining share market as copper.

Table 1.2 - Copper statistics (2003)

	Mine production (Tonnes metal)	Mine reserves (Tonnes metal)
Australia	870,000	24,000,000
Canada	580,000	7,000,000
Chile	4,860,000	150,000,000
China	565,000	26,000,000
Indonesia	1,170,000	28,000,000
Peru	850,000	35,000,000
Poland	500,000	31,000,000
Russia	700,000	20,000,000
United States	1,120,000	35,000,000
Others	2,685,000	116,000,000
Total	**13,900,000**	**470,000,000**

Source: US Geological Survey

Chart 1.3: Copper

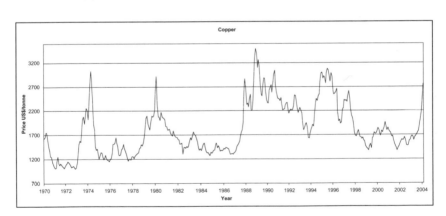

Source: Datastream

Zinc

In an environmentally conscious age zinc is a metal with positive characteristics. It is non toxic and its key uses are in galvanising steel, die castings, construction, the manufacture of brass, pharmaceuticals, cosmetics, and agriculture. The life cycle of many zinc products is long - zinc sheet used in roofing and cladding can last beyond 100 years and galvanised coatings for steel products can prolong the life of the product for up to 50 years. Zinc is also completely recyclable, losing none of its essential properties in the process.

Zinc usage has been rising over the last thirty years at around 3% per annum. Its position as a key metal in the construction and transport industries underlines the likelihood that growth in demand will continue to at least match OECD growth rates. In terms of constant money terms (1999 $US) the zinc price has had two major spikes in the last forty years, in 1974 and then again in 1989. In 1974 its adjusted price in terms of 1999 money values reached US$3,637 per tonne ($1.65 per lb) against a current US$1080 per tonne ($0.49 per lb). Despite the expected growth in usage over the longer term, the poor short term price performance has created problems for many zinc miners leading to production cutbacks.

One of zinc's problems relates to its geological environment where it is often found in ore that is also rich in lead and silver, two metals we discuss below. If the price of one of the three metals goes up that can create problems for the other two metals if their prospects are less rosy than for the other metal. This is because the rising price of the other metal could well encourage an increase in mine output. The mine can then find itself with a surplus of the other two metals, for often it has limited scope to 'favour' one metal over another in its mining plan. This surplus then sends the prices of the other two metals sliding which in due course threatens the economics of the mine and because of this, the production of the strongest metal. Amongst the leading quoted zinc producers are Teck Cominco and Noranda who are also lead and silver producers as well, with Breakwater, Arcon, Ivernia West and ZincOx among the smaller producer and explorers.

Table 1.3 - Zinc statistics (2003)

	Mine production (Tonnes metal)	Mine reserves (Tonnes metal)
Australia	1,600,000	33,000,000
Canada	1,000,000	11,000,000
China	1,700,000	33,000,000
Mexico	500,000	8,000,000
Peru	1,250,000	16,000,000
United States	770,000	30,000,000
Others	1,680,000	89,000,000
Total	**8,500,000**	**220,000,000**

Source: US Geological Survey

Chart 1.4: Zinc

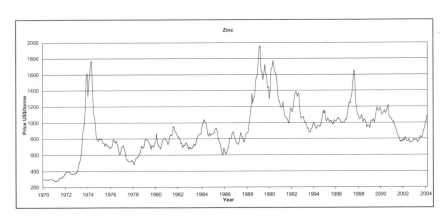

Source: Datastream

Lead

Although in an environmentally aware age lead, with its image as a highly toxic metal, no longer excites much interest, it still has many important applications in construction and transport, but the prime use of the metal is in the manufacture of batteries. Lead, however, is a good example of a metal which has the ability to re-invent itself. Historically it was widely used in domestic piping and petroleum products, its malleability being a key attribute as far as the former use was concerned. When its toxicity became more appreciated it was quickly phased out of piping and finally petrol, but the growth in battery usage more than compensated.

The metal itself is seldom found on its own but usually in a polymetallic (more than one metal) environment along with zinc and silver. This can create problems for investors assessing new mineral discoveries, for if the deposit is heavily weighted towards lead, in terms of percentage of metals present, it is likely that the deposit will be uneconomic unless the lead grade in the ore is very high. This is because the increase in lead consumption these days is so slow; which consequently undermines the metal's price unless there is a matching fall in production which eventually leads to shortages even of lead. As mentioned above, the leading zinc producers are usually major lead producers as well.

Table 1.4 - Lead statistics (2003)

	Mine production (Tonnes metal)	Mine reserves (Tonnes metal)
Australia	715,000	15,000,000
Canada	80,000	2,000,000
China	650,000	11,000,000
Mexico	140,000	1,500,000
Peru	310,000	3,500,000
United States	450,000	8,100,000
Others	550,000	25,900,000
Total	**2,840,000**	**67,000,000**

Source: US Geological Survey

Chart 1.5: Lead

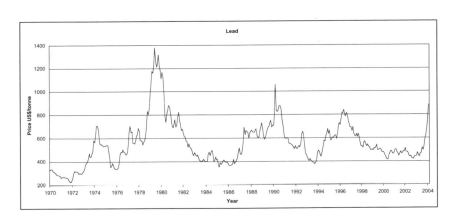

Source: Datastream

Tin

The main producers are in the far east, with China the biggest force in the market. The main uses of tin are the traditional ones of solder in the electronics industry and tinplating. Growth in consumption remains quite brisk over the longer term helped by its importance in electronics. There are few quoted tin mining companies these days. Historically the sector, which in London was dominated by Malaysian based companies, was seen as cyclical with the main rewards for shareholders coming from dividends rather than capital growth. A number of income funds used these stocks and their sister plantation companies to bolster income receipts.

Whilst there is no particular reason why tin mining should not provide investment opportunities the recent record is unexciting to say the least. The old Renison Bell mine in Tasmania was acquired by Australian junior Murchison United which obtained a quote on AIM in London in 2000. Seen as a cash cow for Murchison at the time, the Renison mine is now in the process of being sold. There have also been attempts in the past, all ultimately unsuccessful, to revive the UK's ancient tin mining industry in Cornwall as a result of intermittent surges in the tin price and the perceived appetite for UK incorporated mining companies outside the restraints of the UK's then exchange controls. These controls meant that UK investors had to purchase investment dollars at an often substantial premium to the spot exchange rate (the dollar premium) to invest in foreign mining companies. Investment currency was not needed to buy UK incorporated companies.

Table 1.5 - Tin statistics (2003)

	Mine production (Tonnes metal)	Mine reserves (Tonnes metal)
Bolivia	13,200	450,000
Brazil	14,000	540,000
China	90,000	1,700,000
Indonesia	61,000	800,000
Peru	65,000	710,000
Others	21,800	1,900,000
Total	**265,000**	**6,100,000**

Source: US Geological Survey

Note: Malaysia and Russia are both small producers but have large tin reserves.

Chart 1.6: Tin

Source: Datastream

Nickel

Seen by some as a metal of the future its short term prospects are considered good as well. Its main uses are in stainless steel (around 65% of nickel consumption), and in the manufacture of nickel and steel alloys. Growth is expected to average 5% plus over the next few years which is ahead of general economic growth. Supply which is dominated in stock market terms by Norilsk of Russia, Inco of Canada and WMC of Australia (now primarily a processor of metal rather than a miner), is lagging behind long term growth, although Norilsk does tend to have high metal inventory levels which can overhang the market. The longer term market is also having to grapple with the fact that new Australian nickel production, using historically difficult-to-treat laterite ore and new treatment processes, is struggling to achieve half reasonable levels of production.

The metal, which was central to the Australian mining boom of the late 60s, continues to excite corporate and investor interest. As well as the Australian laterites there are also similar deposits under investigation in south east Europe and the Pacific basin, and Canada. The latter, one of the major producing countries, remains highly prospective for new finds such as Voisey's Bay. Nickel is now established as a metal whose producers can attract strong investor support when the production/price cycle is rising. The metal seems less interesting to investors where it is mined as a by-product, for instance by South African platinum miners who are quite big producers of nickel and where nickel revenues can represent 10% of mine production by value.

Table 1.6 - Nickel statistics (2003)

	Mine production (Tonnes metal)	Mine reserves (Tonnes metal)
Australia	220,000	22,000,000
Canada	180,000	5,200,000
Cuba	75,000	5,600,000
Indonesia	120,000	3,200,000
New Caledonia	120,000	4,400,000
Russia	330,000	6,600,000
Others	355,000	15,000,000
Total	**1,400,000**	**62,000,000**

Source: US Geological Survey

Chart 1.7: Nickel

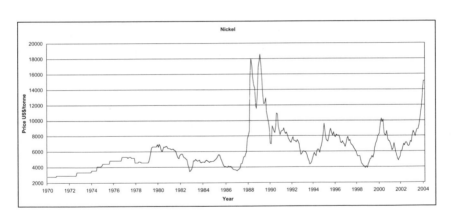

Source: Datastream

Bauxite/Aluminium

There is no doubt that aluminium is one of the most important metals used in the modern economy, its main consumers being the transport, construction and packaging industries. However it is not mined itself but is a product of the mineral bauxite, one of the most common elements in the Earth's surface. Aluminium's key properties of strength and light weight make it an ideal metal in areas like vehicle building where fuel economy is important. This gives it a green angle as does the fact that it is easily recyclable and has a much higher scrap value than steel for instance; in the UK local councils will often collect aluminium cans separately for recycling purposes. The price of aluminium is driven by market forces and the process of producing metal is very energy hungry. This means that soaring power prices from time to time can disrupt production as aluminium plants shut down in response to the crippling increase in operating costs.

The main quoted aluminium stocks, such as Alcan and Alcoa, are to be found in North America and the big diversified companies like Rio Tinto and BHP Billiton also have a big exposure to the metal as does Australia's Alumina Ltd. Most producers of aluminium are fully integrated, mining aluminium's raw material bauxite, processing it into alumina for smelting into aluminium and then making basic aluminium products such as sheet and extruded bars. Some producers even take the process the whole hog and manufacture packaging items such as cans and aluminium foil.

The development of Australia's bauxite/aluminium in the 60s excited wide interest amongst investors who saw it as part of the huge leap forward that that country's mining industry experienced in that decade. However, the integrated industrial nature of aluminium makes it more like the steel industry than the mining industry, and it could be argued that in today's markets aluminium shares are mainly of interest to investors who trade the economic cycle rather than investors whose specific interest is mining.

Table 1.7 - Aluminium statistics (2003)

	Smelter production (Tonnes metal)	Smelter capacity (Tonnes metal)
Australia	1,850,000	1,850,000
Brazil	1,390,000	1,400,000
Canada	2,800,000	2,800,000
China	5,200,000	6,500,000
Norway	1,150,000	1,080,000
Russia	3,400,000	3,400,000
United States	2,700,000	4,120,000
Others	8,810,000	9,050,000
Total	27,300,000	31,100,000

Source: US Geological Survey

Chart 1.8: Aluminum

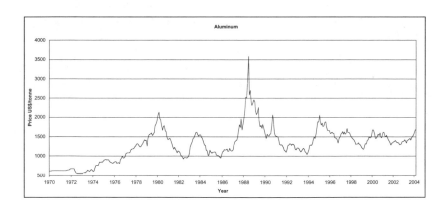

Source: Datastream

Iron Ore/Steel

Although the steel industry no longer is viewed as occupying the commanding heights of any economy, it remains a major industrial sector and is the prime customer of a wide range of metals, some of which, like cobalt and nickel are dealt with elsewhere. Like aluminium steel it is not mined but is the product of iron ore. The price of steel is not driven by market pricing in the sense that the prices of base and precious metals are, but is set on a contract basis between producer and consumer. The price of iron ore, the raw material, is also set on a contract basis.

The major producers of iron ore are China, Brazil, Australia and Russia in that order and the major consumers China, Japan and the US. Well over 90% of iron ore mined each year goes to the steel industry. Because iron ore is a relatively low priced commodity, in 2002 its price averaged around $23 per tonne in the US, an economic deposit these days would have to be pure in iron ore content, and this is particularly the case with the Australian producers in Western Australia, most of whose mines have an ore grade of over 60% ferrous content.

The opportunities for investing in iron ore shares are limited for much the same reason as they are for coal which we deal with later. The major producers are controlled by bigger groups, with the big three UK houses to the fore, and whilst a strong iron ore performance will obviously help Rio Tinto, since it is only around 10% of turnover the influence on earnings will not be overwhelming. The Brazilian giant CVRD is another major listed producer. Also the lack of volatility in the price of iron ore reduces the attractions of listed producers as vehicles for strong share price performance in relative terms during a mining bull market.

Table 1.8 - Iron ore statistics (2003)

	Ore production (Tonnes ms)	Ore reserves (Tonnes ms)	Iron content (Tonnes ms)
China	240	46,000	15,000
Brazil	215	19,000	12,000
Australia	190	40,000	25,000
Russia	92	56,000	31,000
India	80	9,800	6,200
Ukraine	63	68,000	20,000
Others	240	91,200	40,800
Total	**1,120**	**330,000**	**150,000**

Source: US Geological Survey

Chart 1.9: Iron Ore

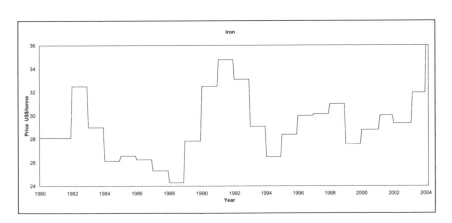

Source: Datastream

Precious metals/minerals

In this section I have excluded gold as its importance justifies a section all to itself. Also included here are platinum group metals such as rhodium that might more appropriately be covered under minor metals. I believe that investors tend to look at platinum group metals (PGMs) as a homogenous metals group when assessing the sector's prospects. I also include diamonds in this section. Precious metals have two distinct characters - they can be used as a store of value (particularly in gold's case) but they can also have wide industrial applications. The use of precious metals in jewellery spans both roles.

The image of precious metals can depend on when investors first started to take an interest in the stock market. Those who first surfaced in the late 70s will remember the huge rise in the silver price when the Hunt brothers, who made their fortune in oil in the US, tried to make another one by cornering the silver market with ultimately disastrous consequences for themselves and others. Before that, gold and diamonds, and their shares, had been very popular as stores of value during the highly inflationary years of the mid 70s. In recent years we have had strong but temporary runs in rhodium and palladium, two of the other PGMs, and in platinum itself, centring on long term shortages in what are seen as metals for a high tech future, shortages that have often proved short-lived.

The classic theory about *precious metals* is that the phrase describes the relative rarity of the metals, their beauty and therefore their often high price. This historic view is partly undermined by silver's fate over the last century or so, for its price now is a fraction of that of gold (currently a ratio of around 60 to 1 down from 15 to 1 in the 1870s), and it is rarely found on its own but rather in the company of lead and zinc.

Chart 1.10: Gold/silver ratio

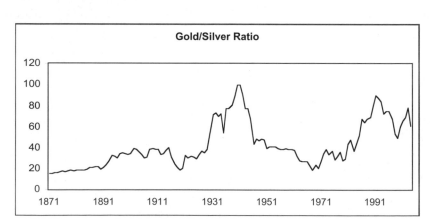

Source: Datastream

Also the historic role of both gold and silver as money, and thus a store of value, has led to substantial stockpiles of both in the hands of central banks in the case of gold and in private hands in the case of silver. Platinum, never having been classed as money, does not have large stockpiles potentially overhanging the market. Indeed for that reason it could be argued that platinum is a much more logical precious metal to corner, i.e. to buy up all stocks potentially overhanging the market in order to force the price up.

Silver

We lead off with silver because of its historic role as a monetary metal, although its current value is hugely below the value of platinum and is likely to stay that way. The metal has a number of industrial uses in photography, electronics, homeware, and jewellery. It is arguable whether it any longer has a role as a store of value, although it is believed that Indians, whose main precious metal interest is gold, still have material amounts of silver hoarded. The growing popularity of digital photography and the downloading of pictures for distribution via the internet is thought by some to herald a serious reduction in demand for silver. Only time will tell and it is not in the scope of this book to argue on such technical matters, our only observation being that digital photography does not always match, in terms of reproduction, the quality of conventionally developed photographs.

Because of silver's position these days as a by-product metal, there are few companies that market themselves as primarily silver miners which means that the prices of zinc, lead and gold are usually at least as important as silver in terms of profitability. There is also the problem of silver metal inventories which are notoriously difficult to calculate because no one truly knows how much is held in private Indian hands. Suffice it to say that newly mined silver production, like a number of other metals, runs well below annual demand, and disposals from stockpiled/hoarded metal is critical in bridging the gap.

There are a few straight(ish) silver plays but they are almost all North American companies, Hecla and Coeur d'Alene, which also produce gold, are perhaps the two leading stocks. They are highly cyclical and speculative shares primarily for the professional risk taking investor. Over the years there have been a number of strong runs in the silver price but stock market profits have been scarce and transitory because of the paucity of silver shares, and the price has ultimately always disappointed, usually giving back all of its advance. Having said that, hope for silver springs eternal with such shrewd businessmen as Warren Buffett and Bill Gates dabbling heavily in the metal and silver shares.

Table 1.9 - Silver statistics (2003)

	Mine production (Tonnes metal)	Mine reserves (Tonnes metal)
Australia	2,100	31,000
Canada	1,270	16,000
China	2,300	26,000
Mexico	2,800	37,000
Peru	2,750	36,000
United States	1,300	25,000
Others	6,480	104,000
Total	**19,000**	**270,000**

Source: US Geological Survey

Chart 1.11: Silver

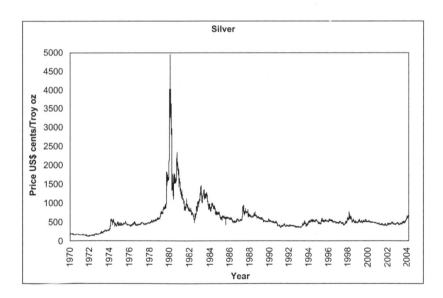

Source: Datastream

Platinum

The main uses of platinum are in car exhaust catalysts, jewellery, glass/fibreglass and petroleum refining, it also has a variety of potential high-tech applications including nuclear medicine and fuel cells. It can be argued that platinum's future is at least as bright as its past, in some contrast to silver, the main future excitement coming from the development of fuel cells which in due course are expected by some to replace petrol as the main method of propelling vehicles. It is important to understand, however, that the concept of fuel cells has been around for many years and progress in developing a commercial product has been very slow. Nevertheless fuel cells have impressive intellectual support from Sheikh Yamani, the legendary ex Saudi Arabian oil minister.

One of the main problems with platinum is that South Africa produces around 80% of the world's annual output and some investors may find that African investment, even in the relatively prosperous and stable South, is more risk than they care to take on. The other major producer is Russia which may not appeal much more than South Africa. There has been considerable effort expended on exploring for the metal in Canada, Australia and in northern Europe, and there is a producing mine in the US although it has a poor record of profitability. Ironically outside South Africa the biggest platinum deposits are to be found in politically unstable Zimbabwe.

In South Africa itself there are four main producers, with Anglo American's Amplats the largest. The other three are Impala, Northam and former UK conglomerate Lonmin. There are also a few smaller independent producers like Aquarius who have developed new mines in the wake of the Government's *use it or lose it* minerals policy. These new deposits are all relatively small and were of little interest to the major South African players who have bigger long term expansion projects on their plates. There is also an international dimension to this South African dominated business, as the marketing of platinum, because it is a strategic metal, exercises the interest of the European Commission which has more than once stepped in to block mergers and asset sales within the industry.

This domination of both production and marketing is reminiscent of the old set up of the diamond industry when De Beers's CSO controlled the market, of which more later. The discovery of a new platinum province, along the lines of the Canadian diamond discoveries of the 90s, would truly be exciting, providing considerable speculative opportunities in the market, especially in the light of the strong platinum price trend over the past couple of years.

Table 1.10 - Platinum/PGM statistics (2003)

	Platinum Mine production (Kilograms metal)	PGM Mine reserves (Kilograms metal)
Canada	7,000	310,000
Russia	36,000	6,200,000
South Africa	135,000	63,000,000
United States	4,100	900,000
Others	4,900	800,000
Total	**187,000**	**71,000,000**

Source: US Geological Survey

Chart 1.12: Platinum

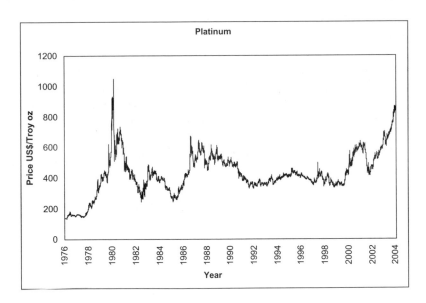

Source: Datastream

Other PGMs

In essence when I talk about other PGMs produced in South Africa (which is the dominant producer) I am referring to palladium and rhodium, although osmium, iridium and ruthenium are also from the PGM group. Palladium and rhodium are primarily used in the manufacture of catalysts for the car industry and price is critical when manufacturers decide how much palladium and rhodium, in addition to platinum, to 'load' into the catalyst. Interestingly, around twice as much palladium is used in catalyst manufacture as platinum, and the loadings between the two are very price sensitive.

The South African PGM mines tend to produce considerably more platinum than palladium, whilst for the Russians the position is reversed. At the start of 2001 palladium reached a price level of $1,100/oz when platinum was around $900. Since then the price of platinum has improved and currently trades around $620/oz; palladium on the other hand has collapsed and now sells at around $240/oz. This volatility in palladium is an historic phenomenon; over the next few years a more stable price environment is expected as new supply comes on stream.

Rhodium, which is used to harden platinum and palladium, also has a volatile price history. In 1991 the price soared to over $7,000/oz as a shortage of supply allowed speculators to squeeze the market. With a price presently around $450 down from a 2001 high of $2,300 rhodium's ability to take metal market speculators on a roller coaster ride is proven. For mining share investors such volatility can really only be taken advantage of through platinum shares as rhodium is not found on its own. Currently a typical SA producer would find that the value of its rhodium output was 12% of its platinum output.

The volatility of both palladium (where Stillwater in the US is the only quoted primary producer) and rhodium, and their by-product position in South African PGM producers, the market leaders amongst quoted PGM plays, makes it very difficult to invest on a sensible basis. Any investment decision would have to pay close attention to quite sophisticated calculations about supply, price targets and substitution, and there is plenty of room for error.

Table 1.11 - Palladium/PGM statistics (2003)

	Palladium Mine production (Kilograms metal)	PGM Mine reserves (Kilograms metal)
Canada	11,000	310,000
Russia	74,000	6,200,000
South Africa	64,800	63,000,000
United States	14,600	900,000
Others	6,600	800,000
Total	**171,000**	**71,000,000**

Source: US Geological Survey

Chart 1.13: Palladium

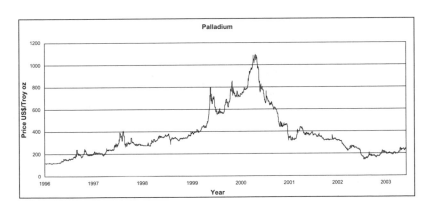

Source: Datastream

Diamonds

There are two prime categories of diamonds - industrial and gem. The former are low in value and as their name implies are used in industrial processes, and although they are naturally mined they can also be produced synthetically in a factory. Gem diamonds, primarily used in the manufacture of jewellery, are considerably more valuable than industrial and also rarer (only 15% of stones can be considered of gem quality). In terms of carats mined (1 metric carat weighs 200 mgs), industrial stones are around half the total, near gem a further 35%, with the balance being gem. Translated into value though, gem diamonds represent as much as 80% of the value of annual mined output.

Diamonds are mined in a variety of countries, the main ones being South Africa, Botswana, Russia, Angola, Namibia, the Congo, Australia and Canada. They are also to be found in Brazil, Sierra Leone and the Central African Republic, and exploration continues in a number of other countries including Finland and India which was the main source of diamonds before the emergence of Africa in the 19th century.

Table 1.12 - Diamond mine production by value (2002)

	US$ BN	%
Botswana	2.3	29
Russia	1.7	21
Angola	0.9	10
South Africa	0.8	10
Canada	0.5	6
Namibia	0.5	6
Australia	0.4	5
Congo	0.4	4
Others	0.5	6
Total	**8.0**	**100**

Source: The Diamond Market & Six Diamond Juniors, WH Ireland

The dominant position of De Beers

The dominant force in the diamond industry remains De Beers, now a private company effectively controlled by Anglo American. In recent years De Beers, which operated the diamond marketing cartel the Central Selling Organisation, has restructured its operations to move up the diamond chain into manufacturing and retailing. It remains the largest diamond miner still and also continues to market diamonds through its renamed marketing arm, the Diamond Trading Company. However the group no longer seeks to operate along monopolist lines as the buyer of last resort, a role it has claimed since the depression of the 1930s when it reorganised the industry to save it from collapse.

Few investment plays

Looking at diamonds from the point of view of stock market investment, the table is rather bare. De Beers, which was a public company and one of the largest quoted mining groups, has been taken private and though Anglo American has a 45% stake in the company, the impact on its diversified profits at around 20% of earnings is useful without being overwhelming. BHP Billiton controls the Ekati diamond mine in Canada but results are hidden in a speciality products segment where that segment represents around 10% of group pre tax profit. Rio Tinto owns the Argyle diamond mine in Australia and has brought the Diavik mine in Canada to production but again its diamond activities are in earnings terms relatively small, less than 10% in 2003.

There remain a number of diamond exploration companies mainly listed in Australia and Canada, some of which like Aber Diamond and Southern Era do have current production. In South Africa, Trans Hex is the only remaining listed diamond miner of any substance. The disappearance of De Beers from the stock market has, therefore, left a very large hole in the sector. But the sector has also lost Ekati discoverer Dia Met to BHP Billiton, and Argyle discoverer Ashton Mining to Rio Tinto in recent years. Unfortunately the discovery of kimberlite pipes, the source of and setting for diamond mines, is a painstaking business and any major new diamond mines even if discovered soon will take many years to bring to production. Still diamonds retain a fascination for mining investors, and if the current junior exploration effort does locate major new discoveries in due course, one would expect an upsurge of interest as happened when the Canadian discoveries were made a decade ago.

Minor industrial metals

As can be seen from the above not all metals historically attract the attention of mining investors. Perhaps, as with aluminium, the mining of the raw material is judged to be far less important than the upstream processing operation. Or perhaps like lead they are judged to be metals with very modest growth prospects and consequently of little interest.

The world of minor metals has these conflicts as well, and other problems to boot. Almost by definition minor metals have lower turnover value than their more weighty peers in the major sector, although the unit value of the metal may be high. That can mean that the sudden popularity of a minor metal can bring so much attention from prospective producers that potential output threatens to drown the market. As an example the price of tantalum in 2001-2, fired by forecast demand from the mobile phone industry, soared only to crash back.

Minor metals, however, are often seen as metals for the future with bright prospects based on high-tech growth industries. Nickel and platinum would not have been seen as major metals at the end of the Second World War, though nickel's strategic qualities no doubt were appreciated by the defence industry as it looked forward, and platinum jewellery had been very fashionable in the 1930s. Today growth prospects for nickel and platinum are counted amongst the most promising of any of the major metals. So looking forward what does the future hold for some of the more prospective minor metals?

Tantalum

Having raised the subject of tantalum earlier it is appropriate that we return to it now as the metal has a number of instructive things to tell us about minor metals. As mentioned above, tantalum is used by mobile phone manufacturers in capacitors which are used to hold electric charges in the phone. As such this is clearly a high growth area, or was a couple of years ago. However, the mobile phone industry represents only 30% of annual consumption, and capacitors can also use niobium as a substitute. Other sources of demand for tantalum include portable electronic equipment, superalloys, cemented carbides, and growing demand from computer memory chips and processors is expected. Also as the metal has a very high melting point it is used in the furnace and chemical process industries.

This is an impressive list of potential high growth industries and the worldwide explosion in the ownership of mobile phones in the late 90s fuelled a rash of tantalum exploration companies seeking funding and a public quote. Whilst tantalum sells at around $30/lb currently, at the height of the mobile phone induced excitement in 2000 the free market or spot price was around $250/lb. Producers with long term supply contracts would however have been locked into much lower prices, perhaps in the $50/lb area. The nature of special minor metals is that customers must have security of supply because there is little or no spot market, unlike gold or copper. Mirroring that, miners must have secure contracts with a price guarantee.

When demand for tantalum, which has a record of fairly violent price swings, started to expand in the late 90s powered increasingly by the mobile phone revolution, it directly led to the incorporation of a number of small new mining companies who had acquired tantalum prospects and needed funds to explore their leases. Most of the projects were already known as prospective for tantalum, and some of them had had work done on them in the past. One of the more robust of these new companies was Angus & Ross, a UK company which had the backing of major tantalum user, Cabot Corp of the US. Its Greenland project gained sufficient market attention to see the A&R share price rise from around 5p to 25p in early 2002 before plunging back to around 4p a few months later as the tantalum/mobile phone bubble burst. More recently its shares have rallied as attention has switched to its newly acquired Australian gold interests.

The world's largest tantalum producer, Australia's Sons of Gwalia, which is also a major gold producer, found that its share price benefited dramatically in the new millennium from the tantalum bubble combined with a sustained run in the gold share market, which saw its price rise from 154p in 1999 to 367p in 2001. Since that peak its shares fell back to 51p earlier in 2003 as the market became worried about both the tantalum price and the state of Gwalia's gold hedge book which had gone heavily into the red due to a soaring gold price.

The lessons of tantalum

The lessons to be drawn from tantalum are applicable right across the mining board. If you are interested in a minor metal, timing is vital, for often the time between price bubbles can be long and the shares you own will at best go nowhere.

It is also critical to understand that some price levels in commodities can become so inflated that they take decades to be reached again - nickel at $8,500/tonne in 1968, sugar at £400/tonne in 1974 and gold at $850/oz in 1980 - are three examples of this, with sugar and gold in the meantime never having been even close to their historic highs.

The other problem with minor metal exploration companies is that after the bubble, to survive the hard times, they have to issue new shares, often at very low prices, with the result that the shareholder who buys at or close to the top, in the end can be diluted down to almost nothing.

All of this may seem obvious in hindsight but greed can be blinding at the time of investment. So, like Ulysses tied to the mast so he could not succumb to the Sirens, tantalum investors (perhaps *speculator* might be a more appropriate name) with good profits should have ignored those that urged them to hold positions for the long term. Quite marginal changes, or prospect of changes, in supply can have a disproportionate effect on the price of the metal and burst the price bubble, bringing the shares crashing down in its wake.

The fact that most business between miner and customer is done at a fixed contract price, so mine tantalum revenues may not be hugely affected by the spot price crashing, is of minor interest to a speculative market where a price bubble may have been seen by some as signalling a new and much higher price when supply contracts are re-negotiated in the future.

Table 1.13 - Tantalum statistics (2003)

	Mine production (Tonnes metal)	Mine reserves (Tonnes metal)
Australia	820	40,000
Brazil	200	n/a
Canada	58	3,000
Congo	30	n/a
Ethiopia	40	n/a
Rwanda	20	n/a
Others	62	n/a
Total	**1,230**	**43,000**

Source: US Geological Survey

Chart 1.14: Tantalum

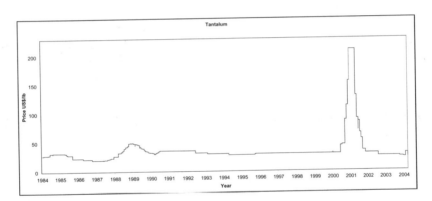

Source: Datastream

Cobalt

Cobalt is usually found as a by-product of copper, and central Africa, particularly Zambia and the Congo, is a major source of the metal. It is an important metal with uses as a strengthening alloy for steel and in magnets; it is also used in inks, paint and varnishes and as an isotope in radiotherapy. Although demand for the metal is linked to the broad economic cycle, its price can be very volatile and the decline of the Zambian and Congo copper industries has exacerbated that trend. In the late 70s and then again in the late 90s the price soared towards $40/lb only to crash back into single figures each time, and in the interim it showed plenty of volatility.

The lesson of Nkana dumps

One particularly vicious example of minor metal fatigue was Canadian incorporated Colossal Resources which had a cobalt re-treatment project in Zambia based on the old cobalt rich dumps at the Nkana copper mine. Its share price soared in the mid 90s to over $20 before the project unthreaded and the shares fell back to mere cents. At the time the project looked highly attractive, with the cobalt price in one of its upsurges. The problem was that cobalt, like so many minor metals, has a paper thin spot market and most trade is done on the basis of long term contracts. Colossal unfortunately had first to offer its output to the parastatal company Zambia Consolidated Copper Mines (ZCCM), which was controlled by the Zambian government. If ZCCM did not want the metal then Colossal was free to sell it to other customers. Unfortunately the structure meant that Colossal could find it difficult to sign up long term customers because of ZCCM's effective pre-emptive right to the Nkana output. In the end, this structure, a falling cobalt price, and a fatal dispute over its ownership of the project, seriously damaged Colossal and its shareholders. A couple of years later the Nkana dumps project was acquired by South African major Avmin, but it had little better luck despite expectations of handsome returns from the operation. Last year Avmin wrote off its investment and has now sold its interest in the project. Some projects are simply fated.

The lesson to be drawn from the above is that cobalt is a typical feast and famine minor metal with high and consistent volatility. It is almost certain that if investors ride the cobalt cycle in a vehicle like Colossal they will need to get out or else their profits will turn to dust. Whilst this seems so obvious, it is an error repeated time and time again in mining booms, and indeed other stock market booms such as the recent internet/high-tech bust.

The differential between mine production and potential reserves

The following table shows a huge differential between mine production and potential reserves. This is due to the large amount of by-product cobalt tied up in nickel laterite deposits many of which cannot yet be mined economically. A large increase in the nickel price therefore could threaten to bring substantial amounts of by-product cobalt onto the market if the nickel price rise leads to development of these currently uneconomic deposits.

Table 1.14 - Cobalt statistics (2003)

	Mine production (Tonnes metal)	Mine reserves (Tonnes metal)
Australia	6,600	1,500,000
Canada	4,700	90,000
Congo	10,000	3,400,000
Cuba	3,200	1,000,000
Russia	5,000	350,000
Zambia	12,000	270,000
Others	5,200	390,000
Total	**46,900**	**7,000,000**

Source: US Geological Survey

Chart 1.15: Cobalt

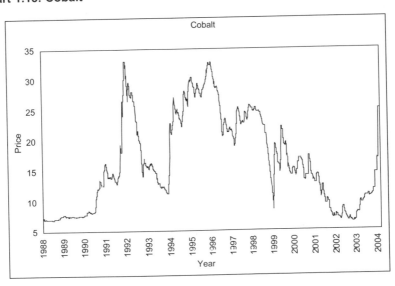

Source: Datastream

Tungsten

A metal with a broad array of uses, many of them strategic, tungsten is an object lesson in the problems that can occur in minor metals. Tungsten has a number of important properties including having the highest melting point of any metal, being exceptionally hard and also extremely heavy. This means that it is the favoured metal to be used in high temperature applications such as light bulb filaments, and as tungsten carbide is used extensively in cutting and drilling tools. It is also used widely in the armaments industry in the manufacture of armour plating and ammunition.

From time to time tungsten, which is mined in the form of *scheelite* or *wolframite* ore, is subject to sharp price fluctuations as is common with minor metals. The tungsten price is measured in metric tonne units (MTUs). In the mid 70s, a time of high international political tension and high inflation, tungsten sold at $175/MTU. Over the next 15 years it slithered lower and lower until in the early 90s it touched $25, before recovering to $45 later in the decade, and it remains around that price today. The price of the metal is materially affected by the large strategic stockpiles held by the US, Russia (and the old CSI states), and China. With western production held back by the poor long term price record a large deficit of demand over new mine supply is common. However, despite comments over the years that stockpile material must be close to exhaustion or of too low a quality to be of interest to consumers, the drawdown of stocks continues to hold back the tungsten price.

Betting on the tungsten overhang

Intermittently mining companies with tungsten interests come to the fore. In the 70s it was Australia's Peko Wallsend which amongst its diversified interests owned the King Island Scheelite mine, and for a time did extremely well from the high metal prices reigning then. More recently the small UK mining group Avocet built up a portfolio of tungsten mining and marketing interests on the back of expectations that stockpile disposals were coming to an end and that the mined supply deficit would lead to a sustained improvement in the tungsten price. The price rise did not come through as Chinese material in particular continued to reach western markets and Avocet was forced to shut down a substantial part of its tungsten operations and eventually sell the rest. Its own situation was made worse by problems at its Malaysian gold mine (now overcome) at a time of gold price weakness.

The lesson that tungsten teaches us is that even the most closely watched metal markets can fail to give up key secrets, and that intelligent and detailed research, as has been available on tungsten for many years, can give the wrong guidance if it is based on incomplete figures. Those who supported Avocet came very close to losing everything as the shares plummeted from around 160p in 1997 to 11p in 2002 when it abandoned its main UK listing and moved to AIM. Avocet added insult to injury when, having re-invented itself as a focused gold miner, it froze existing small shareholders out of an attractive financing in 2003 by changing the percentage of shares it could issue to outside investors without an open offer to shareholders, a ploy that is reaching epidemic proportions amongst small miners. As for tungsten, in the longer term it may well be that the metal overhang will finally disappear and the price rise substantially, but whether one would want to bet on it is another matter.

Table 1.15 - Tungsten statistics (2003)

	Mine production (Tonnes metal)	Mine reserves (Tonnes metal)
Austria	1,400	10,000
Canada	3,000	260,000
China	49,500	1,800,000
Russia	3,400	250,000
Others	2,300	580,000
Total	**59,500**	**2,900,000**

Source: US Geological Survey

Chart 1.16: Tungsten

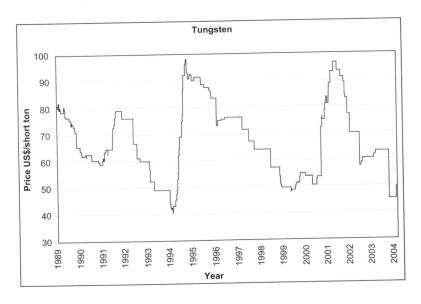

Source: Datastream

Magnesium

We have included magnesium in this review of minor metals because picking the major metals of the future - and magnesium may be one of them - can be enormously rewarding, especially as changes of status amongst metals happen sparingly and gradually. It is also the case that new metals, in the form of newly discovered elements, are extremely rare so an upwardly mobile minor metal will certainly be already known to metal markets. Magnesium has been in commercial use for decades. Its main usages now are in aluminium alloying, iron and steel , and in die-casting, with the motor industry being the main consumer here. It also has a number of other uses in chemicals and wrought products.

A future major metal?

Its prospective role as a future major metal relates to its combination of lightness and malleability. In the past it has been well known for its uses in relieving stomach ailments in the form of milk of magnesia, and in flash bulbs, flares and fireworks, but these are now hardly growth areas. Interestingly it was used by the German car industry in the 30s in the manufacture of engine blocks where its lightness combined with great stability when hot was of particular benefit. That usage, however, died out after World War II and has only relatively recently been revived. One of the metal's growth areas is magnesium sheet metal which is used increasingly in the manufacture of products such as computer casings, digital cameras and mobile phones. It is entirely possible that other, and perhaps more substantial uses will be found for magnesium sheet metal, with car bodies a prime long term target.

Currently the major producers of magnesium are China, western smelters, and Russia and the ex CIS. Of course amongst these three are our old problem children, China and Russia/ex CIS, who so often seem to have surplus metal available when supply tightness threatens, although the latter is only a small producer of magnesium. China, however, is a very large force producing 51% of the world's primary magnesium against 40% coming from western smelters. (The difference between this figure and the one in the following table relates to the fact that magnesite production statistics are used not magnesium. Magnesite goes into magnesium compounds such as oxide used primarily in making refractory products and in agriculture and construction. Magnesium metal is used in alloying aluminium products and also in car and machinery components). Over the last five years western primary production has fallen by half, the resulting market gap being filled entirely by China, demonstrating once more that country's ability to provide substantial new sources of at least minor metals, if the need arises.

The secret for magnesium's future appears to be the application of appropriate treatment technology to new projects. The consequent ability to scale up production at low cost and provide significantly increased supply is particularly exciting in the light of the potential of the sheet metal sector. Two listed Australian magnesium developers, Magnesium International and Australian Magnesium, have been working on two new magnesium deposits for some years, the former with more success than the latter. Could one of these Cinderellas be in the right place at the right time?

Table 1.16 - Magnesite statistics (2003)

	Mine production (Tonnes metal)	Mine reserves (Tonnes metal)
Austria	200,000	15,000,000
China	1,100,000	380,000,000
North Korea	290,000	450,000,000
Russia	300,000	650,000,000
Turkey	580,000	65,000,000
Others	870,000	640,000,000
Total	**2,980,000**	**2,200,000,000**

Source: US Geological Survey

Note: The tonnes metal refers to the amount of magnesium metal present in the ore

Chart 1.17: Magnesium

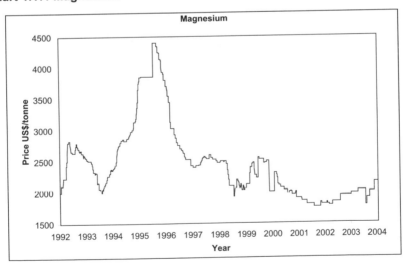

Source: Datastream

Other minor metals

Amongst the other minor metals where publicly listed mining companies have, or have had, significant exposure are manganese, molybdenum, chrome, titanium, cadmium, and antimony. Occasionally there can be an uplift of interest in some of these metals, and both molybdenum and antimony have sparkled in the past. Despite this interest any investor would have to have a high level of knowledge, either of the minor metal or of the mining company involved, to make it worthwhile to have a go in what is a highly specialised area. The level of information attached to one of the major metals like gold and to the big diversified mining groups is extensive; whereas minor metals and their miners are far less easy to follow. We will return later to the issue of information and how well mining is served in this area.

It can also be argued that when the mining sector is having an extended run, as it did in the early 70s and the mid 80s, minor metals as a group will tend to run later in the cycle than their 'elders and betters'. So a promising story may not come to the fore until insiders have positioned themselves and the circumstances are ripe for wider dissemination of the story. It may then be that more general investor attention to a minor metal situation, will come too late for newcomers to make much money if any at all, and that all they will be doing is providing an exit for the insiders. Elements of this were observable in the recent tantalum rise and fall. A great deal of caution is, therefore, required in becoming involved in the minor metal sector.

Non-metals

Energy minerals

The scope of this book does not include oil and gas, huge subjects in their own right, but the main energy minerals which are mined, coal and uranium, have a major position in the world of mining.

We have also left out tar sands, that gluey half liquid, half mineral substance rich in trapped oil, where a possible long term industry is in the making in Canada. Tar sands have been around for many years and progress in economically processing the substance has been the subject of huge amounts of research and development spending, and more of the same is still needed. I have also ignored oil shales, conceptually similar to tar sands and needing further research on the issue of optimising the economics of treatment, although there is some commercial production in Australia.

Coal

Coal is found in virtually every country in the world and a century ago it was the prime source of energy fuelling the rapidly expanding electricity industry, the economically dominant iron and steel industry, and also the heating of homes worldwide. Today the power stations that produce electricity can as easily be fired by oil, natural gas, hydro-dynamics and nuclear as by coal, and there is an increasing green element in electricity production in the form of wind and sea power. The iron and steel industries, although still important, no long occupy the commanding heights of the global economy and coal fired furnaces are now just one way of making steel. Heating homes with coal is now a very minor practice in this age of oil and gas central heating, particularly in the advanced world, indeed domestic coal fires are now being marketed as a *designer concept* in the UK.

Main producers

The main coal producers are China, Russia, the US, Poland, Australia, Colombia, and South Africa, the latter three being substantial exporters as well; but many other countries also produce coal, often for domestic power station consumption. The world's leading diversified mining companies, the UK big four, are all major coal producers, with Rio Tinto being the biggest in terms of turnover.

Coal is produced both from underground mines, some of which are relatively shallow drift mines, and opencast surface mines. Over the years coal has acquired a somewhat negative image with some deep level underground mining having a poor safety record, with additional health risks from airborne coal dust, and surface mining often being portrayed as environmentally damaging.

Coal like so many commodities is subject to cyclical fluctuations, and the links with electric power and steel make it particularly sensitive to economic growth rates. This cyclicality is, therefore, relatively straightforward to monitor and often manifests itself, for example, in the sometimes vigorous price contract negotiations between the Australian coal producers and their prime customers, the Japanese steel producers and electricity utilities.

Independently quoted coal producers disappearing due to industry rationalisation

Some years ago there were a number of interesting independently quoted coal stocks in South Africa, Australia, the US and Canada. If you were able to read the coal cycle, trading the stocks was often very rewarding and they were all accustomed to paying out good dividends. One of the most interesting of these cyclical vehicles was South Africa's Amcoal controlled by Anglo American, then a South African registered company. Amcoal itself had been formed in 1975 from four listed and four unlisted coal companies. It had large export contracts priced in US dollars but had local SA rand costs, and its dividend record was progressive despite the cyclical nature of the industry. In due course Anglo American acquired the whole of Amcoal's capital and the company disappeared from the stock market.

This kind of rationalisation became a global trend and other independently quoted coal producers were also taken over by the diversified giants. In the end the strong distributable cash flows of the coal producers became too juicy a target for the big diversifieds to ignore, and very few coal companies remain separately listed, with just a couple of any size in the US, Peabody and Arch. The stock market abhors a vacuum and at least one new but small South African coal company was looking to float in London in 2003. However, for the moment coal remains a mineral where investors will find it difficult to participate directly, without being in a diversified company like Anglo American, or Xstrata whose historically prominent coal earnings will be diluted by other metal interests following the acquisition of MIM.

Chart 1.18: Coal

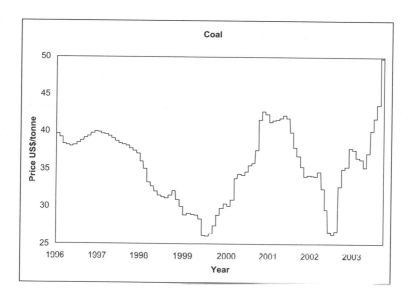

Source: Datastream

Uranium

Energy minerals, including oil, can be highly controversial. Their use is often judged to damage the environment, the mining of them can be both dangerous and also lead to pollution, and in the case of uranium there is the added hazard of risk to health from exposure to radiation as well as the problem of disposing of nuclear waste which is highly toxic.

By far the largest customer for uranium is the electric power generating industry, although it has become very difficult to get planning permission to build new nuclear power stations anywhere due to environmental lobbying. France has the largest exposure to nuclear power as a percentage of its generating capacity. On the whole though the expansion of nuclear power has ground to a halt and few believe that in today's climate it has much of a long term future.

At one time in the early 70s at the end of the Australian nickel boom, as mentioned earlier, uranium discoveries in the Northern Territory ignited a new flurry of excitement first in the shape of Queensland Mines and later Pancontinental Mining. A large amount of money was made and then lost as these promising discoveries fired a speculative mini boom. The boom finally broke on the rock of worries about long term uranium demand and local political obstruction, not to mention in the case of Queensland a rather over-optimistic assessment of the richness of its discovery.

The oil price crisis of the mid to late 70s also prolonged interest in uranium. Then the need was to find cheap sources of power for the beleaguered advanced economies who felt they were too reliant on oil from a region, the Middle East, that was both unstable and unfriendly. For a while nuclear power fitted the bill. Now that sense of crisis has passed and with it the need for the nuclear solution. It is unlikely that uranium will feature again as a stock market star, although Chinese demand may yet surprise us and spark a revival of interest. Indeed in early 2004 the spot uranium price had reached a 7 year high of $16.20/lb. There are a few listed uranium mining companies about; Cameco, Denison Energy and WMC Resources are three but most uranium companies, due to necessity, have other strings to their bows and therefore are not pure plays for the bold investor.

Chart 1.19: Uranium

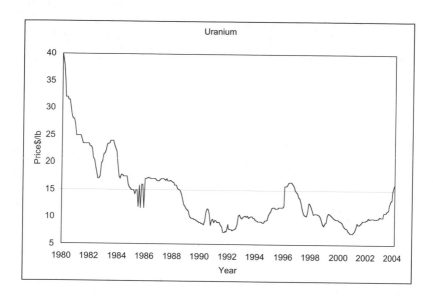

Source: Datastream

Industrial minerals

The last broad category we will look at is industrial minerals. This sector could also include minerals such as sand and gravel, limestone and clay, but these raw materials are most closely associated with the building industry and their value added is often minimal. In addition producers appear in construction share portfolios not in mining portfolios, so they have been left out.

Industrial minerals are often found in the form of 'soft' ore, i.e. crumbly and in many cases having the consistency of sand. These minerals can be used in the manufacture of chemicals such as fertilisers (sulphur, potash and phosphates) or products such as ceramics (zirconium sand), detergents (borax), and oil industry drilling mud (barytes). One of the fastest growing minerals in this general category 30 years ago was asbestos, which had wide application in building, protective clothing, car parts and paper. Today its use is heavily controlled and demand has fallen sharply. It is rarely used in the West, but production and consumption in countries such as China and Russia remains quite healthy.

In the past this area of mining has attracted sporadic investor interest, but it shares many of the same problems with regard to information, and transparency in pricing the minerals, as minor metals. Many of them are, like coal, sold on the basis of fixed contract prices, although these do vary over time and are affected by new producers and the economic cycle. It is not unknown for mining companies to build their long term structures on these bulk minerals. Freeport Sulphur and Texas Gulf Sulphur of the US both became large diversified mining groups on the back of the cashflows generated by their traditional sulphur operations. Texas Gulf in the end was taken over by Elf Aquitaine Oil in 1981 and Freeport eventually broke itself up and distributed its operating parts to shareholders in the 80s.

Because these minerals are often mined/produced in substantial quantities, tens of millions of tonnes in the case of sulphur and phosphates for example, relatively small price adjustments can have a significant effect on a company's profits. But some of these minerals also display greater stability in terms of generating profits than the more glamorous precious and base metals, and Rio Tinto, for instance, has had occasion to thank its unglamorous but steady US Borax operations for countering weak base metal returns a number of times in the past. However, taken all in all I think that, as with most minor metals, the ability of investors to do well out of industrial minerals situations is limited.

Gold

We believe that gold is such a key part of the mining sector that it deserves a section all to itself. Its history is littered with world shattering events like the gold rushes of the 19th century in the US, Canada and Australia; and one of that century's most vicious wars, the Boer War, was ignited by British determination to control the new gold mines of South Africa. Centuries before, the Spanish had raped and pillaged their way through Central and South America in pursuit of gold and silver and the fabled city of Eldorado. Some of the most dramatic stock market scams have centred around gold and some of the greatest triumphs too. In everyday language we use gold allusions like "heart of gold", "good as gold", "it's a gold mine", "safe as Fort Knox" (where the US gold hoard is stored), and "gold plated" to describe situations in approving tones. Banks also issue gold credit and debit cards to particularly well-heeled customers. Yet until recently gold has seemed to sink into a coma, attracting little general interest, sustained only by a tight group of supporters whose knowledge of gold's history, and its frequent relapses, encourages them to exercise patience certain in the knowledge that gold will eventually revive.

Chart 1.20: Long term chart of the gold price

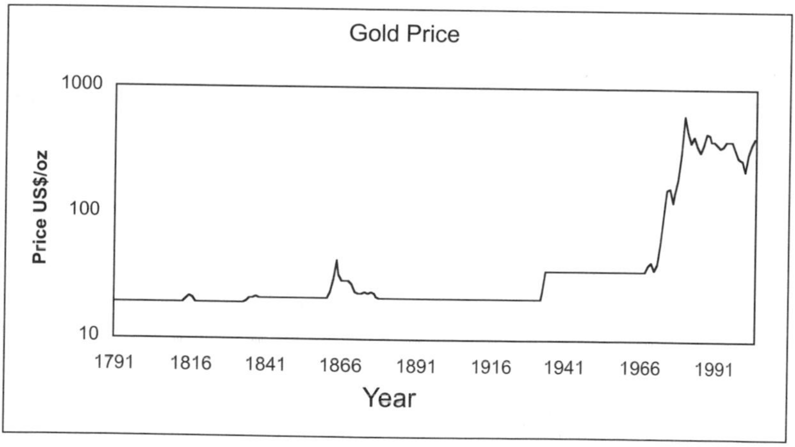

Source: Datastream

Monetary gold

The subject of gold is a large one and over the years many books have been written about the metal which John Maynard Keynes described as a "barbarous - relic". In the 19th century, and for part of the 20th, gold was at the centre of the monetary system because of the gold standard. For centuries it was used as money in the form of coin, and countries stored their monetary reserves in the form of gold bar. In due course gold came to be seen as too heavy, in terms of value, and cumbersome, as commercial activity exploded and personal transactions increasingly required change to be given. Coins using other metals were struck carrying values very much lower than was the case with gold coins, and this provided necessary flexibility for personal transactions. In such an environment the birth of paper was a boon to governments and banks as it enabled them to introduce paper money, although to begin with issued banknotes had to be backed by gold, a requirement long since dispensed with.

The role of central banks

Over the last twenty or so years many (but not all) central banks have begun to sell off their gold reserves and concentrate foreign currency reserve holdings in US dollars, Japanese yen and more recently the Eurozone euro. Included in those central banks who have sold large amounts of gold are the Bank of England (although the decision to sell was taken by the UK government) and the Swiss central bank. Those that have not sold gold, like the effectively defunct German Bundesbank, are thought to have leant out large quantities of their holdings to support the burgeoning derivatives market in gold, of which more later.

However, whilst gold has been downgraded in the international monetary system it has not disappeared completely. The newly formed European Central Bank has a gold component in its reserves, France retains a large gold reserve, and the US has the largest declared gold reserve holding and, perhaps because its currency, the dollar, is the prime reserve currency, it has very little in the way of foreign currency reserves. It is also thought that growing giants like China may be acquiring gold reserves as may Russia, whose gold mining industry, after decades of neglect, is now expanding.

The issue of the future of central bank gold holdings is one that divides opinion. Some gold market observers, including most vociferously Mitsui's London based guru Andy Smith, believe long term that gold will, like silver a century or more ago, disappear from central bank reserves. Other commentators, particularly gold bugs in the US, believe that in time gold will regain its central position in the monetary system as the excesses of money and debt creation over the last twenty years finally undermine the integrity of the system. In the meantime gold, if it is no longer seen as money, is still seen in some quarters as having investment qualities, and its industrial role as the prime precious metal used in jewellery offers steady long term growth potential.

Investing in gold

Our main concern in this book is to steer investors through the mining share market, and the gold share sector has always offered an encouraging number of choices. However private investors in particular have in the past dabbled in physical gold whether by buying gold coins such as *Krugerrands* and *Sovereigns*, or gold in bar form, so a brief mention here is appropriate.

Physical gold

One of the characteristics of gold that makes it an investment vehicle is the fact that it is high value for low weight, as people fleeing revolution with only one (strong) suitcase have found to their advantage. It is also very easy to store as it is very dense, consequently its weight is compacted into a small dimension. So a 400 oz bar measuring, in 'old money', around 7 x 3 x 3 inches, is worth $160,000 (at $400/oz). If you carried the same amount of wealth in the form of copper you would need to plan for a substantial lorry to carry the 50 tonnes - not much good if you're in a hurry to catch the last plane out of Saigon, for example.

Gold broadly can be bought for physical delivery or for storage in a secure warehouse. There are a number of specialist gold and gold coin dealers who will take small orders, although the bullion banks are after wealthy customers only. In the UK in the 70s the clearing banks dealt in gold coins in small numbers for their customers but this service has largely been discontinued. The other method of dealing in gold is through holding *certified gold*. In essence that means that specific gold bars are not allocated to a buyer, but he receives a certificate stating the amount of gold that constitutes the liability of the bank (usually one of the bullion banks) to him.

Gold Bullion Securities

The World Gold Council has launched a new gold investment product, *Gold Bullion Securities*, which is listed on the London Stock Exchange and which should provide smaller, and perhaps also larger, investors with an easy and cheap way of investing in gold. The security is backed by a fixed amount of gold on the basis of one tenth of an oz per share. The gold will exist physically and will be the property of the gold fund shareholders, although there is some debate as to how physical the gold has to be in the hands of the Fund's custodians. Dealing costs are relatively low at 0.5% per trade. The shares are listed in the Financial Times under Speciality and Other Finance and appear to trade at a slight premium to the underlying gold value. The fund of gold was valued at around £100 million in February 2004 and daily volume in value is usually over £2 million. Recently the Council has decided to 'update' the product to make it more attractive to investors. Present holders of the shares will be permitted to switch into shares in the new version when it is launched.

Gold derivatives

Investors in gold can also spice up their exposure by using the derivatives market to obtain greater reward from gold price changes. One route is the purchase of options giving the investor the right to buy (or sell) at a fixed price at some time in the future. The investor puts down a relatively small amount of money to secure the option and if he has bet correctly can enjoy a return far greater than an investment directly in gold itself. Using the options market is, however, very much taking the paper gold route, and there must always be the concern that the counterparty may not be able to honour his side of the trade in extreme circumstances. Although in most cases the option would trade on an exchange and the exchange should guarantee the contract.

There is quite a philosophical divide on the customer side in the gold investment world.

- Some potential investors buy because they think **gold is cheap** and they will make money. They do not intend to hold their gold for ever, and are simply looking for a decent turn on their purchase price. They tend, therefore, to buy gold in certified form which is cheaper than buying specifically allocated gold. It also simplifies the process of buying and selling because a book entry is all that is needed to complete the deal.

- For others, dealing in gold has a much more **mystical significance** and they not only want to deal in physical gold they also want to take delivery and store it themselves. Taking delivery can literally mean having it delivered to the buyer who then holds it in a safe or secretes it somewhere safe; more normally such a buyer will probably put it in a personal bank deposit box. When buying coins it is usual to take personal delivery, and there are also small low weight gold bars or wafers which are mostly purchased for personal keeping.

A matter of trust

The other key point to make about gold is that many investors in gold buy the metal because they no longer trust their government, trust the international financial system, or trust more conventional forms of investment including bank deposits. This latter issue galvanised Japanese citizens to cash in their bank deposits, when government insurance of such deposits was materially scaled down in 2002. In place of their deposits, which under the regime of negligible interest rates were providing little income, many Japanese bought gold bars and coins and took delivery. The withdrawal of government insurance cover came at a time of rising concern about the solvency of Japanese banks, and gold seemed like a solid alternative.

Private investor scepticism about government attitudes to gold is rooted in the past and one example will suffice. In the 30s, as the US government of Franklin Roosevelt grappled with the Depression, it was decided to use gold as a means of bolstering prices at a time of chronic deflation, in particular farm produce prices. To this end the price of gold was raised to $35/oz in 1934. Before that, in 1933, Roosevelt controversially through the Emergency Banking Act ordered all gold, gold coins and gold certificates held by US citizens to be handed in to the Federal Reserve in exchange for paper dollars or dollar deposits. There are various estimates of how much gold actually was surrendered, but any gold known to the authorities, like gold certificates and gold held to customer accounts in banks, would have been automatically handed over. US citizens only recovered the right to own gold in 1975, but in the interim many had clearly bought it and stored it overseas, as the price of gold, strong ahead of the lifting of the ban, fell sharply afterwards as demand failed to materialise.

Gold then has an important role as a safe haven investment and though many governments these days claim to have little or no interest in it, sceptical supporters of gold believe that if financial chaos was to return then the view of governments could easily change. So to avoid the danger of a Roosevelt-style enforced confiscation of gold, the best thing to do is to store your gold yourself. You then have the choice whether to comply with government dictum or not. Of course what you would be doing would be unlawful and there might well be records that could trace the gold purchase back to you. Also if at some time you wanted to sell your gold it would have to be done unofficially with the likely consequence that a discount to the market price would have to be accepted.

What drives gold

Since the great inflation of the 70s and 80s the general investment view has been that gold is a hedge against inflation and that's about it. In fact there are other influences, some financial and some political, which have an historic influence on the gold market, and indeed as we saw above, a period of deflation can also be helpful in certain circumstances.

Although it was the effect of inflation in the 70s that is credited with pushing gold from $35/oz at the start of the decade to $850/oz by January 1980, there were other reasons. Perhaps the most important was the fact that gold had remained fixed at the $35 level since Roosevelt's decision in 1934. The central banks, in effect, as buyers and sellers maintained that price until the US, who had sold their gold reserves down from around 22,000 tonnes after World War 11 to around 8,000 tonnes in 1971, closed their gold sales window. Without central bank intervention the price immediately began to move ahead, a trend that continued for the next ten years. So central bank intervention in the gold market proved in the end to have held back the gold price rather than supported it.

Tension in the Middle East

The effective fixing of the gold price had also inhibited the development of new gold mines, a situation which continued until the 80s. This meant that once the central banks had withdrawn from the market newly mined gold was unable to keep pace with demand, forcing the price higher. The 1973 Arab-Israeli War triggered a major rise in the oil price which had a serious effect on price levels generally, and the rate of inflation, which had been rising for several years, exploded. In such circumstances gold was once more seen as a store of value and a hedge against the falling purchasing power of money. The latter years of the 70s saw further financial and political turmoil. Inflation was still surging along and a string of disturbing events culminated in 1979 with the US Embassy hostage crisis in Iran, and in 1980 with the Soviet invasion of Afghanistan and the Iran-Iraq War. During this time the US dollar was weak against both the German mark and the Japanese yen which further supported the gold price.

The Middle East and near Asia were at flashpoint throughout the period causing great volatility in the oil market and to the oil price. The inflationary implications of a rising oil price and thus the knock-on effect on gold continued to affect the yellow metal's price, and that remains the case to this day, although the actual effect is much less marked now due to investor expectations that any supply threat to oil will be temporary.

Today gold is less affected by political upheavals

Other historic influences have also lost their power to affect the gold price in a sustained manner. The political upheavals of today remain worrying but little of that worry is seen in the gold price. If the World Trade Center had been attacked in the late 70s there would have been a huge rise in the gold price, in 2001 the rise was modest and contained. The actions of the Soviet Union in the gold market were of prime interest to gold analysts in the past, so if there was a good harvest investors would buy gold because gold market supply would be squeezed as the Soviets would not need to sell any of their reserves to fund food imports.

The issue of official sales, which essentially are sales from reserves by central banks, was important in the 70s and 80s and retains its importance today. The difference is that whilst gold demand has risen materially over the years, particularly for jewellery, the combination of the expansion of mine output in the 80s and 90s, which had been stimulated by the 70s price surge and central bank selling and lending, has been effective in capping the gold price. This situation may be changing as demand continues to grow and mine output begins to slip at a time when central bank activity is also showing signs of having peaked.

Chart 1.21: What drives gold?

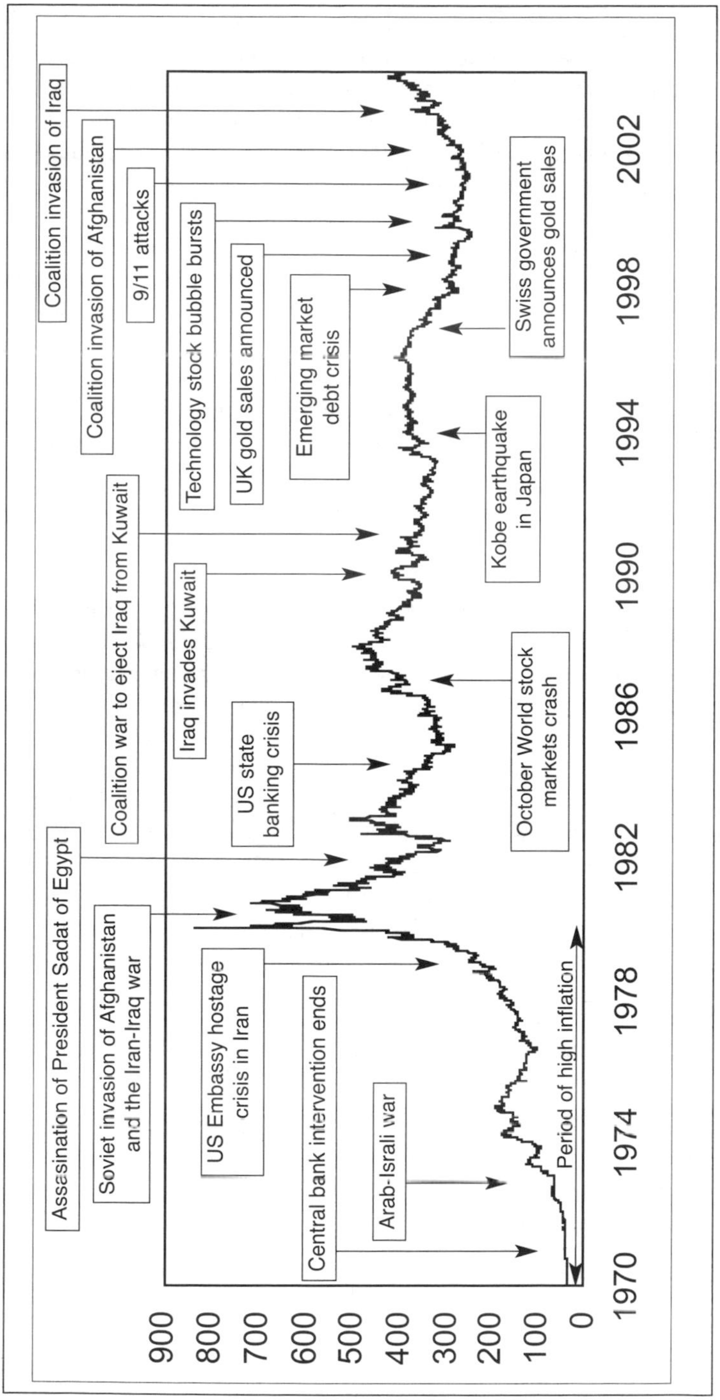

Coalition invasion of Iraq

Coalition invasion of Afghanistan

9/11 attacks

Technology stock bubble bursts

UK gold sales announced

Emerging market debt crisis

Swiss government announces gold sales

Kobe earthquake in Japan

Iraq invades Kuwait

Coalition war to eject Iraq from Kuwait

US state banking crisis

October World stock markets crash

Assasination of President Sadat of Egypt

Soviet invasion of Afghanistan and the Iran-Iraq war

US Embassy hostage crisis in Iran

Central bank intervention ends

Arab-Israli war

Period of high inflation

900
800
700
600
500
400
300
200
100
0

1970 1974 1978 1982 1986 1990 1994 1998 2002

Source: Datastream

Hedging

Hedging, a subject which crops up in other parts of this book, has also had a significant effect on the gold price as mines have often been the final customer for central bank gold lending mentioned above. By borrowing gold and then selling it forward mines are able to lock in a higher future price, the mechanics being that gold borrowing is very cheap and throughout the last decade funds so borrowed could be put on deposit at high interest rates. When the borrowed gold had to be returned the mine could deliver its own gold, keeping the profit it had made on its 'round tripping' of interest rates. Of course this strategy meant that mines were selling hoarded central bank gold as well as their own current production which led to an expansion of supply to the market, and this had a negative effect on the gold price itself. Over time hedging strategies have become highly sophisticated, some would say dangerously so, replacing the initially simple forward sale described above. But with strong signs that hedging is on the wane and central bank selling and lending also much reduced, one of the contemporary gold market's most potent negative influences may reverse itself over the next few years.

Relationship with the US dollar

Perhaps the greatest continuing influence on the gold price has been the US dollar. During the 70s and 80s it was seen as a weak currency against the mark and the yen, the currencies of the then rising economic giants of Germany and Japan, but liquidity in these two currencies was poor and the UK pound, where there was reasonable liquidity, was for the most part as weak as the dollar. Gold was a natural substitute for the greenback, especially when investors realised that it had broken clear of its own imprisonment within the central bank intervention system which lasted from 1934 until 1971. Indeed when Ronald Reagan became US president he strongly believed that the relative economic decline of the US, which could be traced back to the Vietnam War, was mirrored in the weakness of the dollar. Since nothing signified that weakness as clearly to world markets as the countervailing strength of gold, a return to a strong dollar must inevitably lead to the undermining of gold.

Chart 1.22: Gold v Trade-weighted US Dollar

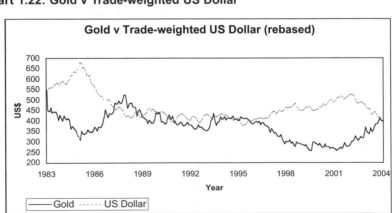

Source: Datastream

So for the last twenty years gold has drifted as the dollar has prospered. In the US there are supporters of gold who believe that over this period the authorities have intervened against gold, lending and selling metal from their own vaults to keep the price low, and even supporting this action in the fast expanding derivatives market. Foremost amongst the groups harrying the US authorities over this issue is the Gold Anti Trust Action Committee (GATA) who believe the weakness in gold has been critical in pointing out the dollar's superiority as a reserve asset. During this extended period of dollar strength the US has, as a consequence, built up a huge deficit on its external account with the rest of the world which now throws into doubt the wisdom of the policy of seeking a strong dollar at any price. With the dollar in retreat the position of gold once more becomes interesting.

Interest rates

Alongside the dollar the level of interest rates is also a consideration when looking at gold as an investment. In the 70s and 80s interest rates were relatively high although inflation was also high which meant that real inflation adjusted rates were not so attractive. In the 90s the rate of inflation initially fell more quickly than did interest rates, with the consequence that real rates began to make cash deposits look attractive. At the same time stock markets were booming everywhere so gold, an investment that paid no interest, looked unattractive. Now that interest rates have fallen back and stock markets have crashed, the opportunity cost of holding gold as an investment is low which has resulted in an increase in interest in gold as an investment. Concern about national, corporate and personal debt levels has also increased interest in gold as a safe-haven alternative to bank deposits as has been the case in Japan.

Chart 1.23: Gold v Interest Rates

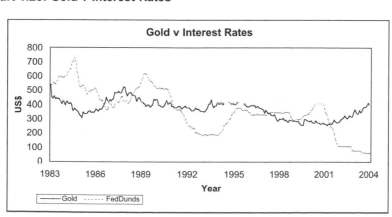

Source: Datastream

Buying gold shares

The threat of getting caught by a sudden ban on owning gold can be avoided by choosing gold shares for one's exposure to the metal. In the 30s US investors did extremely well in gold shares, which enabled them to legally benefit from the rise in the government supported gold price. Those who bought the US's leading gold miner Homestake for exposure to the strong gold price and to hedge against a weak stockmarket would have outperformed both.

The gearing effect of mining shares

One of the great advantages of buying gold shares rather than physical gold is that shares are highly geared to movements in the gold price. By highly geared I mean shares will rise more sharply than the gold price when it moves higher, the opposite being the case, of course, when the gold price falls. This is the result of the effect of marginal gold price gains dropping straight through to the operating profit line. Thus if a gold mine is used to receiving $300/oz for its output and its costs are $250, it will make an operating profit of $50 per oz produced. If the gold price rises $50 to $350, a 17% increase, then the mine's operating profit rises by 100% to $100 per oz. The effect of a $50 increase in the gold price will, of course, depend on the level of a mine's costs, and many mines have costs well below $250 which would mean that the profit gearing to a rising gold price is less than in our example. For instance if our virtual gold mine had costs of $150/oz then the effect of a $50 rise in the gold price would be a 33% increase in operating profits, still twice the rate of the gold price rise.

Opposite are shown two gold shares, Barrick and Bema, plotted against the gold price. Barrick large, expanding and low cost, although still volatile exhibits much lower price volatility than Bema which historically has been a smallish, high cost producer.

Chart 1.24: Barrick Gold Corp [ABX] v Gold

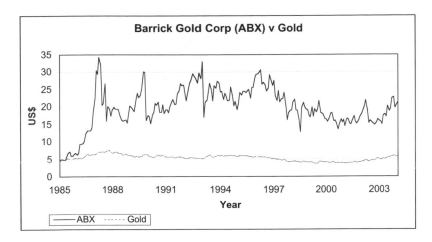

Source: Datastream

Chart 1.25: Bema Gold Corp [BGO] v Gold

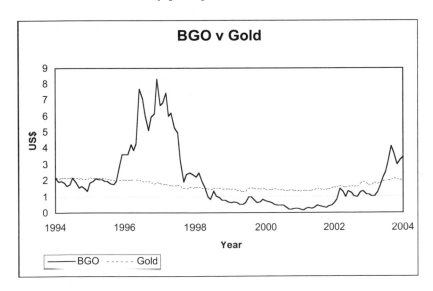

Source: Datastream

Currency factors

The South African gold mining sector provides us with another potentially volatile influence on operating profits which is the dollar/rand exchange rate. The level of the US dollar against the currencies of other big producers like Australia and Canada is also influential but the currency movements tend to be much more modest than those of the South African currency. In recent years we have grown used to seeing the rand depreciate against the dollar which has benefited South African producers whose costs are primarily incurred in local currency. That means that as the rand falls against the dollar a mine's revenue converted into rands will rise even if the dollar price of gold does not change, because gold is sold in dollars. Whilst this is going on, costs which are incurred in rands remain the same. If the gold price rises then mine revenues increase even faster. However, this has never been a one way trend, despite the rand's chronic weakness in the 90s and up until last year, and recently the rand has begun to strengthen materially which has meant that dollar revenues converted into rands have fallen sharply. A rising gold price could mitigate the effect but that cannot be guaranteed.

The controversial issue of hedging

One of the most controversial areas in evaluating gold shares is the extent to which a gold company hedges. The main purpose of hedging is to protect the mine from a catastrophic loss of revenue when gold goes into a cyclical downturn. On the face of it this seems a most sensible thing to do, even if traditional gold share investors tend to want to carry the gold price risk themselves. In the gold boom of the 70s forward selling of gold was confined to the activities of the Winnipeg Commodities Exchange where volumes were thin and the participants were largely market speculators. Arguably the first modern hedging deal was the one contracted by Australia's Pancontinental to develop its Paddington gold mine in Western Australia in the mid 80s. Here the company took out a gold loan from one of the bullion banks where it effectively sold forward gold that it would produce when the mine began to operate. The cost of borrowing gold and selling it to raise mine development capital was far cheaper than taking out a commercial bank loan, and when the loan repayments started they could be made in the form of returned gold from Paddington production.

Since then the gold derivative market has exploded. It has drawn in gold miners, often but by no means always high cost producers, seeking to obtain prices well above the spot market level. It has also attracted non gold miners wishing to exploit the very low borrowing rates on gold to borrow gold and sell it to obtain cash for other investment activities. It is believed that some hedge funds followed this practice, particularly the infamous Long Term Capital Management group. However, in recent years this kind of activity has become less widespread as interest rates on commercial loans have fallen and the gold price has begun to recover.

The gold price rises...and a gold miner nearly goes bust

For gold share investors there is also the complexity of some of the hedge structures put in place by some mines. The 1999 announcement that a group of central banks had agreed to limit their selling of gold had an immediate and positive effect on a languishing gold price, and it soared from the mid $250s to over $300 in a matter of days. What really shocked the market was that two mines in particular, Ghana's Ashanti and Canada's Cambior, almost went bust because of this. The craziness of a gold miner crashing because the price of gold suddenly surged is unarguable until one realises what was going on. In effect some mines had sold all their production forward at prices well below $300, and the structure of their derivative book meant that they were committed to meeting margin calls when the book was in aggregate under water, that is to say that the value of the derivative instruments purchased was below the potential value of the gold yet to be produced.

Whilst all this seems to verge on lunacy, it is likely that part of the explanation for what went on was that the derivative departments of the bullion banks did not understand mining and the mining companies' finance departments did not understand derivatives. Having said that, mines today are much less keen on hedging, some have a policy against the practice, and others, whilst historically committed to hedging, are reducing the scope of their activity. Hedging too has, in many cases, reverted to using what are called plain vanilla hedge strategies. In essence a mine either buy puts or calls which consist of a single payment, betting on the direction of the gold price. Alternatively they could simply sell production for forward delivery with no margin call commitment, thereby locking in an enhanced future price, although one that would not necessarily be above the spot price reigning at the time of delivery.

It is probable that most gold share investors want to retain full exposure to movements in the gold price and not be hedged against a fall in the price. For those gold companies who have management with modern performance-based salary and bonus packages, the volatility of the gold price could play havoc with their rewards. They have in some cases, therefore, collaborated on highly complex derivative structures that aim to preserve a good portion of the upside when gold runs, but also at the same time have in place protections against the possibility of a weakening gold price. Such structures are complex and are not without risk as Ashanti found out. One may also suspect that the way the 1999 crisis was resolved underlines the profitable nature of the gold derivative business to the bullion banks, and the desperate need for them not to see any gold miner go under due to its hedge book. If that had happened the gold derivatives industry would probably have been terminally damaged.

And then there's politics

The other problem that a gold share investor could face is major, politically driven, changes to gold mining on a national basis. There have been many examples of this over the years, and in South Africa black empowerment, apartheid reparations and the introduction of royalties on turnover are but the latest example of how governments can spoil the party for investors. In the early 90s the Australian gold mining industry lost its tax free status having staged a remarkable recovery since the near disappearance of the industry in the 70s. That successful journey back from the dead was too much for the Australian government to leave alone.

There is also the issue of security of the investor's holding. In the apartheid era the subject of nationalising the South African gold mining industry was discussed by the Nationalist Government on more than one occasion, the industry being primarily under the control and ownership of the mistrusted 'English' South Africans rather than the Afrikaners. The power of the 'English' mining houses, however, won the day, but taxes were always hefty, with the effective rate being as high as 65% for the most profitable mines. Since World War II, mining companies have seen assets in Cuba and Chile expropriated without compensation, and part-nationalisation in Zambia eventually ruin the copper industry. On top of these obvious negatives, which frankly are by no means exclusively a problem for mining companies, gold or otherwise, there are the problems of poor management and in the case of the famous Bre-X scam, problems relating to, at best, inattentive and distant management.

For some, the gold mine sector, despite the huge rewards that some have garnered from investing in it, is just too speculative. If the gold price is going up then the right approach for such investors is to buy the metal direct and perhaps spice up their exposure by buying options, again in the metal. The real gearing in a gold bull market, despite the snags, though lies in the gold share market, and many of those snags can be avoided or mitigated by close observation of what is going on in the sector as a whole.

Gold shares in the stock market cycle

Gold shares have an important role in hedging a broad equity portfolio, although these days few equity strategists ever give gold another thought when it comes to weighting asset classes. The claim made by gold share investors is that when industrial equity markets are in retreat gold, and therefore gold shares, are often going in the opposite direction. Certainly this was true during that extraordinary period between 1972 and 1975 when equity markets, on the back of a sustained oil price explosion and subsequent rampant inflation, collapsed, with the UK market for example falling 74% over that period.

Chart 1.26: UK Financial Times Gold Index [FTGMD] v FTSE All-Share [ASX]

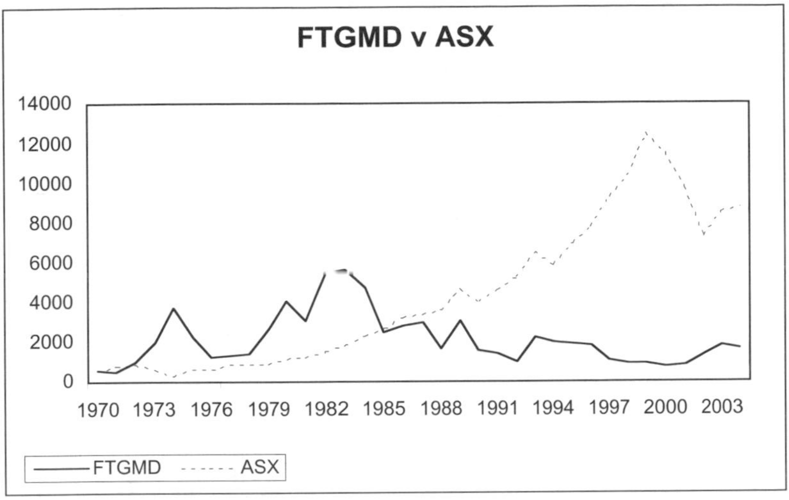

Source: Datastream

Despite tight UK exchange controls then, which meant that UK investors had to buy investment currency (the so-called *dollar premium*) to invest overseas, often at a substantial premium to the sterling spot currency rate, London was the acknowledged global centre for mining securities trading. For UK stockbrokers at this time that was just as well because the collapse of prices and volumes in the UK stock market meant that broker revenues were desperately thin. Fortunately, all the largest brokers and some of the smaller ones had dedicated mining coverage which saved many from financial ruin. It is not clear today, if a similar situation occurred, whether the mining sector, even if it did run counter cyclically, would be able to bail out the securities industry. Certainly the short 2001/02 gold boomlet, which coincided with a sickening fall in industrial equities, suggests not, with many large and small brokers unable to offer even basic gold sector advice.

Gold is inversely correlated with the broad equity market...usually

However, the gold share sector is not solely negatively correlated with the broad equity market, because it can also run strongly when the whole market is rising as happened in the mid 80s. This may sound as if I am trying to claim almost divine status for gold shares, but I am also realistic enough to accept that there are many times when the equity market has risen without gold shares participating in the rise. One could say, though, that there is plenty of support for a view that when ordinary equities plunge gold shares can outperform significantly. Whilst 1973/4 is the most dramatic example of this phenomenon, much more recently we saw the gold share sector racing ahead in 2001/2 as equity markets crashed. Paradoxically, as an added confusion, the market crash of October 1987 brought mining, including gold, shares down as fast as industrial shares.

Chart 1.27: Long term UK Financial Times Gold Index

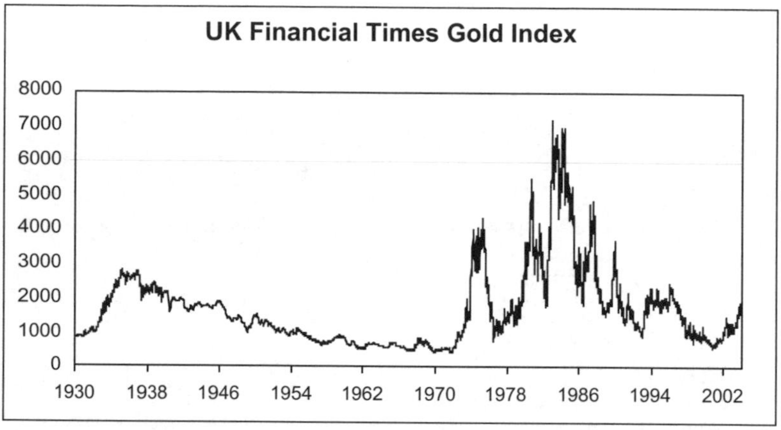

Source: Datastream

The legendary Julian Baring, Head of James Capel's mining team in the 70s and 80s, who we met at the beginning of the book, saw gold shares in the same terms as an insurance policy on your house. You do not buy buildings insurance because you expect your house to burn down, but rather you take it out against the faint possibility that such a disastrous event might happen, because if it did it would have the potential to wipe you out financially. Gold shares have the potential to provide an investor with counter cyclical growth, a tremendous boost to a portfolio when every other sector may be in retreat.

But gold shares have two keys advantages conceptually over straight buildings insurance, they can grow in value over time and also provide an income flow through dividends. It is, of course, the case that gold shares can, when the precious metals cycle turns down, also shed value as fast as they gained it as the cycle unfolded on the upside. As has been said before the need to keep an eye on mining share profits and secure them in due course is not unique to the sector, but the nature of gold shares as a long term wasting asset makes such attention essential.

What do you buy?

Gold shares, as pointed out above, are a classic wasting asset. Mines, and oil fields, once production has depleted them, tend to shut down because the economics no longer work. There may be some mineralised material left, but without further discoveries of substantial additional ore or a sharp rise in the metal price, gold in this case, it may be decided that the capital for expansion could be better spent elsewhere.

There are two broad categories of gold shares these days.

1. There are the **growth orientated** groups like Canada's Barrick Gold who seek primarily to use shareholder earnings to expand the business either through new mines or through increasing output from existing operations.

2. In contrast, there are those groups like South Africa's Harmony Gold which, interested though it is in expanding the group, is also aware that **dividends** are important as a tangible reward to shareholders for the group's success.

Feeding into these broad categories are the smaller, often single mine companies, common in the past but rather superseded by today's philosophy of diversification, and the gold exploration companies. These latter companies are, of course, seeking to become the producers of tomorrow, and hope is a major driver of their market performance. Having usually no production of their own they are reliant on speculative shareholder capital to fund their search for gold, although some of the highly regarded explorers can often get their expenses paid by large producers in joint venture arrangements.

The role of mining houses in South Africa

In the past, when the South African gold mining industry dominated western production, the emphasis for shareholder returns was the dividend. The industry worked through half a dozen or so mining finance houses like Anglo American who in their turn ran a number of individual gold mines which they had initially financed and then floated on the stock exchange. There were, no more than ten years ago, around forty individually quoted South African gold shares - some had substantial ore bases and reasonable gold grade which put them in the long life/low cost category, while others were rather the reverse with a low gold grade and a short life/high cost profile. The idea was that if the gold price went up, as it did in the mid 70s, more ore would come in to play and alter for the better the profile of marginally profitable mines in particular. The issue of new mines was the responsibility of the mining houses who had an extensive exploration programme aimed at finding new gold resources. The South African tax system drove the industry's structure as the mining houses were able to charge exploration as a pre-tax expenditure. Individual gold mines had a unique margin related tax and lease charge system, which meant that only exploration done on the gold mine's individual lease was allowable. For years outside exploration spending had to be carried out by the controlling mining houses themselves not by group gold mines. In this way the houses also had a steady stream of new gold mines to bring to market.

Size matters

In recent years the gold mining industry worldwide has changed structurally. Emphasis is now placed on gold companies building up production to what has become the magic 1 million oz per year mark. Membership of various gold share indices around the world is now driven by annual production levels, and institutional investors still interested in gold will often only look at large producers and 300,000 ozs is often the cut-off. Some of the larger producers are listed in the following table. These large producers tend to sell at a premium to their smaller peers because of this institutional support. However, these large producers do not have the same gearing to the gold price, or to new discoveries, or gold price related increases in production.

Table 1.17 - Gold shares (March Quarter 2003)

Largest producers	Attrib. Production (ozs)	Cheapest producers	Total cash costs (US$/oz)
Newmont	1,780,500	Randgold Resources	88
AngloGold	1,402,000	Meridian Gold	92
Barrick	1,263,238	Goldcorp	99
Gold Fields	1,072,000	Kingsgate	102
Placer Dome	903,000	Rio Narcea	120
Rio Tinto	765,000	Newcrest	122
Harmony	714,096	Hecla	137
Freeport McM. C&G	579,600	Buenaventura	138
Ashanti *	385,592	Glamis Gold	170
Buenaventura	346,734	Wheaton River	182
Others			
Kinross	335,891	Barrick	194
ARMGold	246,000	Newmont	201
Durban Deep	205,302	AngloGold	210
Avgold	105,021	Gold Fields	225
Randgold Resources	95,368	Ashanti *	208
* 2002			

Source: World Gold Analyst, Financial Mail

In a gold bull market it will still pay the more aggressive investor to look for gold miners which have higher costs than average as their earnings will rise faster than those of low cost producers in percentage terms as the metal price rises. The safest stocks will remain the large diversified gold groups like Newmont, AngloGold, Barrick and Gold Fields, and it is this type of gold stock that falls into the defensive insurance category. In saying this I am differentiating between

1. buying gold shares for exposure to maximum growth in a gold bull market, and

2. having a defensive strategy to hold a core of quality gold shares which act as a counterweight when equity markets are weak but also do well when gold rises.

For those investors who really do have nerves of steel and seek maximum performance, the gold share exploration sector, with luck and skilful stock picking, may well provide the greatest returns, particularly in a bull market. The reason for this is straightforward. Successful exploration companies provide two pricing influences – the potential of the newly discovered mine and the prospects for gold itself. Producers, both large and small, are usually just a play on the gold price, although they, themselves, may well discover new sources of gold as a result of their own exploration efforts. However, it goes without saying that great care is needed as exploration prospects will need to be expertly assessed and many investors may not be confident of their ability to steer their way through exploration reports. It is worth remembering that even experts have been duped by misleading publication of exploration results. Amongst the things that need to be analysed are the configuration, size and grade of the deposit, its geographical location, the geological setting and, of course, the likelihood or otherwise of it being developed given the macro and micro-economic circumstances at the time. We go into these key aspects later in the book.

Gold mine classifications

As a loose guide for newcomers to the gold mine sector the table below shows the broad categories that gold mines come under.

1. We have the **large diversified companies** which have a number of usually large operations and these are very often widely spread geographically.

2. The next category is the **large gold miner** with one very large mine or one core operation which overshadows its other interests.

3. The **smaller category** mines may also have one core operation or a number of small operations, and they may be declining forces due to falling production from ageing mines or growing forces with small but expanding operations.

4. In the **exploration and development** category come those companies, who may be small producers, but whose real future depends either upon a promising exploration programme or the successful development of a gold deposit.

Table 1.18 - Classification of gold mining companies

Classification	Example companies
Large diversified	Newmont, Barrick, AngloGold
Large undiversified	Freeport McMoran, Ashanti, Buenaventura
Smaller	Avgold, Randgold Resources, Peter Hambro Mining
Exploration/Development	Centamin Egypt, Moneta Porcupine, Gold Mines Sardinia

We have shown a few examples of each category but these cannot be taken as recommendations in any way. Indeed in the two junior categories literally scores of different companies could have been used as illustrations; our choices were metaphorically drawn from a hat.

As far as how each category differs from the others when the decision to invest is taken, the issues involved in taking that decision are sometimes complicated. Fairly clear is that if you are intending to create a small core of gold mines in a diversified equity portfolio for risk hedging purposes the **large diversified gold companies** are the obvious choice. At the other end of the scale if you are looking at the gold sector with aggressive intent, i.e. you think the gold price is going to rise sharply, then the smaller stocks tend to perform well.

This latter point, however, is not clear cut as larger producers, particularly if their costs are on the high side, may have gearing to the gold price and rise strongly. Certainly when the gold price began to recover in 2001 the large South Africans like Harmony and Gold Fields (not shown above) led the gold sector recovery.

The big **single mine dominated producers** like Freeport are probably not going to perform much out of line with the big diversifieds. The **smaller producers** may offer some outperformance possibilities, especially if they have large potential resources just requiring a higher gold price before they can be brought to account. As far as the **gold exploration sector** is concerned, a strong gold bull market will increase investors appetite for risk, and if exploration success can be correctly anticipated the upside in the share price of the lucky company could be enormous. This latter point, of course, applies to any mining share not just in the gold sector.

When do you buy?

Timing is probably the most critical element in successful gold sector investing. A gold boom is an awesome event to behold and as I have stressed previously it often occurs when more conventional investment sectors have begun to disappoint. The cyclicality of the sector makes it vitally important that gold share investments are not made around the top of the market, unless the investor knows what is going on and is merely seeking a short term trade, something a few people (very few) did profitably towards the end of the internet bubble in

2000. The inevitability of ultimate decline in the gold share market will almost certainly lead to shares bought at the top and held, being booted out in deep frustration at the bottom of the market.

Since there are very few gold experts in the market, either in broking or fund management, investors will usually have to rely on their own advice for timing. Certainly broad consensus that gold has had its day can be a good indicator that sentiment is about to change for the better. Because a rising gold price often signifies a deteriorating financial/economic background there also is a natural aversion amongst many brokers to gold shares as an investment class and recommending them to their clients. The reason for this is that brokers make their living from trading the broad market, not just a small defensive part of that market, and therefore are reluctant to admit that market prospects are poor enough to push them towards the gold share sector. A glance at the relentless bullishness on the broad market of many general research newsletters aimed at private investors written by UK brokers would illustrate the point. When gold shares have fallen a long way and your broker still advises avoidance, a look at the charts, to check on whether the fall has flattened out and the trend therefore may be spent, is essential. If the gold price, itself, has also been consolidating for an extended period and the pace of the downward fall has clearly been exhausted, a long term buying opportunity may be beckoning.

Dividend yields can be a clue

In the past, dividend yields on South African gold shares were an almost foolproof signal of market tops and bottoms. When gold shares historically have yielded in the 12% to 15% range, as they did in 1977, 1983, 1985, 1989 and 1993, they have been a buy and when they have moved to a single figure yield basis, around 4%, this has signalled a sell. These days, following the major consolidation of the South African gold share sector, there are only a handful of stocks to choose from and full distributions have become a thing of the past. However, some timing guidance is still possible from gold share ratings; obviously a higher than average yield and lower PE, if based on sustainable performance, would be well worth consideration, admittedly something that could well apply to other market sectors.

Currencies – as always, watch the US dollar

Currency movements may also provide some clues to gold timing, although short term changes in the broad trend of the US dollar may send out false signals. In the past a fall in the US dollar has often been accompanied by weakness in the other gold mining country currencies - the Canadian and Aussie dollars and the rand. The strengthening currencies have been the German mark, the yen and the Swiss franc. In such circumstances the weak US dollar stimulates the gold price and gold mine revenues start to rise; since the local currencies are also deteriorating in line with the US dollar the increased revenues fall straight to the bottom line. More recently we have seen the US dollar, after a long bull market, beginning to weaken against the mining country currencies as well as the euro, the yen and the Swiss franc. Because of this, some gold shares in 2003, particularly the South Africans, lagged far behind the rise in the gold price. Having said that, we may be witnessing an aberration in the currency market, and in due course the old 'English speaking' currencies may move back into line with the US dollar. At that stage the strength or otherwise of the US dollar may once more become a lead indicator for gold shares.

The equivocal influence of interest rates

Although some commentators view interest rates as a possible timing indicator I would warn against using them for this purpose without very close thought. The problem is that essentially gold does not yield an income return, so reward comes entirely from increases in its value. So when interest rates are low and falling, the opportunity cost of switching from bank deposits to gold is low, i.e. if you invest in gold you give up only a modest income for switching from your bank deposit account. On the other hand if interest rates are high and rising, the opportunity cost of choosing gold rather than putting your money on deposit may be high. The complication comes when you have interest rates rising in an environment of high inflation, in which case the opportunity cost of holding gold appears high. However since gold is a hedge against inflation this may not actually matter. Also if inflation is factored into the interest rate equation the real inflation adjusted return may not be very high, and may even be negative thereby reducing the real opportunity cost.

Over the long term, spotting sustained increases in money supply can be helpful in ascertaining whether and when gold will start to take notice of the inflationary implications of such continuing monetary stimulus. The short term problem is that if in the broad economy the supply of goods and services is rising at a time of weak demand there is unlikely to be any great increase in price levels as producers of consumer goods will have little or no pricing power. In due course, if monetary stimulus continues, this balance is bound to shift as the combined weight of money created finally begins positively to affect demand for goods and their prices. At this stage inflationary influences are likely to begin to make themselves felt, but, as has been happening over the last couple of years, both Japan and the US have been throwing money at their economies without stimulating inflation. This indicates the possibility of long leads and lags in the time it takes inflation to surface in the broad economy.

Pitfalls and pointers in gold

Many of the principles that underlay investing in mining are common to all sectors - costs of production and finance, grade of ore mined, local/national rules on royalties and taxation and on upstream processing, satisfactory local infrastructure and labour availability, ease of access to markets, and scope to operate flexibly to benefit from good times and survive in bad times. In gold mining there are some helpful pointers to ease the task of stock selection.

Ore grade

The grade of ore in gold mining has been on a sinking trend for many years. In the late 60s when most investors were playing in the Australian nickel mining boom, the gold price was into its third decade of being anchored at $35 and some mines in South Africa still mined grades of 1oz (32gms) of gold to each tonne of ore. In 1971 the gold price was effectively freed and as it soared ore grade fell sharply as mines found that less gold per tonne of ore mined was needed to generate economic revenues.

Today gold mine grades tend at best to be in single figures in grams per tonne, a large open surface mine might be mining and processing ore of a grade no higher than 3 grams per tonne. Grade in underground mines varies but in South Africa with development costs sunk many years ago a grade of 3 to 4 grams could be economic depending on the gold price. A new mine in such an underground environment would probably have to grade around 10 grams.

So investors trying to gauge the likely prospectivity of a new gold discovery would have to base their view at least partly on the deposit's grade. When looking at an exploration situation additional care is needed as very high grades may be reported, but they may not be typical of the whole deposit under investigation. Such grades are described as *bonanza gold*, and when a reserve/resource figure is being compiled these bonanza grades are often arbitrarily ignored to give a more realistic overall grade. The high grade ore does not, however, disappear and when the deposit is finally producing gold, the mined grade, as a result of the bonanza gold, may be higher than the stated reserve figure.

Production costs

Gold mines tend to show their costs as a US dollar per oz figure although some Australian producers rather confusingly use Aussie dollars. The most quoted figure is the operating or production cost figure which does not contain central corporate costs, finance costs or depreciation. Production costs show what it costs to keep the mine going at the most basic level but it is clearly important to account for the other costs as well. Some mines become only marginally profitable in operating terms at times of low gold prices, and disguising central and financial costs which come on top could mislead the unsuspecting investor.

Mines have some flexibility as far as costs go, and the weakness in the gold price since the mid 90s has meant that they have had to exploit this to the full. The strength of the US$ over the period has been helpful as mines in countries like South Africa have costs denominated in the weak local currency which means that costs converted into US$ have fallen even though the gold price has also fallen. This has helped the mines maintain their profit margins. Over the last few years they have had to plan their operations on the back of a gold price which has tended to trade around $300 with $250 as a bottom level, although in 2001 it was close to $350 and in 2003 broke through $400 for the first time for ten years. This move has certainly relieved the pressure on a number of high cost producers whose operating margins have soared as a consequence. The South African producers have unfortunately had to contend with a strengthening Rand/US$ rate which has in part cancelled out the advantage of a higher gold price. Against this volatile background, mines have had to get on top of their production costs and use the low end of the established gold price trading range as the target below which these costs have to be forced. At the same time some producers have become very aggressive in the area of derivatives where they have sought to mitigate part of the cost burden by achieving a gold price above the market spot price through a variety of structures planned for them by the banking industry.

Infrastructure at location

One of gold's particular characteristics, as mentioned before, is that it has a very high value for a very low weight. The significance of this is that it is relatively easy to get the gold to market, a helicopter could be used to ship gold from a very remote mine location on a regular basis. A weekly trip, for example, might see a tonne of gold (32,000 ozs) being transported, or 1.6 million ozs annually, which would constitute a very big mine.

For a base metal such as copper a complex transport infrastructure would be required like the Tanzam railway which takes copper halfway across Africa from the Zambian copperbelt to the port of Dar Es Salaam. Of course the establishment of a mine in a remote location is always a difficult matter as plant, equipment, fuel and other mine supplies have to be brought in, although for some of the bigger items such as plant this is a one-off happening.

Consequently a gold discovery in a remote location is unlikely to be a problem and as long as there is water on or close to the property, which is very often the case even in a very dry environment, the only other issue is the proximity of power. Surprisingly often, power lines are found within a reasonable distance of even quite remote locations.

Geographic location

The importance of where a deposit or mine might be found is not limited to just gold mines but it is nonetheless critical in evaluating a gold prospect. In some countries like Zimbabwe it is relatively easy to explore for and develop a mine, even in these difficult times. The problem is that the price that a mine can sell its gold for is controlled by the Government. This happens also in China, where permission to develop a mine is not always straightforward. In Greece, although there is a format for obtaining mining permission, of two major gold mines planned in the 90s one has had to be abandoned for environmental reasons and the other one, the Sappes project of Greenwich Resources, backed by the Government, continues to struggle to secure local support. In Argentina Canada's Meridian Gold, having acquired the promising Esquel gold project, which is strongly backed by state and central government, has encountered very strong local opposition over the twin issues of potential water pollution and spoiling of an area of natural beauty. There are, however, countries where the establishment of a gold mine still continues to command all round support for the jobs and wealth it creates, Mali in eest Africa and Tanzania in east Africa are two such countries.

Table 1.19 - Gold statistics (2003)

	Mine production (Tonnes metal)	Mine reserves (Tonnes metal)
Australia	275	5,000
Canada	165	1,300
China	195	1,200
Indonesia	175	1,800
Peru	150	200
Russia	180	3,000
South Africa	450	8,000
United States	266	5,600
Others	744	16,900
Total	**2,600**	**43,000**

Source: US Geological Survey

Concluding on Gold

Gold generates more emotion than the rest of the metal sector put together. It has its supporters and its detractors, not all of whom are rational. Despite that, gold shares rate, in my view, a position in every portfolio. However, they seldom attract much attention, beyond a professional core of followers, until crisis hits the financial system sending conventional investments like ordinary equities crashing and investors panicking into last resort assets of which gold is perhaps the best known.

The gold story is not always straightforward, and dichotomies such as the bullish effect on gold historically of both inflation and deflation can confuse. Some understanding, though, of how gold interacts with more mainstream assets is worth having as correctly applied it can help to lift relative performance and boost personal wealth.

2. Mining Markets

Having taken the decision to participate in the mining sector the investor has a number of decisions to make, the first relating to the market in which he wants to invest. What is meant by that is the desirability of one market over another in terms of investment products available and the statutory standing of the market in its country context. Fortunately the main mining share markets are all satisfactory from this point of view which enables the investor to concentrate on issues such as service, costs and convenience.

Some investors may be nervous of investing in overseas markets because of the perceived currency risk and prefer to confine their mining investments to UK stocks. In fact, as has been said before, there is always a currency risk in any UK mining stock where, as they usually are, the operations are overseas. This, of course, applies to any UK company with sizeable overseas business (most of the Footsie for instance). Indeed it could be argued that currency rate changes are often very gradual and the effect on earnings is often mitigated by other influences such as rising revenues. Also where the investor is taking an aggressive stance on the mining sector and buying a small speculative share, this action in itself implies far more risk than longer term changes in currency rates. Having said that not all foreign markets, even within the mining-experienced English speaking ones that primarily concern us here, are exactly the same and this should be borne in mind when trading.

London

As things currently stand most of the world's largest mining groups are now incorporated and listed in the UK and are FTSE100 stocks. There are also a number of medium sized UK incorporated miners and a rather larger number of small UK incorporated mining companies. As well as these there are mining companies which are, to all intents and purposes, UK companies but which are incorporated in a UK offshore environment like the Channel Islands. UK (and UK offshore) incorporated mining companies with a full listing appear on the following table.

Table 2.1 - UK mining companies with full listing on the LSE

Anglesey Mining	Greenwich Resources
Anglo American	Lonmin
Anglo Pacific	Randgold Resources
Antofagasta	Rio Tinto
BHP Billiton	UK Coal
Bisishi Mining	Vedanta
	Xstrata

Note: The above companies are incorporated in a UK jurisdiction (UK or Channel Islands); companies with their main listing in the UK but incorporated outside the UK (Aquarius Platinum) are not included.

The UK mining sector is officially represented as one of the FT Actuaries Industry Sectors which are published in the Financial Times each day; the mining sector contains nine stocks. The FTSE series also includes a separate Gold Mines Index containing 18 companies (see following table), all but one foreign, and that index sub divides into separate indices for Australasia, Africa and the Americas.

Table 2.2 - FTSE Gold Mines Index

Company	Country of incorporation
AngloGold	South Africa
Ashanti	Ghana
Avgold	South Africa
Barrick	Canada
Buenaventura	Peru
Cambior	Canada
Durban Deep	South Africa
Gold Fields	South Africa
Goldcorp	Canada
Harmony	South Africa
IAMGold	Canada
Kinross	Canada
Lihir	Papua New Guinea
Meridian Gold	Canada
Newcrest	Australia
Newmont	USA
Placer Dome	Canada
Randgold Resources	UK

There are also a number of foreign mining companies with listings in the UK. Some of these are very historic as in the case of the South African gold mines which are also very much secondary ones now, and there may be other listings elsewhere. In recent years we have seen a new kind of London listing on AIM where primarily Australian mining companies seek a secondary listing to raise capital from UK investors but retain their Australian incorporation. Listed in the following table are the current mining stocks with an AIM listing; it should be remembered, however, that the list is expanding rapidly. A number of mining companies are also listed on OFEX.

Table 2.3 - Mining companies listed on AIM (Mar 2004)

African Diamonds	Eurasia	Ocean Resources
African Eagle	Eureka	Oxus
African Gold	European Diamonds	Palladex
American Mineral Fields	Firestone Diamonds	Palmaris
Angus & Ross	First Quantum	Patagonia Gold
Avocet Mining	GMA Resources	Peter Hambro Mining
Bema Gold	Galahad	Petra Diamonds
Brazilian Diamonds	Golden Prospect	Portman Mining
Bullion Resources	Gold Mines of Sardinia	Reefton Mining
Caledon Resources	Griffin Mining	St Barbara Mines
Cambrian Resources	HPD Exploration	Southern African
Cambridge Minerals	Hereward Ventures	Southern Era
Celtic Resources	Hidefield	Tiger Resource
Centamin Egypt	Highland Gold	Tertiary Minerals
Central African Mining	Jubilee Platinum	Thistle Mining
Cluff Mining	Mano River	Trans Siberian Gold
Conroy Diamonds	Marakand Minerals	Water Hall
Consolidated Minerals	Monterrico Metals	Yamana Gold
Dwyka Diamonds	Murchison	ZincOx

Note: The above AIM listed companies are not all incorporated in the UK, neither is their AIM listing necessarily their prime listing.

Despite the revival of London as a leading centre for mining the sector is not particularly well regarded by the local broking community, something which we touched on earlier and which we will be going into later on. Despite that the London market is a well regulated one, with good investor protection, and the legislative base (including taxation) which rules the activities of UK mining companies is considered both reasonable and secure. Investors can therefore be reassured that investments made in UK mining companies are safe from the point of view of local incorporation and stock market. But in saying this we cannot obviously guarantee that the overseas mining operations of the companies would be protected *in extremis*, say in the event of nationalisation or of radical changes to how a local industry operates.

The other thing to bear in mind is that the current investment research culture in London is to talk up pan-European investment as the concept of the future. Whether that will prove the case or not, it does tend to deflect attention, when looking at British business activity overseas, away from mining which is mainly an activity outside Europe. Despite that, the UK mining sector is back to a size that demands respect.

Chart 2.1: FTSE350 Mining [UB04] v FTSE All-Share [ASX]

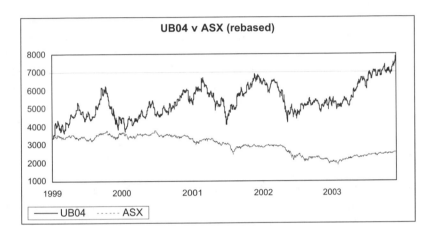

Source: Datastream

Johannesburg

Over the last ten years it could be argued that Johannesburg has lost out to London as mining companies have re-located to the City. It has also lost out to the US in terms of influencing mining share price levels, certainly in the area of gold shares, due to the high level of SA gold share ownership in the US. Although South Africa remains a major mining country it has lost some ground, as mentioned earlier, to North and South America and to Australia and other Far Eastern countries. It also lists significantly less mining companies on the stock exchange than formerly, and of those left, important ones like Anglo American and BHP Billiton only maintain a secondary listing in Johannesburg. Nevertheless the JSE Securities Exchange in conjunction with the FTSE have a number of indices covering mining. In the main index series there is Resource 20 Index covering the biggest mining stocks and a broad index simply named Resources. This latter index is sub divided into Mining, Diamond, Gold Mining, Platinum, Other Mineral Extraction and Mines, Mining Finance and Oil & Gas.

However, the decline cannot be laid at the door of the Johannesburg exchange itself. I am also satisfied that national law and local regulation are reasonably satisfactory as they relate to the operations of the stock exchange, and thus to the financial security of investors. Unfortunately there is the issue of 'goal post' moving, and recent action with regard to black empowerment, the Mining Charter and royalties does act as a warning that the circumstances under which mining companies operate in South Africa can change suddenly. I do remain happy, however, that the regulatory and legislative framework under which the exchange functions is sound, although the new dealing system which embraces a de-materialised (paperless) settlement approach does not pay proper attention to the position of small foreign investors.

The small cloud

If there is one small cloud on the South African horizon it is the political dominance of the post apartheid government by the African National Congress (ANC). Post colonial Africa is littered with the debris of failed democratic structures in the form of banned or destroyed political opposition parties. The complete dominance of South African politics by the ANC means that a less enlightened philosophy than currently pertains in the Party could be very unsettling. There would be very little that foreign investors could do to protect themselves if a future radical ANC leader decided to go down the path that Zimbabwe turned onto three years ago. It is also the case that foreign exchange controls in South Africa, though loosened since the apartheid era, can be used in an erratic manner. An example of this was when Anglo American, South Africa's premier corporation with massive local assets was allowed to migrate overseas but permission to do the same was refused to Randgold & Exploration, a mining group with almost no local assets at the time.

A trend towards big banks, big funds and big companies

The globalisation of securities markets over the last fifteen or so years has led to the emergence of a relatively small number of international investment banks and stockbrokers. Some markets have adapted quite well in that they have kept a reasonably strong layer of purely local firms in the market, albeit below the level of the global giants. South Africa's market is now dominated by a few major globally controlled firms and the country's institutional investors are likewise dominated by a few very large groups. Since the market itself is dominated by a relatively small number of very large companies, smaller companies have a struggle to attract investor attention and interest. This is one of the main reasons that, despite the interest in establishing smaller companies to assist the Government's black empowerment policy, smaller mining companies are still quite thin on the ground. Although the government's 'use it or lose it' lease changes should have led to a surge in new small local mining flotations, and may do so in due course.

Chart 2.2: FTSE/JSE Gold Mining Index

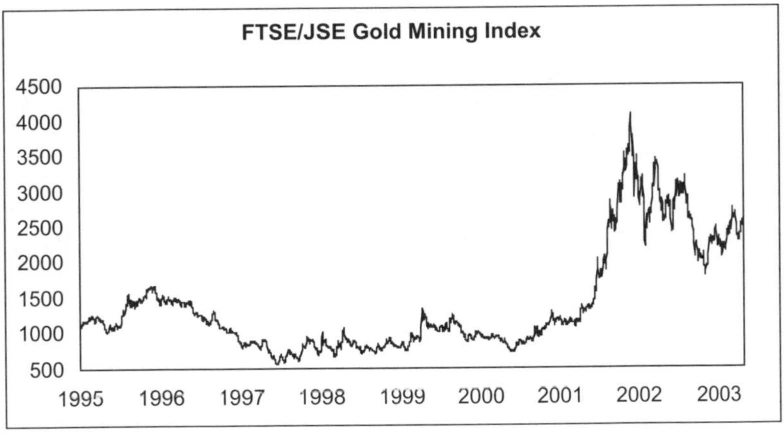

Source: Datastream

Sydney

The Australian mining scene fortunately appears to be well past the nationalistic wobbles of the 70s when the foreign ownership of mining resources was a very hot political issue. The legislative and regulatory background to both stock exchange and country is encouraging towards foreign investment, although Aussie national pride can never be completely discounted. There is also the quirky rule that in takeovers over half the shareholders of a company by number, not by shares owned, must support a takeover before it can go through. The legal framework is familiarly Anglo-Saxon and the needs of both private and institutional investors are well catered for in the stock exchange's Chess settlement system. One of the things that materially helps investor confidence in Australia, and indeed in all the main mining markets, is the fact that English is the native or dominant business language. That means that investors can readily understand the operational basis and cultural backgrounds of these markets.

No longer a key mining market

Looking at the Australian mining market as a magnet for investors, it no longer has quite the array of major investments that it had a few years ago due to the activities of foreign majors and the consolidation through takeovers of the sector. Whilst this confirms that Sydney is a true free market, the contraction in Australian ownership of many mining companies means that it is no longer a key mining market. However, it retains the entrepreneurial character that has fuelled past mining bull markets, and the geological potential of Australia, allied with its investor friendly background, suggests that it is capable of hosting future bull markets. To this end Sydney maintains a vigorous junior mining sector which is active both in Australia and overseas. However the local market does not always give full credit for overseas success, a fact that drove Aquarius Platinum, with its successful South African operations, to move its main listing to the UK. The main Australian indices covering the mining sector are the Metals and Mining sub sector and the Gold index.

There is also some evidence that Australian investors are less enamoured of mining shares these days which means the shrinkage of the sector has led to few tears being shed. Whatever the truth of this it is unsurprising that over the last ten years or so, when mining as a sector has very much occupied the shadows of the market in deference to high tech, telecoms and media, Australian entrepreneurs and investors have sought out new pastures for profitable exploitation.

Chart 2.3: Australia ASX All-Mining

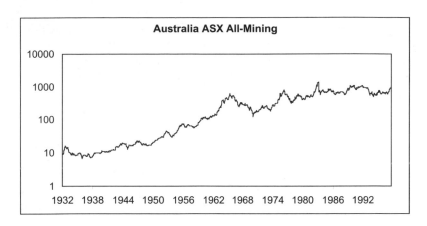

Source: Datastream

Toronto

Over the years Canada has proved its credentials as a major market with a full range of mining companies in which to invest, from giants such as Inco right down to highly speculative exploration plays. Today the country retains arguably the most active junior mining sector of any stock exchange, which is supported by helpful tax reliefs for local investors at the seedcorn level. Canada does have a political tradition of electing left of centre governments from time to time, and some of the provinces have in the past had quite radical, even socialist, administrations, British Columbia and Manitoba being two examples. On the whole though the country's mining industry has managed to prosper despite occasionally choppy political waters. The, at times, fractious relationship between francophone Quebec and the rest of Canada has also on occasions adversely coloured external perceptions about Canada as a place to invest in.

Today Canada's political stability and its adherence to market economy principles underpin its globally orientated mining industry. The Bre-X scandal, mentioned earlier and into which we will go in more detail later, was a wake-up call for the Canadian broking industry. In recent years we have seen the notorious Vancouver market, where the junior exploration companies were almost all listed, metamorphose into the TSX Venture Exchange to improve regulation and investor protection. It is, however, important to note that foreign investors are needed to push on junior stocks after the tax efficient initial financing done by private local investors. Canada's conservative institutional investors only become involved, as a rule, when the ugly duckling has become a high market value swan. This strategy proved disastrous in the case of Bre-X, which became a fully listed TSE 300 company attracting blue chip Canadian institutions just before keeling over. The main Toronto indices covering the mining market are the Diversified Metals and Mining and the Gold indices.

Chart 2.4: Toronto 300 Gold & Prec. Metals Index

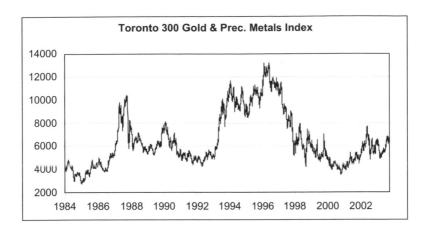

Source: Datastream

New York

The disaster of the Wall Street crash and the depression in the 30s led to the establishment of a securities regime in the US which was highly regulated, and well ahead of the rest of the world. Commercial banks were also separated from investment banks (brokers) due to the conflicts of interest endemic in the consolidation of the two very different kinds of securities business. We see these conflicts of interest again today in the liberalised climate that has slowly evolved in the US since Wall Street's *big bang* in 1975. Theoretically, though, New York is one of the safest markets in which to invest with strong regulators in the form of the SEC and a comprehensive rule book.

The small number of US incorporated mining stocks, of which only a handful are of any size, means that the sector has attracted little attention from either the mainstream broking or investing community in the US in recent years. There have been far more attractive high growth (sic) sectors to get involved in than mining, and those US investors interested in mining have tended to go overseas. There is, though, one great advantage flowing from this lack of interest and that is that the US mining sector has experienced none of the chicanery that has attached to other infamous parts of the US market, particularly high tech and the internet.

Whilst the New York Stock Exchange remains the premier trading floor in the US it is still the case that a number of overseas mining companies have obtained listings on NASDAQ, once almost as big a force in trading South African gold shares as Johannesburg but now world famous as the main market for high tech issues. New York itself has virtually all the US mining groups of any significance listed and a good few foreigners such as AngloGold. It also lists major mining companies from more exotic countries like the Peruvian gold miner Buenaventura. The other exchanges with mining links are Philadelphia and the American SE, which respectively run the main gold share index, XAU, and the Gold Bugs Index, HUI, in the US, the components of which appear in the following tables. The XAU broadly features the largest gold producers and the HUI is composed of companies opposed to hedging. Some small and speculative native US mining companies have trading facilities on the informal OTC (Over The Counter) market in the US.

Table 2.4 - XAU Components

	Market symbol	Country of incorporation
Newmont Mining	NEM	US
Barrick Gold	ABX	Canada
AngloGold	AU	South Africa
Gold Fields	GFI	South Africa
Freeport McMoran Copper & Gold	FCX	US
Placer Dome	PDG	Canada
Harmony Gold	HMY	South Africa
Goldcorp	GG	Canada
Kinross	KGC	Canada
Meridian Gold	MDG	Canada
Agnico Eagle	AEM	Canada
Durban Roodepoort Deep	DROOY	South Africa

Table 2.5 - HUI components

	Market symbol	Country of incorporation
Agnico Eagle	AEM	Canada
Bema Gold	BGO	Canada
Coeur d'Alene	CDE	US
Freeport McMoran Copper & Gold	FCX	US
Gold Fields	GFI	South Africa
Goldcorp	GG	Canada
Glamis Gold	GLG	Canada
Randgold Resources	GOLD	UK
Golden Star	GSS	Canada
Hecla Mining	HL	US
Harmony Gold	HMY	South Africa
IAMGold	IAG	Canada
Kinross Gold	KGC	Canada
Meridian Gold	MDG	Canada
Newmont Mining	NEM	US

Other markets

Although the main mining share markets cover the bulk of the major mining groups, be they locally incorporated or foreign companies, some mining shares do trade in unusual locations as well. Others have listings in foreign markets because of particular interest in their shares in that country. On the whole it is probably better to trade in the main mining markets when you can, but that is a subject that we will be going into in more detail later.

Looking at the non-mainstream markets where mining shares are listed and dealt I would make the following observations. Most of the markets, many of which are new and have been structured along lines agreed with the International Finance Corp, have understandable and relatively robust regulations, offering investors some degree of comfort if they deal in them. However, the example of the Russian market in the later 90s when some companies simply expunged from the register the holdings of some investors which they didn't like, does give investors reason to pause. There is also the problem that despite a strong regulatory background smaller markets in countries with a volatile political history are always at risk from a government simply changing the rules and forcing its stock exchange to comply to the disadvantage of foreign shareholders. History, unfortunately, is littered with examples of expropriation without compensation of foreign shareholdings - revolutionary Russia and maoist China would be two examples. It is interesting to note that at the end of 2003 the Chinese floated Fujian Zijin Mining, a mainland gold mining company, in Hong Kong to huge enthusiasm. China's economic boom and consequent thirst for metals and minerals may well spawn more such issues in due course.

Markets where mining shares are traded and which are open to foreign investors include-

- **Zambia**, where ZCCM Investments (formerly Zambia Consolidated Copper Mines) is listed. The market is small, as most of the shares are owned by the Zambian Government, but around 13% are in private hands, mostly overseas with London, Brussels and New York making a generally thin market and Paris a slightly larger market.

- Kuala Lumpur trades what is left of the **Malaysian** tin mining industry and is a serious Far Eastern market. However its response to the near Asian market meltdown of the late 90s was to lock foreigners into their holdings by denying them the right to repatriate sales proceeds for a couple of years. This action undermined its free/liquid market status.

- **Mexico** has, in Grupo Mexico, a mining giant, and in the wake of the North American trading zone the market there is reasonably well regulated, but investors nervous about Mexico's past might be more comfortable with the ADRs listed in New York.

- The same might be said for investors interested in **Peru's** Buenaventura but perhaps uncertain about the standard of regulation in the Lima market.
- In a similar vein, black Africa's leading gold mine Ashanti, now merged with AngloGold, had listings in both **Ghana** and **Zimbabwe**, but London, the location of its primary listing, or New York probably again provided a more re-assuring dealing environment for most investors.
- Both the **Philippines** and **Indonesia** have stock exchanges with mining sectors but much of the exploration and development of major mines in the latter country in recent years has been carried out by foreign groups.
- Both countries have continuing low level civil unrest which is something of a turnoff for foreign holiday makers let alone investors, and this volatility has to be weighed against the relatively rapid economic growth which both countries promise.

Many, particularly South African, mining companies have listings on European bourses with Paris, Brussels and Frankfurt/Berlin being leading centres. Indeed some stocks trade better on the Continent these days than in London, the other, less flattering side of the coin which on its face has London as the centre for the mining industry's giant groups. Some mining groups have been active on the takeover front and in acquiring the target company in exchange for their shares have found themselves listed in another market as a result - AngloGold and Placer Dome in Australia are two examples, a third was Ashanti in Zimbabwe. It is unlikely that a foreign investor would want to deal in these stocks outside their main markets, but there might be pricing advantages, and therefore arbitrage opportunities, from time to time in so doing.

3. Mining Shares

We now come to the meat of our look at the broad mining sector, mining shares themselves.

We have already touched on a number of mining companies when we looked at the metals sector, and in some detail in the case of gold. The following part of the book is divided up into several segments relating to mining shares. Firstly we look at the various categories of shares from large diversified companies like mining houses down to the small mining company sector. This categorisation of the sector by size allows investors to choose the degree of risk they are prepared to tolerate in what can be a highly volatile investment area. Mining share funds are also considered. We also look at mining market cycles, how to build a mining share portfolio and what to look for in results and exploration announcements.

Pre-flight checks

To begin with, however, it is important that anyone contemplating an investment in the mining sector should go through a few 'pre-flight checks'. Having identified a mining company that is of interest it is worthwhile collecting together some background information.

1. First establish the country of incorporation of the company and where it is listed with particular attention to the issue of the best market to deal in.

2. Get hold of the company accounts and other relevant investor information either through the internet and the company website, or through company report distributors (explained in a later section).

3. Using the published information calculate some basic ratios to determine whether the shares are still good value (see final section on company valuations).

4. Check details on the company's directors, brokers/promoters and also the longer term history which might not feature on the company's website.

Having done this you should be in a better position to make judgements about the mining companies that have caught your attention.

Mining finance houses

The term, *mining finance house*, was originally used to describe the structure of the great South African mining groups, i.e. groups who financed exploration and the initial development stages of bringing a mineral deposit, once discovered, to production. Now the phrase is used to describe many diversified mining companies operating, usually, in a number of countries and producing a broad spread of metals. Some describe these groups as *diversified mining companies*. Whichever description is used, these companies are generally perceived as the safest group of mining stocks for those investors looking to spread the risk of being in the sector. However investors must bear in mind that the more they try to reduce or spread risk the less upside they will experience should a metal or a country start to attract market attention.

Do you really want diversification?

A particular example of this was seen in the gold share market in 2002. After many years of underperformance gold and gold shares began to attract interest, and at a time when other equities were in a downtrend. Some brokers with no expertise or interest in gold recommended that clients, if they wanted exposure to gold, should buy Anglo American rather than one of the straight gold producers in Australia or South Africa. Although Anglo controls one of the largest gold producers in the world, AngloGold, it also has interests in a number of other very large undertakings including platinum, diamonds, forest products and coal. Gold consequently only contributed around 14% of its earnings. The result of buying Anglo American was that the typical 200% increase that an investor would have seen in a South African gold share, like Gold Fields or Harmony, between mid 2001 and mid 2002, would have been replaced by a thoroughly pedestrian 4% increase in the 'safe' Anglo. Of course when gold shares, having overreached themselves at that stage, suffered heavy profit taking and plunged in value the diversified nature of Anglo in contrast should have provided protection against that. Unfortunately as gold shares fell back they did so in step with broad equities which had a very weak summer. The result was that Anglo, Gold Fields and Harmony each fell by around 45% until the market erosion slowed right down in late July.

This highlights a problem for diversified mining groups in the current economic climate, for as they get bigger and more diversified they increasingly move in line with the broad index, thus in part losing their counter cyclical hedging characteristics. What we do not know is whether a repeat of the market conditions of the mid 70s, when metals were all the rage because of a massive surge in the rate of inflation, could detach, say, the major UK mining houses from negative movements in the FTSE100, and send them spiralling upwards in a counter cyclical direction to the rest of the equity market.

Chart 3.1: Rio Tinto [RIO] increasingly tracks FTSE100 [UKX]

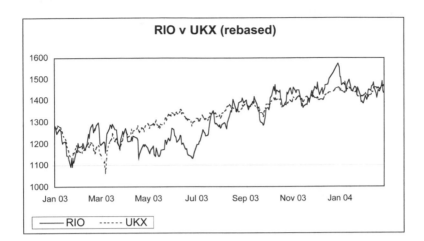

Source: Datastream

What has been said so far about the diversified mining houses suggests that they may have lost their ability to perform outside the confines of the market itself. However, whilst the performance of Anglo American above was disappointing last year, one must not forget that after the 1998 financial turmoil of Russia and LTCM, the UK mining finance sector was one of the best 'Footsie' performers as investors gambled on an economic recovery stimulating metal prices. Perhaps the most interesting thing about this performance, for someone brought up in the markets of the 60s and the 70s, was that the mining finance sector ran relatively early in the recovery cycle. This, however, was also what happened in the 80s when mining stocks, which had risen immediately and in line with the economic upturn, provided no protection from the October 87 crash, and indeed in Australia, for example, fell more sharply than the industrial index.

The number of big diversified mining companies is getting smaller

Given that the typical investor these days can buy shares in any market he chooses, the choice of big diversified groups is limited as amalgamations have created a handful of giants and a few growing groups whose ambition unsurprisingly is to get bigger and become giants. By now we will all be familiar with the three large UK houses - Anglo American, BHP Billiton and Rio Tinto - and to them must be added the smaller Xstrata.

All are FTSE100 stocks, and the first three are also ranked in the FT Global 500. Recently admitted to the FTSE100 is Antofagasta, and corporate activity may also in due course push Lonmin towards the 100, of which it was a constituent in its

Lonrho days. Using the FT Global 500 as a guide, other mining giants are CVRD of Brazil, Newmont Mining of the US and Canada's Barrick Gold, (the latter two being gold not diversified groups), and that is that!

Table 3.1 - Profile of diversified mining companies

	Market Cap (£bn)	Earnings from metals (%)	Geographic earnings (%)
Anglo American (Finals Dec 2003)	18.4	Platinum 25, gold 11, diamonds 23, coal 14, base metals 12, industrial minerals 14, paper & packaging 16, ferrous metals 6,	South Africa 36, Africa 17, Europe 25, South America 18, Australia/Asia 6, North America (2)
BHP Billiton (Interims Dec 2003)	28.0	Petroleum 27, aluminium 14, base metals 15, carbon steel 23 diamonds & special products 9, coal 3, stainless steel 9	Australia 45, Europe 15, North America 7, South America 8, South Africa 8, Rest of World
Rio Tinto (Finals Dec 2003)	23.0	Copper/gold 28,iron ore 31, energy 10, aluminium 13, industrial minerals 10, diamonds 7 gold 1	North America 25 Australasia 52, South America 11, Africa 1 Indonesia 13, Europe & others 9,
Xstrata (Finals Dec 2003)	5.0	Coal 28, chrome13, vanadium (2) copper 56, lead/zinc 4, forestry-technology 1	Americas 39, Australia 35, Europe 9, Africa 17,

Source: Last reported figures

Note: The market capitalisation figures are as of March 2004 and the BHP and Rio Tinto figures incorporate the capitalisation of the Australian arms of the two companies. Figures for Xstrata include MIM on a pro forma basis for the whole 2003 financial year, although the merger was only completed in the second half.

How the big companies are diversified

BHP Billiton

The largest of the diversified mining groups is **BHP Billiton** but the makeup of its operations is rather different from those of Anglo American and rather more like Rio Tinto's. The importance of its oil earnings gives it a very different flavour from its two main peers. It is also heavily orientated towards bulk metals and minerals - aluminium, iron ore (hiding in the carbon steel category) and coal - a characteristic it shares with Rio Tinto. It has important copper interests in Chile and an expanding diamond mine in Canada. This gives it some exposure to direct consumer demand trends and the more volatile world of spot metal pricing, where prices are set not through long term contracts but change daily as a result of trading trends on a metal exchange such as   the   LME (London Metal Exchange). Its major geographical area of operations is Australia, with South America its second most important operational area and North America not far behind. What is interesting about BHP Billiton is that it does not have any gold or platinum exposure, although it is involved in diamonds.

Chart 3.2: BHP Billiton [BLT] v FTSE100 [UKX]

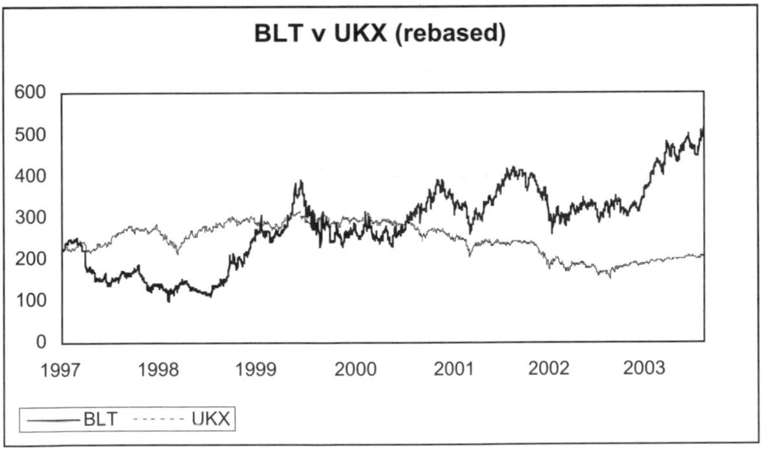

Source: Datastream

Rio Tinto

Rio Tinto has some gold interests and is developing a diamond mine in Canada, but like BHP Billiton it is primarily involved in producing bulk metals and minerals like industrial minerals, iron ore, coal and aluminium. It also has modest exposure to the spot metal markets where the mining sector as a whole gets its main earnings leverage. In terms of geography Rio Tinto is operationally heavily linked to Australia and the US.

Chart 3.3: Rio Tinto [RIO] v FTSE100 [UKX]

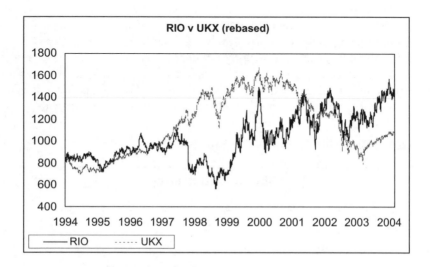

Source: Datastream

Anglo American

Although it is a value judgement, **Anglo American** has the more interesting metals/minerals spread with significant exposure to paper and packaging, platinum, diamonds, coal, industrial minerals and ferrous and base metals. Spot metal prices have a greater influence on its earnings than on the earnings of the other two UK giants. Geographically Anglo is still skewed towards South/southern Africa/Africa, with 53% of earnings coming from the continent in 2003, although South Africa at 36% of the group slipped back in importance as Europe and South America gained.

Chart 3.4: Anglo American [AAL] v FTSE100 [UKX]

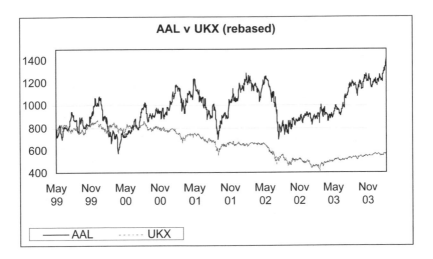

Source: Datastream

Xstrata

Xstrata's position as a coal producer, with a strong leaning towards Africa, has been transformed by the merger with Australia's MIM, and base metals have become very important to the group as a result. It is now better balanced as to products and countries of operation, although if current high copper prices are maintained it may become rather top heavy in that direction.

Chart 3.5: Xstrata [XTA] v FTSE100 [UKX]

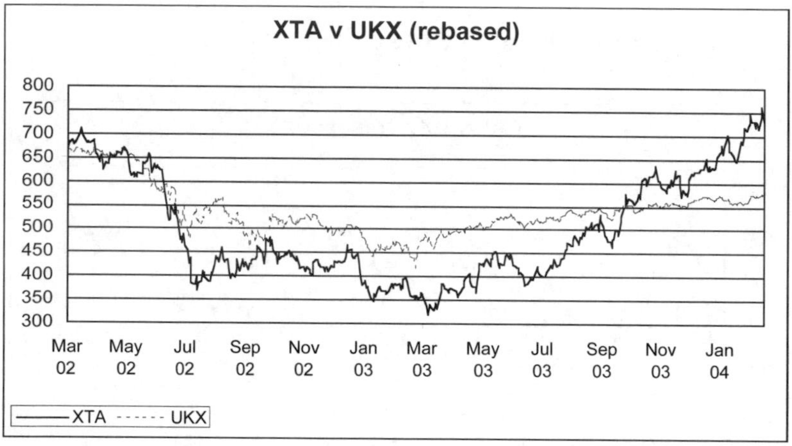

XTA v UKX (rebased)

Source: Datastream

The previous charts demonstrate that investing in a large mining finance house may not always provide the expected diversification of risk, and may also divorce the investor from the spot market metal price action that drives a mining bull market.

Certainly an investor in BHP Billiton (ignoring the further complication that its major oil production earnings may run in an entirely different cycle), or Rio Tinto, will be looking to volume increases from the bulk minerals side for the lion's share of any earnings advance.

Anglo American offers a much wider diversification with good spot metal price exposure; however, it does retain its historic African focus although that is now somewhat reduced having been 70% plus a couple of years ago.

Xstrata is by far the smallest of the group and may well be interested in further mergers or tie-ups because of this. At this current stage of its development it is also heavily influenced by the base metal cycle which increases the volatility of its earnings. At the moment with base metals strong that is a plus, but when the cycle turns down its earnings will come under pressure.

Antofagasta

This point can also be made about FTSE100 newcomer, Antofagasta, whose earnings are entirely drawn from Chile, 90% of which are in respect of its copper mining operations there, giving it no risk diversification whatsoever.

Chart 3.6: Antofagasta [ANTO] v FTSE100 [UKX]

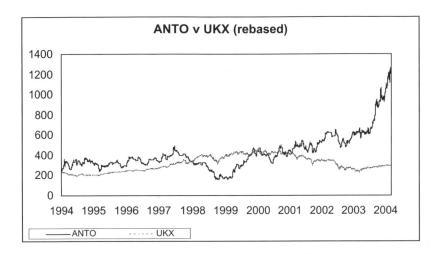

Source: Datastream

Results reported in US dollars

An additional point to be aware of is that though these companies are incorporated in the UK they report their results in US dollars. Since a large proportion of their operations are in countries like Australia, Canada and South Africa where their costs are in local currencies exchange rate movements can be important. US dollar metal/mineral prices may be rising but if the US dollar is weak, as has been the case in 2003, then margins at these foreign operations may be squeezed as local costs when converted into US dollars for the results may be rising faster than revenues.

A hand-picked portfolio of mining shares

One of the other key ideas behind buying a mining finance house share is that it can act as a substitute for a hand picked and balanced portfolio of individual mining shares, and thus take the strain out of investing in a sector with perhaps too many potential pitfalls for those not familiar with how it works. Historically this was not a bad idea, and when one looked at the old Anglo American of South Africa you were effectively buying an investment trust consisting of many separately listed South African mining shares, and often at a discount, although most of the companies involved were controlled by Anglo.

Volume more important than price

Today we are faced with a small number of large mining houses with predominately 'safe' structures built around bulk metals and minerals where price is less the issue than volume. That means that when economic growth slows the main problem facing earnings is the prospect of a drop in volume. Whilst that leads inevitably to lower profits, as does a drop in the price of spot priced metals like copper and zinc, the prices of the latter are much more volatile than prices of industrial minerals where contract prices are more prevalent, and changes are often less dramatic because customers foremost value security of supply. An example of this would be a comparison of the range of Rio Tinto's historic earnings through the cycle, when it was primarily driven by spot metal trends, and its earnings today as a bulk mineral producer.

The point is illustrated in Tables 3.2 and 3.3 by showing the percentage changes in Rio Tinto's earnings per share since 1970. Up until 1995 earnings expanded and contracted sharply, the recessions of the mid 70s, early 80s and early 90s showing up quite clearly with periods of rapid growth in between. This growth was a consequence of both the company's sustained operational growth and the favourable expansion of world economies over the twenty plus years since the near catastrophic inflation of the mid 70s. Since 1995, earnings have become structurally far more stable which has enabled the group to ride out the difficult economic climate since 2000.

Table 3.2 - Rio Tinto earnings volatility

Source: Datastream

Table 3.3 - Rio Tinto earnings volatility (underlying figures)

Year	EPS (%)	Year	EPS (%)	Year	EPS (%)	Year	EPS (%)
1970	10	1980	4	1990	-18	2000	17
1971	-30	1981	-34	1991	-39	2001	-7
1972	57	1982	-2	1992	20	2002	8
1973	137	1983	50	1993	42	2003	-10
1974	-11	1984	15	1994	59		
1975	-44	1985	22	1995	8		
1976	107	1986	-5	1996	-15		
1977	1	1987	14	1997	11		
1978	19	1988	50	1998	-10		
1979	52	1989	25	1999	19		

Source: Financial Times - RTZ annual results.

Becoming core holdings

The importance of stable earnings to the UK mining finance houses relates to their position in the FTSE100 which puts them on the buying lists of index tracking funds and the major UK institutions. Whilst market value will obviously change over time, when the FT Global 500 list was compiled at the end of May 2003, BHP Billiton was the 11th largest UK company, Rio Tinto the 14th and Anglo American the 16th. These stocks are no longer just a conservative way to play the commodities cycle, they are core holdings for portfolios which have no particular remit to invest in the mining sector. This means that market capitalisation, which is often a function of earnings trends, could be critical to demand for mining finance shares in the FTSE100. The greater the market value, therefore, the greater weight a mining finance share will likely have in portfolios, particularly in tracker funds. If mining house earnings are too volatile, share prices, and of course market capitalisation, will probably reflect that, a trend which will be further exacerbated by tracker activity.

The role of mining houses in portfolios

This is a recent consideration, driven partly by the development of tracker funds and partly by the growing importance of mining houses in the FTSE100. The consequence though is to throw some doubt on whether investors looking for leverage to an upswing in metal prices should buy mining houses in preference to more focused individual mining companies. One consideration to be borne in mind, now that the UK mining houses have become major FTSE100 components, is that it is likely that UK investors will have indirect exposure to the sector already, in part due to these stocks being in pension funds, life funds and general managed UK PEPs and ISAs. There is also the problem that in pursuit of reduced earnings volatility some groups may want to try and hedge their more volatile earnings sources. Anglo American, for example, owns 50% plus of AngloGold, a gold company that is still a substantial hedger.

There is no question that the big mining houses are well run organisations, and in a notoriously, and excitingly, cyclical sector like mining the relative stability of their earnings is not to be ignored. Also there is often good price volatility providing opportunities to achieve good trading returns for the nimble investor. In each of the last six years Rio Tinto has recorded yearly share price volatility of over 50% measured on a year low to year high basis, although the share price trend may have been a falling one rather than a rising one in some of the years. Nonetheless this demonstrates good price action in the shares.

Medium sized miners

The medium sized category of mining companies, which it can be argued would cover companies with a market capitalisation of between £250 million and £1.5 billion, contains both single metal companies and diversified groups. This sector has been squeezed in recent years by the rise of the predominantly UK houses, as they have acquired some of their smaller brethren. Returning briefly to the big houses, it is worth just looking at the listed companies they have acquired or merged with in recent years, in so doing removing from public listing some interesting companies with good metal price leverage.

Table 3.4 - M&A in the mining sector

Company today	Swallowed up companies
Anglo American	Amcoal, De Beers, Amplats (steadily being mopped up)
BHP Billiton	BHP, DiaMet,
Rio Tinto	CRA, Peko, North, Ashton Mining,
Xstrata	MIM

Defining a medium sized mining company is somewhat subjective and looking at the list of lost stocks above neither De Beers, BHP or CRA could be considered medium sized, their disappearance merely underlining the fact that the big are simply getting bigger.

This desire to get bigger is also influenced by the size of new mining projects today and the need to get them financed effectively. Clearly the bigger the balance sheet the more comfortable the banks will be when assessing how a new mine is to be financed. However, medium sized companies are often interesting as investment propositions because new projects can have a substantial and positive effect on earnings, and financing may not be a problem if the project is robust and the mining company in question is soundly structured.

More focus can result in out-performance of the larger mining houses

For the investor, the medium sized mining company may also offer returns, even if the metal price scene is quiet, as a result of having new, high margin and expanding mines under development, and where a metal price rise would be icing on an already fairly rich cake. An example of this would be UK incorporated miner Antofagasta ('Fags') whose Chilean copper operations have grown enormously over the last three years with a consequently positive impact on its share price during a period when the copper price until recently has done very little. In the table below we can see the respective share prices of Fags and Rio Tinto at the calendar year end starting at 1998 when Fags copper mining expansion began to have an impact on market perceptions of the group. The out-performance of the more focused Antofagasta is clearly seen and over the whole period shown Fags appreciated by 249% and Rio Tinto by 75%. In fact capitalised at over £2 billion Antofagasta is one of the larger medium sized miners, and was recently admitted to the FTSE100, although market liquidity can be sticky sometimes due to the dominance of the controlling Luksic family on the share register.

Chart 3.7: Relative price performance of Rio Tinto [RIO] and Antofagasta [ANTO]

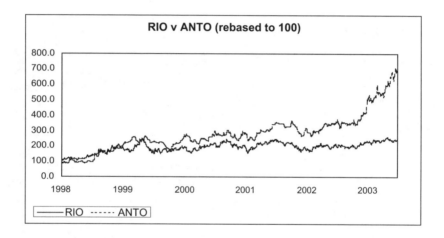

Source: Datastream

Table 3.5 - Relative price performance of Antofagasta and Rio Tinto (underlying figures)

	1998	1999	2000	2001	2002	2003
Antofagasta	177	433 (+145%)	442 (+2%)	530 (+20%)	618 (+17%)	1060 (+72%)
Rio Tinto	699	1495 (+114%)	1178 (-21%)	1314 (+12%)	1220 (-7%)	1556 (+28%)

The steady disappearance of the serious medium sized miner, as said earlier, often occurs because a bigger group wants to increase its product range and thus the diversification of its earnings. This inevitably leads on to a loss of focus, and in the case of the recent Xstrata/MIM merger, the loss of focus has cut both ways as Xstrata has surrendered its total coal focus and MIM has surrendered its perceived position as a classic play on spot base metal prices. The side issue of nationalism, not quite dead in this age of globalisation, which led to some Australian shareholders of MIM voicing disquiet about the effective loss of another mining company to the UK, did not spark any action with regard to a competing bid for MIM in the board rooms of the shrinking group of Australian medium sized miners such as WMC Resources (the old Western Mining). Such a merger would have created a sizeable local champion, although it would have done nothing for investor choice as the market would have still lost one company.

In its own right WMC is an interesting example of the problems that some almost (but not quite) large mining companies experience. At one stage in the last decade WMC was one of the most diversified of the Australian mining groups, with base metals including nickel and copper, gold, oil, uranium, fertilisers, and alumina amongst its interests. In recent years it has exited from gold and oil and de-merged its alumina interests; its next major development is an industrial minerals project in Mozambique, taking it into Africa where Australian investors in the past have shown little appetite. Today WMC is a medium sized player, as is its former subsidiary Alumina Ltd. It still has the ability to finance and develop major new mines, as per its Mozambique project, but whether it could now do a mega project is open to question. Certainly its old rival, MIM, now nestling in the Xstrata bosom, would be capable of something very big again. This is an important issue now, for WMC, like MIM, has a fine exploration record and still operates at Kambalda and Olympic Dam where its historic nickel and copper operations were developed.

A medium sized mining company then could be said to be in one of three key stages of development.

1. It could be growing fast on the back of one or more projects which might appeal to investors wanting exposure to a possible future giant, but one that currently combines growth with relative security.
2. It could be a mature company but with high quality operations that one of the giant miners might be interested in.
3. It could be a mature group whose interests may be a little too small, or old, to attract a bid from a major. Equally a merger with a like-positioned miner might be possible, even though it is probable that a merger of equals would not generate a market premium for shareholders.

A possible attraction of the, perhaps, slightly faded third category company is that its earnings, coming from older operations, might be quite leveraged to metal price movements which would increase its market standing during a period of rising metal prices.

So with medium sized miners we can, if we are lucky, find growth companies, takeover targets and focused and leveraged plays. We can have some security in addition, certainly in the first category, and we may well find good dividend prospects in the third category from time to time. However, we cannot just leave these holdings to their own devices, as could possibly be done with the giant diversified houses, they will need to be managed which probably means traded. It is, therefore, important to stay on top of the fundamentals to avoid suffering sudden and sharp declines in share prices, these stocks in many cases being very sensitive to changes in the metal price environment. They may also be subject to strategic change which may also have a bearing on how the investor views them.

Case study: Avmin

Management within these medium sized groups striving for the big league is also very critical. Errors in strategy will be magnified and uncertain management objectives can confuse shareholders, with a detrimental effect on both short and long term prospects for the share price. One of the smaller South African mining houses, Anglovaal Mining (Avmin), which is now controlled by Harmony Gold and ARM, is a case in point.

In the heyday of the South African mining sector in the 70s, when gold was the big story, Avmin's predecessor, Anglovaal, was a broad based mining orientated conglomerate not unlike, although rather smaller than, Anglo American. The group was dominated by two families, the Hersovs and the Menells, the former loosely looked after the group's industrial interests and the latter were responsible for the mining interests. With the end of apartheid, as we already know, there followed a major restructuring of the South African mining industry, which in part concentrated ownership into bigger groupings for the purpose of competing more effectively as global entities. In the case of Anglovaal the group decided in 1998 to split itself into separate mining and industrial companies with the Menells taking on the running of the dedicated mining group named Anglovaal Mining.

Anglovaal's strategy, therefore, was to increase the focus of the old group's interests, the industrial side having been big enough to deter investors looking for mining market exposure. However, in its position as a mining company, Avmin was on the small side, definitely no more than a medium sized company, although it had diversified holdings encompassing gold, diamonds, nickel, copper, chrome and manganese - all of which had growth possibilities. So in order to increase the focus of the old group, a medium sized mining group with growth assets was brought into being. Initially it linked its longer term growth hopes with a progressive dividend policy, creating a vehicle which looked rather attractive as an investment opportunity.

Two bites of the cherry

Born into a difficult mining market at the end of 1998, Avmin's share price disappointed to begin with, but in due course staged a spirited recovery which culminated in mid 1999 with De Beers announcing that it had acquired a 22% stake in the company. Those who had picked up Avmin early for its interesting mix of assets were clearly looking clever, confirming that undervalued medium sized miners gave investors two bites of the cherry - either the broad market would eventually acknowledge the shares' attractions or a bigger player would; both would lead to a sharp advance in the share price in due course.

De Beers piles on the pressure

The original Anglovaal asset split had been accompanied by a promise that the Menell family, whilst maintaining a share structure which gave them effective control of Avmin until 2001, nonetheless were committed to an eventual capital re-structuring that would lead to them ceding control. With De Beers on the prowl and clearly interested in Avmin's half share in the rich Venetia diamond mine, where De Beers had the other half, the chances of a bid for Avmin could not be ruled out even taking account of the family control issue. Early in 2000 Avmin agreed to sell its Venetia stake to De Beers and De Beers agreed to sell its Avmin shares to a group of institutional investors. The proceeds from the Venetia sale were substantially distributed to Avmin shareholders via a return of capital. However, the resulting Avmin looked rather different from its original structure, shorn as it had been of its diamond earnings which were large and an important component of the company's progressive dividend payment policy.

Avmin, however, was confident that its new projects would in due course more than make up for the loss of Venetia, and much store was put on the cash generating abilities of the Chambishi cobalt development in Zambia, which was referred to earlier on in the book. In the meantime a more conservative dividend policy was to be followed. The Target gold mine, developed by Avmin's subsidiary Avgold, promised further medium term earnings growth. In the event the group was overly optimistic about its Zambian investment and has now, at some expense, withdrawn from it.

Then Anglo buys a stake

Before that, the Menell family entered into a new arrangement over the structure of the group which meant that the release of family control was less open-hearted than had originally been expected. If shareholders and the market were beginning to become confused by Avmin's strategy, the acquisition in 2002 of a near 35% stake in the company by Anglo American only added to this confusion. Especially as Avmin had specifically stated earlier, as part of the Venetia deal, that De Beers' stake in Avmin could not be sold to Anglo. Also with Anglo now on Avmin's board it looked as though the Menell family had changed their minds on the issue of control once more and reverted to loosening their grip on the group.

Elsewhere the obvious reason for Anglo's interest in Avmin, the Target gold mine, a growing operation with significant long term, expansion prospects, held out little prospect of providing cash to the centre in the short term. Needing to fund the cost of the withdrawal from Chambishi, Avmin sold down its Avgold holding from around 60% to around 42%.

And finally, almost, the curtain

In a final twist Anglo, seeing their effective stake in Avgold and therefore Target much reduced, decided to sell their Avmin stake to Harmony and ARMgold in May 2003. Following this the new owners launched a full bid for Avgold.

The, at times, frenetic corporate and operational activity at Avmin had certainly provided the nimble investor with plenty of opportunities to trade the shares profitably since the Anglovaal restructuring in 1998. Having said that some of the corporate activity has been contradictory, particularly the question of control which has had the Anglo group, in the shape of both De Beers and Anglo American itself, in and out of the shares three times. The new owners throw up the prospect of yet another twist to the tail. Clearly being an Avmin shareholder is rarely dull, but it can be confusing in terms of the overall strategy and this is not conducive to maximising share price returns. Also I would argue that the loss of the diamond income flow boxed Avmin in, particularly when the Zambian cobalt project went wrong. Although shareholders got a return of capital from the sale of Venetia they also ended up with a weaker company. The chrome/manganese side has done very well, but these metals do not send the pulse racing, and the Target gold project, a long term winner, now needs a bigger player to bring out its full potential as demonstrated by the bid for Avgold.

The lessons learnt from Avmin

Avmin is an instructive example of the attractions and weaknesses inherent in investing in medium sized mining companies, where mistakes in strategy, if not fatal, can nonetheless undermine a promising situation. These errors are far more difficult to hide in a company worth £420 million like Avmin, than a £18 billion company like Anglo American. However if Avmin had been able to fire on all cylinders, the spread of its mining activities and the leverage afforded by the growth prospects of most of them would have potentially provided the sort of out-performance that theoretically the medium sized miner should be able to offer over its much bigger peers.

The smaller mining companies

The old adage that nothing in this life is for free is something that the investor drawn to the smaller mining company sector is trying to overturn. Mostly he fails to achieve his aim of turning a sow's ear into a silk purse, but there are sufficient successes over the years to keep hopes alive and bring back the speculator to the small company sector when the natural resources cycle starts to turn up again. A little further on we will look at a few examples of this.

One of the continuing aspects of stockmarket investment is that when a sector becomes hot, it is quite easy to raise new money for new small participants, and the late 90s high tech boom which culminated in the internet bubble is a case in point. The most recent example in mining of this sort of thing was the boomlet in small Canadian gold stocks exploring in developing countries in the mid 90s, led by the infamous Bre-X and included stocks like Carterway and Timbuktu. Rather more typical was the Canadian diamond boom which was built on the very real discoveries made in the North West Territories and which unleashed a wave of well supported new issues. This boom lasted for over two years before it ran out of steam and investors, particularly those who came late to the party, retired to lick their wounds.

If prospective investors are prepared to be more realistic about what they are trying to achieve in the small mining sector it is possible to find and follow very decent stocks that do deliver over the longer term. These are often companies with potentially viable projects at a very early stage of exploration/development which require financing and patience on the part of long sighted investors.

A good example - Aquarius Platinum

A good example of the genre is Aquarius Platinum, a once Australian company which arrived in London in 1999 with a platinum mine in South Africa being developed on the back of the new *use it or lose it* policy in that country. Australian investors had shown only limited interest in the company, and as it needed serious development capital it made the decision to seek a listing in London on AIM, which it converted to a full listing on the London Stock Exchange last year, and eventually re-incorporated itself in Bermuda. It has also done deals which have brought new assets into the company and made Impala Platinum a major shareholder, and recently it signed a joint venture agreement with Amplats.

Chart 3.8: Aquarius Platinum [AQP]

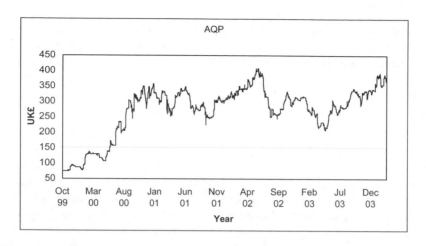

Source: Datastream

From a minnow capitalised at £19 million when it listed on AIM in 1999, Aquarius has made the sort of steady and substantial progress that small mining company enthusiasts dream about and now has a market value of £300 million. However it is important to remember that Aquarius's march to the edge of the medium sized miner category has been as a result of hard work and probably a bit of luck. Investors prepared to put in the research time to identify these kinds of opportunities could well find winners, especially if they are patient.

Those looking for the kind of dramatic returns that can be made in boom conditions will not only have to wait for such a boom to turn up, but they will have to hope that they will be lucky enough to pick out a winner from a pack of often look-alike chancers. In a fully fledged boom like the Canadian diamond boom or the famous, and much earlier, Aussie nickel boom you do not have to be quite so discriminating in your choice of speculative vehicle, but you do have to remember to take profits. In the end if a speculative small/junior mining company does not find a viable deposit to mine, its share price will more than likely collapse.

The rate of attrition in the small company sector is also high, for without an economic discovery a company will have to keep coming back to its shareholders, or to the market, for funds to keep going. This is not difficult to do when mining markets are strong as long as the company's story is compelling enough, but when markets are weak doors tend to clang shut and speculative capital dries up. However, despite the failure rate a surprising number of small companies manage to limp on through the hard times and live to fight again when resource markets swing back into favour.

Getting the minerals out requires different skills from finding them

However, if finding an economic mineral deposit is difficult enough, and achieved by only a small number of hopefuls, turning the deposit into a mine is hardly easy either. One of the problems that smaller companies face is that the management skills required to achieve the metamorphosis from exploration hopeful to mining company are not the same skills as are required to keep a company going during the speculative exploration phase. The approach, perhaps somewhat promotional, that has been highly successful in raising small amounts of equity finance may be quite inappropriate for raising the much larger financing required to bring a mine to production. Many mining entrepreneurs find it hard to relate to the banking industry to which they must go for the mine development money, and bankers, once sure a mine is viable, want to talk to someone who understands the economics of the project rather than just the geology and the engineering.

Small companies are less able to cope with disaster

Another related issue that has to be faced when looking at small mining companies is their robustness. The giants and even the medium sized company may have to deal with a disaster whose scale would probably overwhelm a smaller mine owner. The flooding at Mufulira on the Zambian Copperbelt in 1970/1, and the flooding at West Driefontein on South Africa's West Rand in 1968, were two such events. The expertise and financial strength that, in the case of Mufulira, the Amax managed RCM and, in the case of West Dries, controlling finance house Consolidated Gold Fields, were able to bring to bear on these two near catastrophes was critical to saving the mines. More recently the well regarded UK gold explorer, Navan Mining, collapsed after expanding its interests away from its very promising Bulgarian gold leases into zinc mines in Spain. When the zinc price crashed, Navan's operating losses and its highly indebted balance sheet sunk it, even after a rescue equity financing. In the mid 90s Australian junior gold miner, Mount Burgess, was only saved from disaster when it lost the orebody at its Butchers Well mine in Western Australia, by using its highly prospective Red October gold deposit as bait for a rescue joint venture with Sons of Gwalia. Though Mount Burgess survived, shareholders, who bought before Butchers Well got into trouble, will be lucky ever again to see the price they paid at the time.

An eternal problem - financing the stage from dream to reality

The financing of small mining companies is never straightforward, although because hope springs eternal small scale equity finance, particularly when mining shares are in a bull market, is often readily on offer through stockbrokers with a mining specialisation. It can be costly, but high risk capital seldom comes cheap unless it is raised at the peak of a boom. The real problems for a small company start when it begins to look for longer term project development capital. At this point shareholders in a successful small miner need to pay very close attention to the cost of this later stage capital. If they have taken on significant risk to steer a prospect through the inevitably uncertain early phases of exploration and development, they do not want to cede too much equity at the point when the dream begins to become a reality.

This then is the eternal problem for those few small mining companies that find an economic mineral deposit - *how to develop it without giving too much away*.

One solution - joint ventures

One of the most common, and obvious, ways to develop a new mine is to seek a joint venture with a bigger group (not necessarily one of the giants though). The problem with this approach is that if the prospective mine is likely to be a large producer of whatever metal, the market in the initial stages of exploration will have probably bid the small explorer's shares up to extremely elevated heights following the discovery and the first few *exciting* development/drilling reports. This was certainly the case with the great Aussie nickel boomer Poseidon in 1969/70, of which more later. That old investment adage - *it is better to travel than arrive* - holds a lot of weight in the circumstances of a fully fledged mining boom.

Sometimes, if a company joint ventures at an early enough stage, the share price may actually be boosted by the new partner. That was certainly the case with DiaMet during the mid 90s Canadian diamond boom, which took on giant BHP to carry the expensive Arctic drilling programme required to prove up what has become the Ekati diamond mine.

Sometimes the market has more information on a project involving a small miner but still ignores pertinent facts, such a situation can be very dangerous for the investor who, sensing an interesting opportunity, plunges in believing that the market has fully discounted any potential problems.

Zambia Copper Investments (ZCI)

A good example of this trap would be Zambia Copper Investments (ZCI), then an Anglo American subsidiary and the now disbanded Konkola copper participation. When Anglo finally won the privatisation bid for the Konkola mine and deep level project in 1999, it assigned its interest to ZCI. At that stage the market capitalisation of ZCI was around £90 million with a net worth of just $30 million, and the Konkola Deep project was likely to cost more than $750 million with ZCI having an 80% stake in it. When in 1997 Anglo had had its original bid to buy Konkola conditionally accepted its stake was to be 40%, and with interest high in Zambian privatisation at the time, ZCI's market capitalisation was a heady £250 million (against its modest net worth).

Clearly on the basis of these valuations the market was paying little attention to the fact that ZCI would have to engage in a huge fund raising to follow its interest in Zambia, the effects of which would have been a huge dilution of then current shareholders stake in the company. Indeed at the end of 2001 when the Konkola project was still live and Anglo American had leant ZCI $190 million with interest to be rolled up into the loan, ZCI's debt/equity gearing ratio was a massive 1250%. Before any long term bank development finance could have been raised for the project the potential lenders would have insisted on a major re-capitalising of ZCI. Of course when the shares were standing at 200p in 1997 the market was expecting that Anglo would make ZCI its African mineral vehicle using Zambia as its starting point, or take over the company at a massive premium to its net worth. Neither happened and now ZCI is no longer part of the Anglo stable and its market worth at 7p in mid 2003 had fallen to a mere £9 million, although more recently the shares have traded near 50p as the copper price has improved.

Perhaps the complexity of the above serves as a reason for investors to concentrate on the big diversified miners with their powerful balance sheets and healthy profitability, and eschew the risks endemic in many smaller mining companies. It would be wrong, however, to leave the subject of ZCI without pointing out that since Zambia abandoned the centrally planned economy in the early 90s, the share price of ZCI has moved in wide bands providing a number of opportunities for very profitable trading. This was also the case with the other Zambian copper play, ZCCM Investments. Playing the small mining sector can be dangerous for your health, but as with all stock market investment, those who know what they are doing can make a lot of money, particularly if they are not too greedy.

The days of equity financing have passed

We have touched on the issue of financing of potential new mines owned by smaller companies. The days when South African gold mines, for example, were financed entirely by equity (still common in the early 70s) have passed, and banks through their specialist corporate finance departments, now regularly seek to provide the required finance. Most mines these days are financed on a non recourse basis, which means that if, for example, the mine becomes uneconomic before the loans are repaid there is no recourse for the balance of the loan to the developing company In the case of new gold mines the lenders will probably insist that protection is taken out by selling gold forward or through some other derivative structure that will protect the mine's revenue stream whatever the gold price does. This is less easy to achieve with other metals where forward selling is only available for a short period. It is also becoming less easy with gold as the contango (forward net interest rate), which provides the enhanced price, shrinks in today's low interest rate environment.

Small scale finance is of little interest to the big banks which look to get involved in big projects where big fees can be charged to pay for those banks' big overheads. Big projects these days probably mean that the small discovering company has brought in a substantial partner, so the project financing process should be relatively straightforward with the relevant bank likely to know and be comfortable with the larger mining group involved. It is difficult today to conceive of a mining junior being able to take a large project right through to production from discovery without the help of a bigger entity, so daunting are the financing issues and the associated banking due diligence requirements.

Mining company life cycle

It would perhaps be useful at this stage to look at a virtual life cycle for a mining company to provide some guidance to investors wondering where a company that interested them might have got to in its development.

The growth of a typical mining company

Early stage – private company...

In its very early days the company would probably be private, financed by a small number of linked investors as a result of the acquisition of promising mineral properties by the founder shareholders. The now AIM listed ZincOx Resources is a recent example. These properties might be already known, either as promising prospects like Aquarius Platinum's original South African leases or as old mines now closed. There are plenty of examples of the latter – Australia's Sons of Gwalia, for example, built its gold operations around the old Sons of Gwalia gold mine in Western Australia. The company might also be looking for minerals in a greenfield environment like Poseidon in Western Australia during the 60s Aussie mining boom.

...leading on to further financings, and then a stock market listing...

At an early stage, if the market environment is right and the company's projects are considered promising, an unlisted company would probably seek further finance and a stock market listing to increase the shareholder base and crystallise value for the original shareholders.

...concentrate on the most promising mineral leases...

At this stage it would then prioritise its projects and concentrate its new resources on exploring and drilling its most promising mineral leases. If it was looking at a known mineralised area it would have more obvious drill targets and be able to work in a more focussed manner and more quickly. The next stage would be either the starting of detailed work if the deposit looked economically viable or the abandonment of the project as uninteresting or uneconomic.

...bankable feasibility study, leading to development finance...

If the detailed work indicated a potential mine then a bankable feasibility study would be undertaken, with the aim of seeking development finance from the banks. It is also quite possible that the company would seek to joint venture development of the project with a bigger mining company who would be better able to secure development finance. Such a course was taken by Randgold Resources over the development of its Morila gold mine in Mali, where AngloGold acquired a stake. It is also quite likely that our small mining company might have joint ventured the project earlier during the exploration stage. Indeed the company could be taken over at this stage as happened to Reunion Mining when Anglo American launched a bid to get control of the Skorpion zinc project in Namibia.

...through the development stage to receiving a cash flow from the mine...

We will now fast forward to the point where our steadily growing mining company has brought its project through the development stage and is now receiving cash flow from the mine. It is consequently much less of a speculation and more of a serious, if still probably quite small, mineral producer. It has cash which it can use in a number of ways. It can start to pay its shareholders a dividend but it will probably want to conserve some of its cash to pursue other exploration programmes. It could delay dividend payments so that it had the use of all its earnings to follow an aggressive growth strategy, both in terms of exploration but also corporately, where it could itself become a financing joint venturer or even a takeover predator.

...choice of cash cow or capital investment in further exploration...

At this stage our virtual mining company has arrived at a crossroads. It can become simply a cash cow for its shareholders through the dividend route, spending a little on exploration in the hope that it will discover another economic deposit. If it took this route it would not be impossible that it could be taken over by a larger group attracted by both the mine and the exploration areas. It is unlikely that the company, at this stage of its life, has the option of doing nothing, a luxury enjoyed by many mining companies in the distant past when corporate activity was the exception rather than the norm. So it is unlikely that our company will stand still, it will either grow or disappear into a bigger group, two outcomes that would benefit the shareholders in due course. There is one exception to this which is a growing company where there is one shareholder with a large enough interest to block any unwelcome approaches. In mining Antofagasta would be an example of this, as it was able to bring its copper projects in Chile to fruition, lifting it from market minnow to the Footsie, without fear of an approach because of the control exercised by the Lucsic family.

...to stay independent, the company must move quickly...

Having chosen to stay independent our virtual company then probably has to move fairly quickly to secure its position before it becomes a corporate target. It is important to realise these days that there seems to be no limit to the size or structure of mining companies that may get taken over, although the medium sized companies like MIM, Avmin and Ashanti seem to be the likeliest targets. The reason for this is probably that they are too small to resist a takeover but large enough to have a significant effect on the predator's figures. Having said that we have also seen in recent years giant mergers such as Anglo/De Beers and BHP/Billiton, although in the latter case we had a merger of equals rather than, as with the former, a cash takeover at a premium.

Few companies now graduate from explorer to diversified giant

Investors have to be realistic about the chances of getting in right at the start of a mining company's rise from explorer to diversified giant. Almost all the world's leading mining groups have been around as important companies for several decades. They have, of course, grown to a substantial size over the period, but there are very few around today who will remember them as hopeful juniors. Barrick Gold may be an exception, although some would argue that its strategy of growth by merger and acquisition hardly puts it into the category of a junior explorer that made the big time. Looking around today's mining markets, there are a number of smaller companies that have moved beyond the junior stage having developed a mine and started to flex their muscles both corporately and operationally. Amongst these companies would be Randgold Resources, First Quantum, Aquarius Platinum, and Antofagasta. Whether any one of these will make it to giant status in due course is quite another matter.

It is understandable, if a trifle optimistic, for investors to hope that they might be lucky enough to chance upon a future mining giant in the very early stages of its life. If one or two do they will be lucky indeed, but investors have the consolation of knowing that there are many opportunities to follow a junior out of the lower reaches of the sector onto a somewhat larger, if not giant, stage and make very good money in the process.

Managed investment vehicles

For those investors who find making choices in the mining market difficult, there are always managed funds to be considered. This is a very fluid area where the available choice is not quite what it used to be due to the lack of popularity of the mining sector over the last few years. In the 70s and 80s there were a considerable number of specialist mining/natural resource funds in London, but over the years these have tended to either be amalgamated with other similar funds or disappear completely. The funds are usually listed and take the form of open ended funds such as unit trusts or mutual funds, and closed end funds like investment trusts. Managed mining funds can also be found in a number of countries apart from the UK, including the US, South Africa and Switzerland. Mining funds in the US are likely to be aimed at investors interested in gold mining, whilst mining funds in the UK are mainly generalist in shape.

Fund managers vary in their knowledge of the sector

Although managed mining funds allow the investor to leave the choice of mining company, big or small, to a professional fund manager, it is often a value judgement as to whether the fund manager, whose expenses the investor is paying for through the annual management charge, actually has superior specialist knowledge of the sector. A number of funds do have very experienced specialists running or advising the funds, others use knowledgeable but not particularly specialist managers who have other non-mining responsibilities. These latter generalists may actually have a good grasp of the sector and a good track record, but are unlikely to be able to give the sector the sort of attention that is critical if their stock picking is going to include high risk/high reward situations.

There is also the issue of company access and specialist broker support. The specialist mining fund managers probably are on the early call lists of the most interesting smaller companies, and would also tend to see the best investment propositions from what is left of the specialist mining broking fraternity. It may be that the more generalist managers are not so well served in this area, or if they are their judgement may be less reliable due to their non specialisation.

Since this area is a very fluid one I am neither naming names or dropping hints about whom we are talking, but if investors are planning to use a managed fund for mining sector exposure some research will be necessary or they may end up no better off than if they had used a pin. The following table shows some of the mining funds available in the UK.

Table 3.6 - Mining funds in the UK

Fund name	Fund manager	Fund type
World Mining Trust	Merrill Lynch Fund Managers	Investment trust
City Natural Resources High Yield	Midas Capital	Investment trust
Resources Investment Trust	Resource Services	Investment trust
Baker Steel Gold	Ruffer Investment Management	Unit trust/OEIC
Gold & General	Merrill Lynch Fund Managers	Unit trust/OEIC
Natural Resources A	JP Morgan Fleming Asset Management	Unit trust/OEIC
ARF Global Resources Fund	Martin Currie Investment Management	Unit trust/OEIC
Global Basics	M&G Securities	Unit trust/OEIC

The final point that should be made is that using a managed fund does at least mean that a less confident investor will get the company spread that he may not be able to achieve for himself either because of lack of resources or lack of knowledge.

Chart 3.9: Merrill Lynch World Mining Trust [MLW] v FTSE All-Share [ASX]

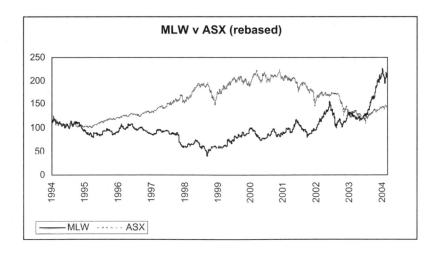

Source: Datastream

Stock market cycles

We have talked earlier about mining shares in relation to stock market cycles for industrial equities. I now want to look at mining share cycles over the last thirty years and to see where they sit in terms of overall market cycles, and whether there are any pointers we can find that could be applied in the future.

The situation that any investor wants to avoid is tying too much of his money up for long periods of time in a sector which is under performing. Having said this I am not backtracking on my view that every portfolio should have a core of gold shares because of their counter cyclical role when industrial shares come under pressure. In that context the gold content acts as insurance against a general equity bear market, and the gold core, when the general industrial market is in a bull phase, will in any case represent only a small percentage of the portfolio's value.

Australia, late 60s - the first modern mining boom

The first modern mining boom was that which 'infected' the Australian market in the second half of the 60s and which eventually ran out of steam following the rise and fall of Poseidon. The bull market lasted from 1966 until 1970, and until the last year or so marched in step with strong industrial bull markets, particularly in the US, the UK and South Africa. When these markets started to collapse in 1969 the Aussie mining market, led by the nickel explorers, took over the running. So seamless was the handover that stock market strategists theorised that the whole mining share sector could be seen as counter cyclical. Thus general investors, having run with the industrial bull market, could extend their profit making opportunities by switching into mining stocks at the appropriate moment. Those who got out of the 60s equity bull market and switched into Aussie mining shares would have hugely enhanced their capital gains, as long, of course, as they got out of their mining shares in time as well. Few did, in the UK partly because of the penal rates of tax on short term capital gains.

Attention turns to gold with the fear of inflation in the 70s

So strong had been the 60s equity bull market that in the UK it experienced another leg in the early 70s, topping out in 1972 at a level it didn't see again for many years. At that stage, although interest in mining shares had revived, it was taking a different shape to the base metal led late 60s boom which had come about partly as a result of the Vietnam War which boosted base metal demand and prices. Attention, stimulated by fear of rising inflation, had fallen on gold, and it was South African gold shares that now took the spotlight. This emphasis was to continue, off and on, well into the 80s, pushing non-precious metal stocks into the background.

In fact gold shares had begun to run late in 1971 following the closing of the US Government's *gold window*, at which foreigners had been able to present surplus dollars for conversion into gold at the fixed price of $35 per oz, for many years. This uptrend continued, accompanied by intermittent pullbacks, until the gold price, having started at $35, touched $200 at the end of 1974. Between 1971 and 1974 South African gold shares rose 600%, although they actually peaked ahead of the gold price in the spring of 1974. From 1972 until the beginning of 1975 equity markets around the world, particularly the UK and US, were in free fall. In December of 1974 the UK market plunged to a level in inflation adjusted terms not seen since the fall of Norway in 1940 in World War II. Gold shares had proved their worth as a hedge against general market weakness. Other non precious metal mining shares did less well in what was a market desperately trying to hedge the effect of runaway inflation. As an example between 1971 and 1974 RTZ (Rio Tinto Zinc) fell from 270p to 73p.

Gold enjoys another run in the late 70s with renewed fears of inflation and geopolitical problems

As industrial share markets began to recover in the mid 70s diversified mining houses also rallied on the back of hopes that the return of economic growth would revive metal prices and their earnings. In fact the next big run in mining share markets was once more in South African gold shares after they bottomed out in mid 1976 in parallel with gold itself which, having hit $200, had halved. A further pressure on gold shares was the fear of race riots in South Africa spilling uncontrollably over into the gold mines of the Witwatersrand. By the beginning of 1979 the political situation in South Africa had calmed and with gold itself rising through $200 for the first time gold shares began to run again. Between 1976 and the end of 1980 South African golds rose by 360% with the lion's share of the rise coming in 1979/80; gold itself rose over 700% over the same period. The revival of inflation and a chronically weak geopolitical situation described earlier in the section on gold led to a growing interest in commodities as real assets, and other non precious metal stocks also attracted attention alongside the golds. However, whilst base metal prices strengthened, as in the mid 70s the spotlight was primarily on gold, and this spilled over into silver.

Following the topping out of gold at $850 in January 1980 gold shares fell back, but by the second half of the year another gold bull run was building up as the Iran/Iraq War threatened stability in the oil rich Middle East. This was short lived and the bears returned in force, so by early 1982 gold shares had fallen back to the level at which they started their last decade run in 1976. Suddenly in barely six months South African gold shares rose by 300%. Other non gold mining shares were also strong on the back of a sustained recovery on Wall Street supported by optimism about growth prospects for the advanced economies. After this sharp surge gold shares retraced two thirds of the rise over the following two years, bottoming out in the first half of 1985.

Gold shares soared in 1986/87 in line with broad equity market, but...

This fall was followed by another bull run in 1986-7 with South African gold shares rising by around 200% to record levels. This happened against a background of industrial equity bull markets around the world. Consequently the mining bull run was a broad based one and other non gold mining companies ran strongly until the October crash in New York led to near meltdown in global markets.

Gold shares de-coupled from the gold price, as gold shares followed the equity markets down

There was also a de-coupling of gold shares from the gold price itself which saw gold, in the wake of the October crash, piercing $500 on the upside for the first time in four years even as gold shares slumped. The gold share market continued to be very volatile even as it worked its way cyclically lower throughout the 90s. There were big runs in South African gold shares in 1989-90 and then again in 1993-4, but these were not counter cyclical movements as equities generally were in a bull phase, albeit one with the ubiquitous *wall of worry* attached.

Gold shares recover their counter-cyclical nature in the wake of the high tech crash

In the later 90s and early in the new millennium industrial equity markets were very strong and this helped to sustain the share prices of the big diversifieds, with Rio Tinto for instance rising by over 180% between 1998 and 2000. During that period gold shares wallowed, almost in despair as the gold price sunk below $300 for the first time since 1979. But as the equity bull market capitulated on the back of the collapse of high tech stocks in 2000, gold shares came back into their counter cyclical own. Over the period from late 2000 until mid 2002 gold shares, unloved and heavily oversold by the end of the tech/internet boom, rose by as much as five times.

Platinum bull markets

Although above I have tended to concentrate on the bull runs in gold shares, there have been instances of strong markets in other mining groups. One example would be platinum shares which are confined primarily to the major South African stocks. These have enjoyed strong cyclical runs over the last thirty years, sometimes in association with gold shares, but not always. Indeed since platinum is used mainly in the car industry and in jewellery its price often moves in line with economic growth trends, partly as a result of being a non monetary precious metal in contrast to gold. Thus most recently we experienced robust growth in platinum shares in the late 90s when between 1998 and 2000 prices rose by almost four times. This run coincided with a rising equity market and a dull gold share market.

Canadian diamond boom 1992-94

It is also important to note that mining exploration booms can have a quite separate life of their own; the Canadian diamond excitement of 1992-4, which has been mentioned before, was a relatively recent case in point. The background in terms of economic growth was poor in the early 90s, and by 1992 the industry's leader, De Beers, was suffering from a sharp fall in demand for diamonds which further soured the atmosphere. That, however, did not seem to worry grassroots Canadian investors and Continental European investors who gobbled up the stream of new issues coming to market to take advantage of the diamond rush in the North West Territories. Of course critical to this was the large BHP/DiaMet diamond discovery at Lac de Gras (now called Ekati), and this provided the incentive for further speculation that other large discoveries might be made.

Sometimes mining share cycles run in line with the broad market as investors conclude that economic growth will feed quickly through to demand for metals, raising production and prices. In the late 90s the UK diversified mining groups performed strongly even as the broad stock market powered to record levels. It may be that the position of these companies within the FTSE100, arguably the third most important index globally after the Dow Jones and the Nikkei Dow, is now so central that they may become less counter cyclical than might have been the case thirty years ago.

Delving back into the more distant past one of the classic examples of mining shares outperforming industrial equities was the experience of US gold shares, led by Homestake Mining, in the 30s following the Wall Street crash of 1929. The driving force behind this out-performance was due, as it was in 1974 when gold shares also outshone equities, to a complete loss of faith in the economic/financial system which drove equities through the floor and the gold price in the opposite direction. Slightly more recently, and mirroring the Canadian diamond boom and the Australian nickel boom was the development of the Orange Free State gold field in the late 40s after the end of World War II. The substantial increase in interest and activity generated by the opening up of a major new gold field was as a result of an event unrelated to any other, and occurred during a period when equities generally were churning sideways because of post-war austerity.

Chart 3.10: Homestake v Dow Jones

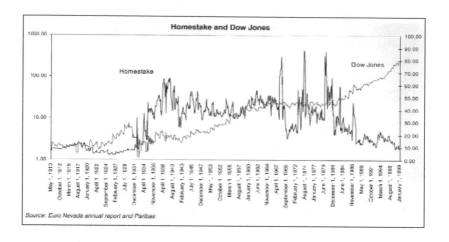

Portfolio strategy

The sort of volatility which has been described above also raises the question of portfolio strategy. Until quite recently the expansion of private pension schemes and the advent of tax sheltered investment vehicles in the form of PEPs and ISAs in the UK led to a rising stream of savings coming into the market, and not dissimilar trends were also to be found in the US. Europe, too, began to pay more attention to equities as an asset class for pension funds, and optimists began to speculate that share prices perhaps had entered a new era when share market weakness would be all but banished. In such an environment the need, indeed the wisdom, of trading shares, of taking profits, could be called into question. However, the cyclical nature of metal markets, and therefore of mining shares, is unchanging even in a new paradigm for stock markets, so those who ride the cycle and take profits will end up satisfied investors. More importantly they will surely want to return when the cycle beckons again. Participating in the cycle and making and taking profits should be the investment aim, not trying to make a lifetime's fortune in one go as many have tried to do, seduced by the prospects of the great scams that sweep across the mining market from time to time.

Building a mining portfolio

Obviously there has to be a portfolio before an investor can develop a strategy to manage it, and here we need to consider how to construct such a portfolio.

To begin with it is obvious that an investor could simply buy a group of mining giants – Rio Tinto, BHP Billiton, Anglo American, Xstrata, Newmont, Barrick, CVRD, and Alcoa – and leave it at that. He would have covered the mining waterfront but as a result he would have simply purchased a tracking portfolio. However once an investor has caught the mining bug it is unlikely he will be satisfied with managing his risk solely through investing in big diversified miners like these. He will surely want to maximise his returns through building his own mining sector exposure. In doing this there are a number of issues to be considered.

The portfolio needs to be dynamic

The first thing that we need to understand is that a personal mining portfolio cannot be a static thing. It seems an obvious thing to say, but if gold is the flavour of the month then it is pointless having little exposure to that metal but for historic reasons be loaded up with, say, copper producers. On the other hand any portfolio should in part be trying to anticipate trends, so it is little good slavishly following the trend and consequently too often buying near the top. Whilst any mining portfolio needs to be actively managed, it also needs a structure.

Core holdings

Above I have cautioned against buying only diversified leaders, but a couple of core holdings in the portfolio is probably sound.

Diversify by metal and not by country

If an investor is going to divide up his holdings into sections they should done by metal and not by country. Doing this should lead to a better balance in the stock list. Along with the core holdings should come a group of more focused shares directed towards backing the investor's call in the metal market. In this focused group there should be a balance of producers and explorers. If nickel is strong then exposure to producers will lead to sharply rising revenues, and hopefully earnings, dividends and share price as well. The explorers provide the hope factor that could turn a piece of desert into a mine and lead to a multiple increase in the share price. If the portfolio is metal orientated rather than country based, this will enable the investor to compare and take advantage of differential price movements between countries in a bull market. To explain, the developing gold bull market that started in late 2001 was led by the South African gold stocks with North American and Australian shares trailing in their wake. This was partly a function of a weak Rand. When gold, after a breather in the middle of 2002, took off again it was not the South Africans that ran most strongly this time but the North Americans and Australians. The South Africans trailed because the Rand was strengthening against other gold mining currencies, and additionally the SA government had announced their intention to accelerate the black empowerment process and also introduce mining royalty payments.

Don't be afraid of holding cash

I would also recommend that investors running personal mining portfolios should never be afraid of holding cash if they don't like the market. They are not specialist institutions running a mining fund for outside investors. In that situation the investor is expected to make the decision about being in or out of the mining market by selling the fund's units or shares not by encouraging the manager to go liquid. The manager is expected to concentrate on getting his stock picking right within the fund. But if a directly invested mining portfolio does go very liquid the investor must not consequently lose interest in the sector. If we assume that he has booked good profits in the course of selling some of his holdings we would expect him to return to the fray in due course, emboldened by his past success and ready to use the experience gained to repeat that success.

A balanced portfolio

So I am advocating a balanced portfolio with a core of big diversified companies perhaps representing between a quarter and a third by value. These stocks will also provide a useful income flow. I would also look for mining fixed interest opportunities in the convertibles area which would further improve the income stream. Perhaps these stocks could represent a further 10% of the portfolio. The rest of the portfolio would be divided between large metal specific mining companies (Inco for nickel exposure would be an example of the type of company), smaller diversifieds where there may also be takeover prospects mixed in, and smaller mining companies with growth potential and this would also include exploration companies. Because I am advocating a growth approach the emphasis in this 60% or so segment of the portfolio would be on selecting the most promising metals and then making sure that at least part of the exposure was fairly aggressive.

Riding the cycles

In the end because of the cyclical nature of the mining market it should be possible to make money from an actively managed mining portfolio on a regular basis. Also because of the sector's cyclicality active investors should not worry about hitting the top and the bottom of the market, except of course if you are buying at the top and selling at the bottom in which case you are only going to participate in a mining boom once. The aim should be to start securing profits relatively early, riding the market up with a diminishing number of positions, until you are left with just your core big stocks. And because of the sector's cyclical element I don't believe it hurts to return to the sector early, just as long as you retain enough liquidity to add shares as the market turns to the upside.

Company announcements

Once an investor has become involved in the mining sector he will undoubtedly be on the look out for regular news from the companies he has invested in. Later in the book we look at the range of information available on mining companies and the sources. But before we do that it would be helpful to have a look at a results announcement and an exploration report from two medium size mining companies. Investors will be looking out for such shareholder releases to check the progress of their investments, and the following comments will hopefully be useful in interpreting such company statements.

Reporting results

Profit/loss account

Below are the unaudited earnings figures for Randgold'sthird quarter to the end of September 2003.

Table 3.7 - Unaudited earnings figures for Randgold

	Sept 2003 (US$ 000)	June 2003 (US$ 000)	Sept 2002 (US$ 000)
Gold sales revenue	29,254	30,679	50,487
Cost of sales			
Production costs	9,265	5,243	5,353
Transport and refinery costs	104	113	201
Transfer to deferred stripping costs	(1,978)	929	(914)
Cash operating costs	7,391	6,285	4,640
Royalties	2,042	2,138	3,571
Total cash costs	9,433	8,423	8,211
Profit from mining activity	19,821	22,256	42,276
Depreciation and amortisation	2,162	2,224	2,630
Merger transaction costs	711	-	-
Exploration and corporate expenditure	3,454	4,554	5,503
Profit from operations	13,494	15,478	34,143
Interest received	254	445	49
Interest expense	(432)	(476)	(869)
Gain/(loss) on financial instruments	591	(52)	493
Other income and (expenses)	(332)	960	(3,357)
Profit on ordinary activities before taxes and minority interests	13,575	16,355	30,459
Income tax	-	-	-
Minority shareholders' interests	77	195	23
Net profit	13,652	16,550	30,482
Basic earnings per share (US$)	0.48	0.59	1.10
Fully diluted earnings per share (US$)	0.47	0.58	1.08
Average shares in issue (000)	28,754	28,074	28,181

Interpretation

A glance at the previous table shows that Randgold's quarterly profits are on the slide, gold sales revenue, profits from operations and net profits fell in the September quarter from levels achieved in June and also in the corresponding September quarter in 2002. If one was looking at the figures blind and knew that Randgold was a gold miner, the conclusion would be that the gold price was on a declining trend over the period or that the mine itself was in decline, producing less in each quarter. That last view would be, on the face of it, confirmed by looking at the segmented information in the statement on the operating results of the Morila mine in Mali in which Randgold has a 40% stake.

Table 3.8 - Morila results for the 3rd quarter to the end of September 2003

	Sept 2003 (US$ 000)	June 2003 (US$ 000)	Sept 2002 (US$ 000)
Mining			
Tons mined (000)	6,170	5,389	5,548
Ore tons mined (000)	602	1,273	849
Milling			
Tons processed (000)	822	771	546
Head grade milled (g/t)	8.24	10.50	27.7
Recovery (%)	91.8	90.9	88.1
Ounces produced	199,585	236,449	428,421
Average price received (US$/oz)	348	337	310
Cash operating costs (US$/oz)	85	70	28
Total cash costs (US$/oz)	111	93	49
Cash profit (US$000)	49,553	55,640	105,690
Attributable to RR (40%)			
Ozs produced	79,834	94,580	171,368
Cash profit (US$000)	19,821	22,256	42,276

With the mine operating results which appear on page 4 of Randgold's results statement it becomes clearer what is going on. Indeed a close read of the statement text would also have explained the decline in Randgold's earnings, but in a hurry the investor might not have had the time to read the statement immediately, relying only on the numbers for his first impression.

Fall in the ore grade

The true picture as shown in the operating results is that over the period shown the gold price had been improving steadily and the mine was increasing the tons of ore it was processing, and this last item would be what one would expect from a very young mine still in the expanding phase. Randgold's problem was a sharp fall in the gold grade of the ore mined which meant that total ounces produced fell back, undermining revenues despite the rising gold price.

The reason for this is not particularly sinister and had been flagged in previous quarters. The situation is that Morila has a very high grade core where mining has been concentrated. Since the mine is operated by AngloGold which has a 40% stake, the Mali Government has the residual 20% stake, this decision was a joint one, but we can assume it was done for cash flow reasons. Over a period of time the grade is expected to fall and Morila's production rate in ore terms is being increased to counter this.

Looking at costs

Returning to the income statement, we can see that production costs rose sharply but that was in line with figures in the mine operating results which showed a major increase in ore mined to counter the fall in grade. We can also see that the stripping cost figure rose sharply further raising operating costs. This latter figure relates to taking off the non mineralised material that overlays the ore, and in September expenditure in this area ran at a high level. This is quite a volatile figure and can provide surprises quarter on quarter. Another important deduction is the figure for royalties paid to Mali; these move closely in line with gold sales revenue. Depreciation is a relatively stable item and is an accounting concept which does not require any cash payment to be made, but exploration and corporate expenditure can seesaw all over the place. There was also a one-off item relating to expenditure on Randgold's failed attempt to take over Ashanti Gold; such items are rare but can distort analysts' forecasts.

Interest figures

As far as the interest figures are concerned, interest expense, following a steady build up of cash from dividends from Morila paid to the joint venture partners, was lower than in June as bank loans to the project continued to be repaid. The fall when compared to last year's September figure was substantial, in line with the reduction in debt levels (see following table). Interest received was surprisingly lower than in June, as it would have been expected that the build up in Randgold's cash balances (also see opposite in the balance sheet) would have led to a figure no worse than in June. This is the sort of item that the investor, if it concerns him, may have some difficulty finding an explanation. He can try his broker but his broker may well not know who to go to. If he does have a copy of Randgold's results where there is a telephone number for investor relations enquiries he could call the company, but, a quick answer may not be forthcoming. There is also a further complication as the statement refers to a sharp increase in interest received, but this is over the nine month period. In fact there may be a quite innocent explanation for the unexpected fall in interest received. Perhaps there are timing differences regarding the crediting of interest or perhaps market activities by Randgold's treasury department led to a temporary fall in the figure, or perhaps simply interest rates fell or cash was moved into more conservative deposit accounts giving a lower interest return.

Balance sheet

Below is the unaudited balance sheet for Randgold's third quarter to the end of September 2003.

Table 3.9 - Unaudited balance sheet for Randgold

	Sept 2003 (US$ 000)	Sept 2002 (US$ 000)	Dec 2002 (US$ 000)
Assets			
Cash and equivalents	107,842	56,331	59,631
Restricted cash	4,555	4,507	4,526
Receivables	11,316	10,027	14,262
Inventories	12,927	11,188	11,601
Total current assets	136,640	82,053	90,020
Property plant and equipment			
Cost	172,043	167,314	168,540
Accumulated depreciation	(98,803)	(89,773)	(92,104)
Net property, plant and equipment	73,240	77,541	76,436
Other long term assets	8,824	5,760	7,402
Total assets	218,704	165,354	173,858
Liabilities			
Bank overdraft	1,245	1,407	1,170
Accounts payable and accrued liabilities	15,568	34,136	20,564
Total current liabilities	16,813	35,543	21,734
Provision for environmental rehabilitation	5,308	4,556	4,972
Liabilities on financial instruments	6,475	6,193	7,530
Long term loans	14,786	23,393	19,307
Loans from outside shareholders in subsidiaries	958	1,445	1,330
Total long term liabilities	27,527	35,587	33,139
Total liabilities	44,340	71,130	54,873
Shareholders' equity	174,364	94,224	118,985
Total liabilities and shareholders' equity	218,704	165,354	173,858

Interpretation

Check the periods being compared

One thing to note is that Randgold in the case of its balance sheet compares its end of September figures with the comparable month in 2002, and does not give a figure for the previous quarter, although that figure is available if you have a copy of the June results. It is important when looking at these figures to understand what quarters are being talked about and compared. There may also be seasonal issues such as wet periods when mining activity naturally falls, and this sort of thing may provide quarterly operating differences that are outside the ability of the company to influence.

An expanding, cash rich company with a highly profitable mine

The balance sheet broadly confirms the position of Randgold as an expanding, cash rich company with a highly profitable mine. One of the items that it would pay to keep an eye on if Randgold was an old and dying company is the net property, plant and equipment figure which could shrink away to a very small figure as spending slowed and depreciation continued to eat into the cost figure. As it is, Randgold's small reduction in the net value is likely to reverse itself as expansion at Morila continues and spending on new projects picks up.

Very cash positive

Randgold's balance sheet is very cash positive which would not be the position of a mining company with limited or no operational cash flow but with exploration and development commitments.

Navan Mining, a UK company with mining interests in Spain and gold interests in Bulgaria, went under recently as its base metal mines in Spain bought with loan finance suffered a sharp reduction in revenues as metal prices crashed. Its balance sheet became hopelessly over geared (borrowings far exceeded the realisable value of the assets) and revenues were unable to cover the cost of financing the debt liabilities. What would have thrown doubt on the balance sheet value of the company's assets was the substantial losses on the income statement.

In Randgold's case all is extremely healthy. It is also interesting to note the provision for environmental rehabilitation which in recent years has become a defined item in more and more mining company balance sheets.

Position of the hedge book

The liabilities on financial instruments, essentially the current position of the hedge book, is a reflection of the fact that many gold mines hedge (sell their gold forward at a fixed price). Randgold has a very small hedge book but some gold miners retain considerable books and the liability figure for them may be a large and growing one if their gold is sold forward at a lower price than the current spot price of gold.

Summary

In conclusion investors need to keep their eyes on the reported results statements as mining can be a highly volatile business, and changes in the wind can show up in the figures before the storm sets in. The main thing is for investors to watch out for anomalies. Revenue figures can mislead as mines may be temporarily producing above budget due to high grades or stockpile sales. Net profits may contain special unrepeatable profits or one-off losses. Cost figures may also oscillate due to temporary problems such as a sharp fall in output or for more fundamental reasons like accelerating labour costs. If there is a cash flow statement that may also be revealing. Net generated cash may not be sufficient to cover bank borrowings needed for group expenditures for example. If something is not as it should be it should come out in the results report, and a sharp eye will hopefully spot it.

Exploration reports

The perception of news

When mining markets are buoyant some of the most eagerly awaited news can be the release of drilling results from companies with enticing exploration projects. A good result will usually lead to great market excitement. However, in a mining bull market even ordinary drilling results can be greeted with unwarranted enthusiasm, and if the market is really hot downright dull results can receive a mystifyingly positive welcome also. In stark contrast in a mining bear market you could find King Solomon's Mines themselves without raising the remotest investor enthusiasm.

Example: drilling results for First Quantum

In the next table, we can see some recent drilling results from First Quantum, a Canadian company with mines and highly prospective exploration projects in Zambia and the Congo (DRC). The project is the Lufua prospect just on the DRC side of the border with Zambia where First Quantum has a number of operations. The company operates a mine in the DRC at Lonshi which is about 60 kms away.

Table 3.10 - First Quantum results from Lufua (Nov 2003)

Hole no. LURC	Depth	Ore type (metres)	From (metres)	To (metres)	Interval (metres)	Total Copper %
40	102	Oxide	16	35	19	1.25
41**	78	Oxide	40	66	26	0.80
			66	78	12	awaited
42**	104	Oxide	23	104	81	1.79
43*	101					
44**	107	Oxide	64	97	33	1.90
45 **	134	Oxide	48	107	59	1.98
(46 redrilled)		Oxide	119	134	15	0.51
46	195	All	36	130	94	1.75
		Oxide	36	86	50	2.01
		Mixed	86	130	44	1.46
47**	144	Oxide	10	21	11	0.71
		Sulphide	60	144	84	2.10
48	197	Sulphide	61	75	14	1.25
		Sulphide	116	197	81	1.00

* No significant mineralisation found
** Hole abandoned in mineralisation

There are a number of important conclusions to be drawn from the previous figures.

Oxide ore treatment

First Quantum operates an SX-EW treatment plant at its Bwana Mkubwa plant over the border in Zambia around 45 kms distance. This allows it to treat oxide ores, which were very difficult and very expensive to treat before the SZ-EW process was developed, very cheaply. The Lufua ore appears to be primarily oxide although there are some sulphide shows, particularly at depth in a couple of the holes. The widths are large, the deposit is shallow and the grade is highly satisfactory for what, if developed, will be an open cut operation using earth moving trucks to mine the ore. The sulphides are not a problem either in that conventional treatment capacity exists over the border in Zambia to smelt and refine sulphide production.

Significance of a dead hole

As regards the drill results themselves it will be noted that one of the holes shows no mineralisation. Is this a worry? The answer in this case is no, although it might be in cases where there have only been a few holes drilled and a dead hole might signify that mineralisation on the property in question is sparse and therefore probably uneconomic. In the case of First Quantum the drill hole in question lies in the north west corner of the deposit (see the drilling map) and may well shut off the mineralisation in that direction, although in a situation like that the company will have to do more interpretation of the geology, and possibly more drilling, to confirm whether that is the case. At the time First Quantum released these drilling results it was awaiting more figures from holes 49 to 68 and some of them like 53 and 57 are probing quite a long way from the centre of the drilling programme. Followers of First Quantum would be waiting with some anticipation for these results.

Figure 3.1: First Quantum Drilling Map

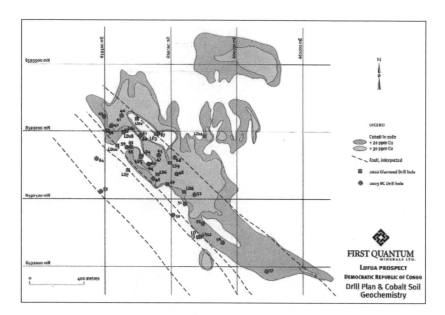

Terminology

When an exploration programme has been successful in discovering mineralisation and has done a fair amount of drilling, reports may use some of these terms – open at depth, open along strike, open to the north/south/east/west, open in all directions. Exploration results may also talk about dip, the angle that the orebody lies at and its thickness. What these terms are telling us is, in the opinion of the explorer, that the deposit has further potential for expansion in the direction indicated

Drill types

The First Quantum results we are looking at talk about the work being done by a reverse circulation drill. This method of drilling is used when drilling relatively shallow exploration holes and it is a relatively cheap and quick way to drill, and the rock can come out in the form of chips or a more conventional core. Two other drills sometimes used, which also deliver chip samples, are rotary and percussion drills. Below 300 ms, and perhaps in certain circumstances much shallower than that, a diamond drill will be used to bring out the ore for assaying. Although more expensive, diamond drilling provides a conventional core which avoids the possibility of contamination. Chip samples in the hands of unscrupulous promoters can be easily salted.

The Lufua drilling results look good

The Lufua figures suggest the possibility of a substantial future mine in the making. If the results from the other drill holes are good then we could be looking at 1 km of strike length, mineralisation down to at least 200 metres with orebody widths up to 80 metres with potential to expand on the flanks of the deposit. At this stage, though, any attempts by investors to come up with a possible size figure, in tonnes, for the orebody is fraught with danger. Such calculations are best left to the company to do and then announce with guidance notes. However, ahead of such announcements, there will be mining analysts who do have a go at a 'back of envelope' calculation.

Rough calculation – take care!

The sort of calculation that they might try is based on assumptions and therefore would provide only a very tentative possible figure. So they might assume that after the announcement the orebody had 500 metres of strike length and a width of 50 metres on average to a depth of 200 metres. That could give us 5 million cubic metres of mineralisation and the contained material could weigh 2.5 tonnes per cubic metre, providing us with a figure of 12.5 million tonnes of mineralisation. Whilst calculations like this may be fun, and may give a possible order of magnitude for the size of the orebody, they are far too provisional and speculative to allow much certainty. However, in mining booms people will give them house room and if the market is very bullish some credence will be given to even the most sketchy calculation (see later section 'Valuing an exploration play').

Don't be distracted by too much technical detail

Many reports, particularly in the early stage of exploration, will contain a lot of technical details that will most probably not be very price important. There will be talk about geophysical and geochemical surveying, an important part of a proper exploration programme, but part of the work that needs to go on to identify targets for drilling, and thus very much an early stage procedure. There may be talk of identifying anomalies which sounds exciting, but these guide drills to potential mineralisation and it is only drilling that will prove whether there is anything economic around. During the programme it is likely that the exploration team will take soil samples. These may turn out to have no mineralisation present or may have promising amounts in the sample. Since these are usually taken from very shallow depths, follow-up drilling will have to be done. Sometimes promising surface sampling can indicate economic mineralisation below, sometimes there is nothing there, so investors need to be wary about jumping to conclusions too quickly. Sometimes, as we saw a lot in the Australian mining boom, excitement can be engendered by one good looking drill hole which to the detriment of the particular company's share price is not repeated in subsequent reports.

Summary – handle exploration reports with care

Exploration reports should always be handled carefully. Like so much in the mining sector a higher risk approach probably pays off in a bull market, but interpreting exploration reports, more than any other aspect of mining sector investment, proves the point in the end that a little knowledge can be a dangerous thing.

4. Valuing Mining Shares

We now come to the vexatious issue of the appropriate method for valuing mining shares.

In the last ten years or so as the long industrial equity bull market, which started in the mid 70s when despair was at its deepest, entered its final stages, market strategists sought to attach some precision to valuing shares in order to underpin the new paradigm of perpetually rising equities. Part of this search for new valuation techniques was in response to a rising dissatisfaction with the conventional measurements of dividend yields and price earnings ratios, something that veterans of past mining bull markets will have some experience of. Of course cynics might suggest that the stock market needed new valuation markers to sustain share prices that when conventionally measured by PE and yield had clearly left 'terra firma' well behind. Two of the valuation indicators that we will be considering - ROCE/WACC and EVA - were particularly fashionable at the peak of the equities bull market in 1999.

The issue for mining shares is whether conventional valuation and measurement methods, such as the PE and yield, are really applicable to such a volatile sector which exhibits certain unusual, if not quite unique, characteristics.

For example, as we have mentioned before, the fact that a mine has a finite life means that when all ore is exhausted it ceases to have any value. A mining finance house must always then be spending money on finding new mines to replace those coming to the end of their lives and these new mines will often be far distant from the old operations. When a factory becomes old it can be knocked down and a new factory, perhaps making a different product, can be erected on the site of the old one. Also the price of mined products, metals, are extremely volatile compared with the output of a factory, be it cars, electronic goods, food products or whatever.

In the following section we will consider some of the most widely used valuation techniques as they apply to mining shares. We will first look at valuation methods for producers, and then techniques for valuing exploration plays.

Valuation methods for mining companies

Sector PE ratios

The PE, or price earnings ratio, where the earnings per share after tax are divided into the share price, can be useful as a quick guide for comparison of peer group stocks. Within the UK mining finance sector it gives investors a guide as to which stocks are out of line with the mean, enabling them to seek reasons for the ratings difference.

In basic terms-

- A **high PE** for a mining share might be signalling anticipation of a substantial uplift in earnings in the future due to new mines coming on stream. For a more mature mining company a high PE might simply be indicating that current earnings have dipped sharply, probably due to lower metal prices which are expected, nonetheless, to recover quickly.
- A **low PE** will usually signal the reverse of the above, and also possibly the market's view that a country risk may attach to the share.

Since a mining finance house or group is expected to replace its historic production over the longer term the wasting nature of its assets, its mines, does not preclude the use of the PE for valuation purposes.

The PE works less well for single mine companies, but following the consolidation of the South African gold mining industry, which used to be made up of predominantly single mine companies, most listed mining companies now seek to develop a suite of mines and build a long term future. The dividend yield, by which the declared dividend per share is divided by the share price, provides a current guide to the cash return to shareholders, enabling comparisons to be made with risk free returns from bank deposits and gilts. The problem with dividend yields is that a low return might indicate either of two quite different things-

- that only a **small dividend can be afforded,** or
- that the **return is likely to grow very rapidly** in the near future and the market is pricing in the prospect of rapid dividend growth.

The above relates substantially to other market sectors as well, but in certain cases mining PEs and yields can be flashing sector specific warnings.

In particular where a forecast PE is low and the yield high this may well not be signalling an attractive buying opportunity if the stock in question is a single mine producer. What may be happening is that the mine has only a couple of years profitable life left and is planning to pay out all its earnings in the form of dividends, hence the high yield. The share price is low, thereby generating the low PE, because whilst the earnings are healthy the very short life of the mine makes their amortisation by the shareholder essential. In such circumstances the share price can only really match the expected flow of income to the end of the mine's life. Now, some investors may want to gamble that the mining company will be able to find new sources of ore, often possible if the relevant metal price is increasing at the time, and therefore the attractive short term income flow is some compensation for the risk that no more ore will be forthcoming from the exploration effort. But this is a decision requiring great care, as the risk is that an investor will end up with a couple of years of nice dividends and a worthless piece of paper at the end.

In terms of where mining sector PEs stand in relation to the broad market the sector's historic volatility is the key. So in a metals downturn PEs of sector leaders will fall below the market average, and vice versa during a metals upturn. Part of this relates to the trailing nature of often highly volatile earnings, with high historic PEs often signalling a sharp upswing in the next reported earnings. But when the sector is running strongly, high PEs often simply reflect investor enthusiasm for mining shares.

Below we can see the PE range for the main UK mining companies over the past five years (Xstrata only listed in 2003). Looking at Antofagasta we can see some interesting influences at work – the high PEs for 1999 and 2000 underline the major expansion of production underway at the time and the high PE for 2003 reflects the developing strength in the copper price.

Table 4.1 - Annual PE range for selected UK mining companies

	1999	2000	2001	2002	2003
Anglo American	29-8	14-9	14-8	16-9	21-10
Antofagasta	40-11	71-17	17-13	29-13	30-14
BHP Billiton	36-8	36-15	18-11	16-14	29-13
Rio Tinto	32-14	31-15	20-10	18-11	22-13

Source: Financial Times

Discounted cash flow/net present value

For a more explicit valuation of diversified mining groups the *net present value* (NPV) based on the forecast future discounted cash flows has a respectable following.

Here the value of a mining group's after tax earnings over ten to fifteen years is calculated, and then discounted back using an appropriate interest rate, these days between 5% and 10%. It might be argued that operations in high inflation countries like South Africa and some Latin American countries should carry a higher discount rate. However it must be remembered that virtually all metals are priced in hard currencies, particularly the US$. This means that if local currencies are consequently weak because of high inflation, operating margins may not be affected as revenues, and thus returns, may keep pace with rising costs. Whatever the rate used, the discounted results in today's money are then aggregated to give a final net present value per share of the group's earnings potential which can be compared against the current share price.

Using this measurement does entail making heroic decisions about the metal prices to be used in calculating the stream of income, but it does in the end give a calculated value for the group's shares which can be compared against the market value of the shares. An NPV, however, can end up giving a result materially higher or lower than the market share price, and it may be that whether the result is higher or lower relates to where we are in the mining sector cycle.

Example: Net present value calculation

Using internal management earnings figures from a small UK mining company, which will remain nameless, developing a mine in the Far East, below we can see the forecast cash flow (taxed earnings) discounted back to give us the NPV of the mine. The mine may have a longer life than ten years and the effect on the cash flow of using a relatively low discount rate of 5% is much more gradual than if a higher rate had been used. For instance if you wanted to be conservative and use a 10% rate, which would be rather drastic today bearing in mind that interest rates and the rate of inflation are well below 10%, the sort of effect that that would have on the figures below would be to reduce the current NPV of Year 10's cash flow to around £4.5 million rather than £8.1 million. In relation to the NPV the company's market value suggests that there may still be value in the shares.

Year	0	1	2	3	4	5	6	7	8	9	10
Cash flow (£m)	(8.8)	(1.6)	8.5	18.9	16.7	14.8	14.1	11.6	9.4	13.2	13.2
NPV (5%) (£m)	(8.8)	(1.5)	7.7	16.3	13.7	11.6	10.5	8.2	6.4	8.5	8.1

Total cash flow (£m)	110.0
Total NPV (£m)	80.7
Company market value (£m)	49.3

Internal Rates of Return

Internal rates of return (IRR) represent the reciprocal of the NPV. The IRR that the NPV gives us as a percentage of the share price can then be measured against the discount rate used in arriving at the IRR. If the IRR is higher than the discount rate the share is good value, but that does, of course, beg the question as to whether the correct discount rate has been used. In a period of very low inflation a low discount rate can be used and vice versa, but mining companies operate in a variety of countries with often differing inflation rates and this will need to be borne in mind when selecting the appropriate discount rate.

Rough and ready methods

Two rough and ready methods frequently used in valuing mining shares are *net assets per share* and *metal value per share*.

Net assets per share

This relates primarily today to historic conditions that used to rule in the glory days of the old South African mining houses when the great percentage of their assets were in listed associates and subsidiaries. It was thus possible to calculate the market value of their listed assets and the result, with the directors value of unlisted subsidiaries and balance sheet items added in, would give a value for the company that could be compared to the market value of the mining house. Today, however, even traditional mining groups like Anglo American have most of their assets in the form of unlisted wholly owned operations.

Metal value per share

Metal value per share has been widely used over the last few years in the gold sector to try and calculate an overall value that can be used for sector comparisons for operating and developing gold mining companies.

There are difficulties with this approach as some gold groups have high cost resources and others have low cost reserves. If the exercise is being carried out at a time of low gold prices, and so a low gold price is used for valuation purposes, the result can give a false impression of the relative attractiveness of a company with high cost resources. The share price of the company will be low because the market knows that its gold resources are uneconomic at the time. However unsuspecting investors will see that the underlying gold value per share of its assets looks very interesting when compared to its far more robust low cost peers. The answer is to apply a discount to the high cost resources, but the problem is how big a discount. Some would ignore such companies in those particular circumstances, but a rise in the relevant metal price could well pitch these companies right back into consideration.

In short, metal value per share could work quite well as a forward looking tool but anyone using it must be aware of the pitfalls. Julian Baring used a rough and ready formula for the discount which simply applied a value to the reserves and resources of 10% of their contained metal. Others vary the percentage discount figure and even make it two tier as between reserves and resources. Neither approach is scientific, or ever likely to be, but results do enable relative value calculations to be done against other companies in the peer group.

As a variation on this many analysts and mining companies, particularly in the gold sector, draw up peer group comparisons by dividing a company's market capitalisation by either its annual production, its measured reserves or its indicated and inferred resources. The upshot of this is that a current value per oz of gold in the three categories can be calculated and then peer group comparisons can be made. The problem with this kind of approach is that the figures must be precise and exactly comparable or comparisons and consequent conclusions may be unsound.

Example: Metal value per share

For an example of how this would work in practice we can look at the latest (Feb 2004) figures for Russian gold miner Peter Hambro Mining.

The calculations are simply done by taking the market capitalisation of the company (converted into US$) and dividing that to give us a per oz figure for production, reserves and resources. The result can then be compared with group companies. Whilst a gold miner has been used for the purposes of illustration any metal producer could be compared in a similar way.

Table 4.2 - Example mkt cap per oz calculation for Peter Hambro

Market cap US$m	Production ozs/yr	Reserves ozs	Resources ozs	Market cap per oz		
				Production	Reserves	Resources
618	170,000	3,400,000	19,900,000	3,635	181	31

In a similar vein you could also take the number of shares in issue and divide them into production, reserves and resources to give a figure for ozs per share. The analysis could then be extended to value that oz per share figure and then compare it with the share price as in the table below.

Table 4.3 - Example metal value per share calculation for Peter Hambro

Share price $	Issued shares	Ozs per share			Value ($400) of ozs per share $		
		Production	Reserves	Resources	Production	Reserves	Resources
9.65	64,000,000	0.002656	0.053125	0.310938	1	21	124

Looking at the results of that exercise one can see that Peter Hambro looks expensive on the basis of its current production, with a gold revenue value per share well below its current share price. The reason for this, however, is that production is expected to rise sharply over the next few years on the back of a large and still expanding resource figure.

Some analysts like to use a front end measurement figure depicting value per oz in the ground. So if they are looking at a Canadian gold miner they may take the view that the value of Canadian gold in the ground should be US$50/oz. If they find a company where the value of its gold in the ground calculated by dividing its market capitalisation by total resource ozs comes out at, say, $25 then that company is cheap. This has the merit of being simple but as we said earlier in this section the estimated costs of producing that oz of gold must be taken into account, so crude valuations based on metal value can be misleading.

ROCE/WACC

We next come to ROCE/WACC - a company's return on capital employed compared to its weighted average cost of capital. Although this concept was all the rage in the 90s it is not a new concept at all, and stock market commentators and economists were aware of it decades ago. The basic thesis behind the concept is that companies destroy shareholder value if the return (crudely, operating profit minus tax) on their capital employed (equity plus debt capital) falls below the weighted average cost of that capital.

How well this works, particularly for mining companies, is open to question but its supporters proselytise aggressively in its favour. Unfortunately it is quite possible to adjust one of the WACC factors, the cost of debt, to a company's advantage as Anglo American did when it moved its incorporation from South Africa to the UK. Using long dated gilt rates for the calculation, Anglo's theoretical WACC fell sharply as UK gilt rates were in the 5-6% range against South African gilt rates in the 12-13% range.

The thesis of destroying shareholder value, however, can be too theoretical, and during bear markets even if the ROCE/WACC ratio is above one, i.e. the company is supposedly creating value for shareholders, the chances are that the company's share price, in line with the market, is falling in value which is the most painful manifestation of capital destruction, particularly at the portfolio level. In some contrast a few years ago in an unpublished look at ROCE/WACC and the mining sector, the global mining research team at French bank Paribas discovered that in the 90s Canadian aluminium giant, Alcan, had consistently posted a ROCE/WACC ratio below one; its share price, however, steadily improved throughout the decade.

Enterprise Value (EV)

Another valuation measure much used is enterprise value (EV) which is simply the aggregate of a company's market capitalisation plus the market value of all non-equity finance (debt, convertibles, warrants) either on or off the balance sheet and minus any cash holdings.

This is a possibility for valuing large mining groups where an appreciable percentage of the assets are fully developed and providing steady cash flow, but where there are enough new projects to enhance that cash flow over the medium term represented in part by the non-equity finance. In order to get a multiple that can then be compared with peer group companies a profit measure, often EBITDA (earnings/profits before interest, taxation, depreciation and amortisation), can be selected and divided into the EV. Theoretically the higher the multiple the more expensive or, conversely, the more highly rated the share.

Example:

Taking the example of the BHP Billiton group-

1. we have a **market capitalisation** of $57.3 billion,
2. **net debt** at the interim stage (December 2003) of $6.4 billion,
3. giving an **enterprise value** of $63.7 billion,
4. the interim **EBITDA** figure was $3.12 billion and for the purposes of this example we will annualise it to $6.25 billion, and
5. if we then divide the EV by the annualised EBITDA for BHP Billiton we get a **multiple of 10.2**.

This can then be compared with other peer group companies such as Rio Tinto whose current EV is $48.4 billion and EBITDA of $3.7 billion (December 2003 final results) to give us a multiple of 13.1 which makes Rio Tinto either more expensive or more highly rated that BHP Billiton.

A number of conclusions could be drawn from the different multiples –

* the market prefers Rio Tinto,
* Rio's earnings upturn is lagging BHP,
* Rio is more expensive for a particular reason, etc.

The difference could provide a switching opportunity if a look at both companies reveals no obvious reason for the value differential.

Economic Value Added (EVA)

Economic Value Added (EVA) is another measure which was widely used in the 90s. Then market movements seemed to be under the perpetual control of the new investment banking giants and their expanding technical analysis departments as they churned out, with growing confidence and authority, theoretical share valuations. EVA recognises that invested capital expects a return for its use and that genuine profit is the excess left over, after the allocation of a charge for its use, to invested capital. So EVA comes out as net operating profit less adjusted tax minus the return on invested capital as calculated by using the company's WACC (%).

The thinking behind this measure is that a company only deserves a value in excess of its invested capital if it generates a return above the cost of that capital. I suspect that EVA, though conceptually reasonable, may be a little too complex for easy use. It may, though, offer some help in assessing mining share value, in that the sharp swings that metal prices experience, and the inevitable effect on mining company earnings of those swings, could be useful in a cyclical sector in pointing out moments of potential under and over valuation. The point being that mining shares returns on capital can at times swing wildly. In what is sometimes a contra-cyclical sector that could mean that when the return has slipped below the company's WACC that could be a clear buying signal despite the likely claims that the company was destroying value. One must also remember that in a low interest rate environment a company's WACC will reduce.

Valuation should not be dogma

The construction of valuation tools is understandable as investors from all levels attempt to provide themselves with the comfort of a little certainty in their sector and stock picking. It is also true that the tightening up of insider dealing rules and other regulation has taken away some of the tried and trusted methods of the past. However, too much dogma in this area may well lead to a hardening in the investment arteries, particularly of private investors, whose investment style has historically always been more intuitive than that of the professional institutional investor. In short the interested investor should establish a body of knowledge on the mining sector and then trade momentum on a short, but hopefully profitable, rein.

Valuing an exploration play

The above valuation methods depend on the mining group having earnings, dividends or reserves and resources to be used in any calculation or peer group comparison. In the case of an exploration share the process of evaluation is much harder but, bearing in mind what we said earlier about calculating the size of First Quantum's DRC prospect at Lufua, we might proceed by creating a virtual company for the purposes of demonstration.

Our virtual company may or may not have some mineral production and therefore income, but its value will be materially affected by a big mineral discovery. Our company has a wide ranging exploration programme, and for the purposes of this example its copper exploration looks particularly promising.

Results from the first drill hole are encouraging

Following a programme of exploration, the company announces it has struck copper on one of its properties. The discovery is based at this early stage on just one hole; others are being drilled but results are not immediately to hand. The hole itself goes down 100 metres and has mineralisation from 20 metres down to 100 metres at which point the drill was stopped. Over the 80 metre intersection the sample assayed a very healthy 2.25% copper. Since the hole was stopped in mineralisation at a relatively shallow depth the prospect of a low cost open pit copper mine beckons (an open pit operation can work down to 300 metres, and depending on ground conditions, even deeper than that). But first results from the other holes being drilled are needed. In due course other fairly widespread holes report similar results to the first hole.

It is worth noting here that the grade of metal in the ore can be economic even when it is low (0.5% would be low), if the deposit was both large and shallow and the ore could be easily mined and treated. Rio Tinto's Bingham Canyon mine in the US, which has a reserve grade of 0.6%, would be an example. Conversely a high grade project like Konkola Deep in Zambia, where the grade is 3% plus, maybe uneconomic due to the depth and the huge water inflow.

The shares surge, but what value should be given to the company?

The shares take off in excitement. At this stage the issue of valuation comes in. A ready method of applying some value to the prospective mine would be by using a 'back of envelope' technique. Since an investor rarely has access to the property, even if he could get there, and no exposure to the inside chatter going on about the find, he must make do with his own devices. He could proceed thus;

He has results from eight holes. The mineralisation runs east/west and four of the holes have been drilled along this strike – one every 100 metres. Four holes have been drilled 50 metres to the south as the exploration manager believes that the mineralisation dips in that direction also, and he is correct. It will take a few months to formulate and carry out further drilling but the idea will be to drill some holes outside the present grid of mineralisation and probe whether the orebody extends beyond. Other holes will be drilled within the grid to confirm the mineralisation has continuity along its strike length.

Calculating the mineral value

For the moment investors or potential investors have no idea whether the company's rising capitalisation spurred by the discovery is reasonable. A few heroic calculations are needed therefore for holding purposes.

1. The current extent of the deposit is 300 metres by 50 metres by 80 metres or 1.2 million cubic metres.
2. That last figure multiplied by 2.5 tonnes per cubic metre weight gives us a rough guide as to the volume of ore indicated so far, 3 million tonnes.
3. The grade is 2.25% copper, suggesting an situ figure of **67,500 tonnes** (149 million lbs) of copper.

A nice start but unlikely to be big enough to be developed without more ore being found. At a copper price of US$1.00/lb the value of the deposit, using Julian Baring's 10% of value yardstick, is just short of **$15 million**.

But the orebody may be larger…and the shares surge forward again

Now since this is a virtual or make-believe company we will imagine that in all the excitement of the discovery its market value, which was a modest $9 million at the start, has risen to $37 million, well ahead of the imputed value above of the new find as it stands. But, of course, the drilling programme is in its infancy and rumours are circulating that the strike length could be over 1000 metres and the ore goes down at least another 100 metres. The orebody also may also extend 200 metres to the south. If this rumour proves true and the grade holds up then the size of the orebody could be over ten times the size of the presently indicated 3 million tonnes. The market gets the bit between its teeth and the shares double for a market capitalisation of $74 million.

But our virtual investor is in a quandary; is this a fair valuation for the company at such an early stage of its life?

Introducing more precision, calculating the net present value

To get a better idea of what we might have we now return to our 'back of envelope', but replace the value of metal in the ground with a more precise valuation method – the net present value. We have, though, to make heroic assumptions again. However, since we are in a highly charged market there is a need to try and establish some valuation level to avoid investment decisions regarding our virtual company being made completely in the dark. Looking at other similar deposits that have been brought to production the investor can come up with a possible, if speculative, structure for the deposit based on the, also speculative, belief that the deposit will turn out to be at least as big as the market rumours suggest. We have, incidentally, assumed that we are in a metals bull market where optimism drives the market for the moment. We fix on the parameters of a possible mine as below.

Table 4.4 - Parameters of the virtual discovery

Annual production	80,000 tonnes (176 million lbs) copper/year
Total development costs	US$300 million
Year of first full production	Year 4
Copper price	$1/lb copper
Revenue/year	$176 million
Operating costs @ $0.45/lb/year	$79 million
Financing @ 7%/year	$21 million
Depreciation over 10 years/year	$30 million
Net profits until year 7/year	$46 million
Tax from year 7 @ 25%/year	$11.5 million
Total undiscounted profits over 10 years	$414 million
NPV discount rate	7%
NPV over 10 years	$239 million
Current market capitalisation	$74 million

But we must question the assumptions made

If we are confident of the rumours of a much bigger orebody which might allow an operation of the size shown above, then the shares may still be cheap. However since the possible mine will not produce for four years the shares are really a long term situation and additional discounts could be applied to the earnings flow to take account of this. Some analysts would apply a larger discount rate than 7% for the period of development until first production, others might arbitrarily cut the value of the cashflow being discounted during the development period. We must also not forget the knotty problem of what metal price assumption we want to make. Usually it is appropriate in speculative situations to use a price comfortably below the current market level for reasons of prudence. In a roaring metals bull market the shares may, however, reflect a far more optimistic mood and the metal price used may well be based on the cyclical peak level. Judging the valuation level of an exploration share on this basis will almost certainly lead to tears.

Be wary of irrational exuberance

All this has to be taken into account during the exciting early stage of exploration drilling when calculating what the new mine might reasonably be worth if brought to production. Of course excitement about the discovery can, indeed often does, lead to gross overvaluation of the shares. During the course of this excitement experienced mining analysts may produce valuation matrices that support the market madness. On occasions their work may be correct but in many cases it will not, being more akin to the wish being father to the thought. Sometimes this may be due to enormous pressure from the company (Bre-X for example), sometimes it may be due to the current position of the analyst's employer (i.e. corporate activity).

The problem with exploration is that it is exciting in the beginning but, following a decision to develop a new mine, the next stage, which in some cases can last several years as the mine is built, is often a quiet one in market terms. So in the end dabbling in mining exploration shares has to carry a *caveat emptor* warning, but it is great fun, and it can be rewarding if you are not too greedy and you have created a credible valuation measure which you are comfortable with and to which you are going to stick.

Defining reserves and resources

Throughout the book I have talked a lot about *reserves* and *resources*, terms that historically have often been bandied about in a reckless manner. Today the terms have a very specific definition and in explaining them I will quote extensively from a paper given by Steve Vaughan of McMillan Binch and Sonja Felderhof of Aird & Berlis (both of Toronto) to a Mineral Law seminar in Nevada in July, 2002. The definitions given draw heavily on the guidance of Australia's Joint Ore Reserves Committee (JORC), the Canadian Institute for Mining (CIM), the US Society for Mining, Metallurgy and Exploration (SME), and the South African Code for Reporting of Mineral Resources and Mineral Reserves (SAMREC).

Below are Vaughan and Felderhof's definitions for the main categories of reserves and resources.

Mineral/ore reserves

"The guidelines provide that Mineral Reserves result in an estimated tonnage and grade which can be used as the basis of a viable project in the opinion of the Competent Person. The term *Mineral Reserve* need not signify that extraction facilities are in place or operative or that all governmental approvals have been received."

Mineral resources

"A Mineral Resource is a concentration or occurrence of material of intrinsic economic interest in or on the Earth's crust in such form or quantity that there are reasonable prospects for eventual economic extraction."

Measured resources

"A Measured Mineral Resource is estimated in the same manner as an Indicated Mineral Resource (see below MC), except that (1) it can be estimated with a high level of confidence; (2) the information must be detailed and reliable; and (3) the locations (drilling MC) are spaced closely enough to confirm geological and/or grade continuity."

Inferred resources

"An Inferred Mineral Resource is that part of a Mineral Resource for which tonnage, grade and mineral content can be estimated based on geological evidence and assumed, but not verified, geological and/or grade continuity"

Indicated resources

"An Indicated Mineral Resource is that part of a Mineral Resource for which tonnage, densities, shape, physical characteristics, grade and mineral content can be estimated with a reasonable level of confidence."

Exploration results

"Exploration Results (described as 'Exploration Information' in Canada and the US) are estimates which cannot be classified as Mineral Resources or Mineral Reserves. If an entity reports Exploration Results, estimates of tonnage and grade must not be reported. The CIM Standards on Mineral Resources and Mineral Reserves (the 'CIM Standards'), however, do permit such reporting as long as it is clearly stated that such estimates are conceptual or order of magnitude. Similarly, A Guide for Reporting Exploration Information, Mineral Resources and Mineral Reserves (the 'SME Reporting Guide') allows the weighted average grade of specified assay intervals to be reported."

It depends on the amount of drilling

In essence the difference between reserves and resources, and between the various categories of each, relates to the amount of drilling that has been undertaken on a mineral deposit. The closer the spacing between the drill holes the more certain will be the estimates of the deposit's size and ore grade and therefore whether an economic mine can be established.

Resources, a term which incidentally the Securities and Exchange Commission (SEC) in the US does not recognise, are those parts of the orebody which have not been sufficiently drilled for there to be complete confidence on size and grade – measured resources having had more and closer spaced drill holes than inferred resources which may have only been very lightly drilled. It is worth having some familiarity with these definitions as mining companies frequently refer to them, particularly when they are developing a new mine, and annual reports will often contain group reserve and resource tables.

5. Madness in Mining Markets

This section looks at a few examples of the sort of madness that can infect mining share markets. Such events are sometimes loosely described as scams, although often what happens is far more an issue of wild over-enthusiasm on the part of investors. However, we start with a genuine scam, and a recent one at that, with plenty of lessons to teach about market navigation - Bre-X an its gold project on Kilimantan..

Bre-X Minerals

The company was incorporated in Canada in 1988. The two key personalities in Bre-X were John Felderhof and David Walsh, the former a geologist and the latter a stockbroker. Both men had been short of money in their early professional years, and in its early days Bre-X seemed infected with the same problem. Interestingly Felderhof and Walsh's first venture together was a trip to the island of Kalimantan in Indonesia some five years before Bre-X was founded. Following its incorporation by Walsh (Felderhof did not become actively involved with the company until 1993) and the initial small scale financings, the company pursued gold prospects in Canada's North West Territories near to the Lupin mine of Echo Bay. When that failed to turn up anything Bre-X turned to Quebec's Joutel gold area and then in 1992 it was back in the NWT this time chasing diamonds in the wake of BHP/DiaMet.

The background to Busang

Felderhof, who much earlier in his career in the late 60s had, as a field geologist, found OK Tedi, a big copper/gold deposit in Papua New Guinea, was re-contacted by Walsh in 1993 as Bre-X seemed to be heading for extinction. Walsh flew to Indonesia where he and Felderhof went to visit some prospects that Walsh had asked Felderhof to look out for. The approach of Bre-X so far had been unfocussed to say the least, but opportunism is often the driving force in exploration companies and Bre-X's gadfly actions were not abnormal for mining's junior sector. In due course Bre-X acquired the licence to work on the Busang gold prospect, and at this stage things began to get interesting. Busang had first been surface sampled in 1988 by an Australian group called Westralian where interesting values between 6 and 27 grammes of gold per tonne had been assayed. Westralian joint ventured Busang with another Australian company, Montague Gold, who did some shallow drilling on the prospect in 1989. Some reasonable values were found but they were thought to be too inconsistent and the drilling programme was ended.

Bre-X takes off

So it was in 1993 that Bre-X became involved in a discarded gold prospect in Indonesia. Although the company was short of money, personnel were hired including a Philipino exploration manager, Michael de Guzman. De Guzman was experienced with a good professional reputation and had worked for Benguet, the Philippines gold group, and Australian junior, Pelsart. The further financing, drilling and promoting of Busang by Bre-X was spread over three years between 1993 and 1996. During that period it moved from the tiny, but lively, Alberta Stock Exchange to Toronto's main board. Its price moved from a low of C$0.10 in 1992 to the equivalent of C$330 in late 1996, with various share placements along the way, some of them well below C$5.00. This incredible increase catapulted both Walsh and Felderhof, whose careers and circumstances were at a very low ebb when they went to Kalimantan in 1993, from poverty to enormous wealth.

The problem was that whilst the share price powered ahead, and Walsh, in particular, was promoting the story of a fabulously rich gold deposit at Busang to a very interested public, work at the prospect under the direction of de Guzman was, as we now know, finding only minor traces of gold in the extracted drill core. Despite that, a number of Canadian brokers with experienced mining analysts became enthusiastic followers of the stock. Also over the three years, the developing story, combined with the extraordinary share price performance, attracted several major mining groups, including CRA, Barrick Gold, Placer Dome and eventually and fatally Freeport McMoran, interested in doing a deal with Bre-X.

Despite the limited drilling done on Busang before Bre-X's involvement, and the unreported lack of success of Bre-X's own drilling programme, the company's promotion of the deposit escalated the size of the gold resource until it appeared to be the largest undeveloped gold mine in the world. In 1993, on the basis of the earlier drilling by Westralian and Montague, David Walsh projected a 20 million tonne orebody with a grade of 2 plus grammes per tonne, mining costs of US$155 per oz of gold recovered to yield a prospective annual cash flow of US$10 million. The grade was unexciting but clearly the expectations were that the ore would be both easy to mine and to treat, which would make the project robustly economic particularly as it would be an open pit operation. The following year the company had increased its Busang resource target to 30 to 60 million tonnes grading over 3 grammes per tonne. That tonnage and grade represented a gold resource of 3 to 6 million ozs. By the middle of 1996 Walsh had raised his Busang target resource figure to 30 million ozs, and later in the year he began to talk about 47 million ozs of gold. Early in 1997 Bre-X raised this resource estimate to 71 million ozs, even as the storm clouds gathered.

By then attention had turned to the potential of other parts of the Busang lease, and from time to time the company also let drop that other exploration areas in

Indonesia and elsewhere in the region were also extremely promising. Bre-X made regular presentations to investors in North America about progress and the potential of Busang. It played host to a number of Canadian brokers on the site itself, although such visits were carefully managed.

The experienced mining consultants, Kilborn Engineering, carried out an audit of work done on Busang which confirmed the prospect's promise. Kilborn remained active on Bre-X to the bitter end, but it is important to understand that though Kilborn were on site at Busang it was their job to see that the work being carried out conformed to expected standards, not to do the work themselves. They expected that the results coming back from the assay laboratories away from the site were correct. On that assumption was Kilborn's support for the project based.

Meanwhile, behind the scenes...

The potential of the deposit was so enormous that not only did Bre-X find itself pursued by major mining groups, the Indonesian Government and the family of President Suharto were also anxious to be involved in the Busang phenomenon. Behind the scenes, as we now know, things were much more fragile. Michael de Guzman had taken to salting the cores before they were delivered to the assay laboratories; *salting* was a technique whereby shavings of outside gold were added to the core to boost the gold values during the assay process. When the results were released the gold grades gave the impression that Busang was a consistent gold orebody with economic gold content. In fact as Westralian and Montague had shown much earlier it was anything but an economic prospect.

The other problem with Busang was that John Felderhof, who was the executive in charge of the operation, was not a natural paperwork man and the status of the Busang lease was sometimes not clear because of this. There were also strange omissions in the drilling work which raised questions, particularly as the area being drilled expanded.

As far as the pursuing mining groups were concerned it seemed that CRA's interest was inflamed by the fact that it had turned its back on Busang when Montague brought it to CRA first. CRA was also prepared to leave Bre-X as a majority holder in the project and undertake to raise all the finance for the project. Its only requirement was that it wanted to do a full due diligence on Busang to confirm Bre-X's work. It was an attractive deal for Bre-X but the company for reasons that we now understand was reluctant to agree to CRA's terms.

If Bre-X's attitude to the CRA offering was puzzling so were its discussions with Barrick, the Canadian gold giant. Bre-X wanted Barrick to take an equity stake in Bre-X to secure its short term funding needs, with a right to back into the venture on a joint basis when a development decision was taken. The Barrick discussions dragged on, with Barrick seeking much tougher joint venture arrangements than CRA had wanted. Around the same time, another Canadian gold giant, Placer Dome, came into the picture. Ultimately Barrick put a joint venture proposal on the table and both parties agreed in principle to proceed, but Barrick needed, like CRA before, to drill a few of its own holes; the data it had been looking at and the samples it had been working on had all been provided by Bre-X. The deal was never consummated as Felderhof refused permission for Barrick to do their own drilling. Placer Dome's keenness led the company ultimately to propose a $6.4 billion merger with Bre-X which would have made David Walsh the largest shareholder in Placer.

Local participation

The Indonesians, unsurprisingly, were as interested as Bre-X in the arrangement because the growing size of Busang meant that a 'new' local participation had to be inserted. Bre-X's two original local partners who had 10% each did not constitute the local interest that would satisfy the authorities. As the joint venture negotiations dragged on Walsh became increasingly agitated as did Felderhof, and even the group's camp followers of analysts and investors began to ask the odd pertinent question. It also became clear that Bre-X was going to have to cede a substantial part of the deposit in any joint venture arrangement. The Placer Dome merger partly protected Bre-X shareholders because they exchanged a slice of Busang for a slice of Placer's established gold interests, but the Indonesians did not want the deal, so Placer was forced to withdraw. This let in Freeport McMoran, owner of the Grasberg copper/gold mine situated on the outlying island of Irian Jaya, and a powerful and efficient organisation well known to the Indonesian authorities.

The check holes show insignificant gold

The rest, of course, is history. Freeport's participation was on generous terms; to allow Bre-X to keep a 35% stake Freeport's own stake was just 15%, although it was to be operator of the mine. The stock market did not like the sharp reduction in Bre-X's stake in the project, but it liked even less the announcement in March of 1997 that Freeport had drilled seven check holes alongside Bre-X holes and all of them had insignificant amounts of gold in them. In May, Strathcona, the mining consultants, drilled their own holes on the property auditing Freeport's work. Again the gold shows were insignificant. Strathcona believed that Bre-X had constructed the biggest mining scam in history, the tampering with core samples and the precision of that tampering were unprecedented in their scale and scope. Also during this period, just before the announcement from Freeport of the dud holes, disturbing news had come out, that Michael de Guzman, the Busang exploration manager had fallen to his death from a helicopter. A badly decomposed body had been found in the jungle, it was thought to be de Guzman's. Certainly de Guzman was never seen again after that helicopter ride. The circumstances of his death remain a mystery to this day with some believing he committed suicide, some believing that he had been murdered and others that the body was not his and that he had disappeared. Certainly the bad news from Freeport would have turned the spotlight on de Guzman, if he had lived, as questions began to be asked about the quality of Bre-X's work on the property.

The lessons learnt from Bre-X

The story of Bre-X is complex and complicated, and the potted version above is not intended to be comprehensive. However, it does cover the key points and allows us to draw some conclusions as to how investors should act when faced with a phenomenon like Bre-X. There are, of course, those who would suggest never becoming involved in such speculative situations. But when a share performs as Bre-X did it is difficult not to be drawn in. Also when some of the biggest mining groups in the world are fighting to negotiate a joint venture over Busang, and one of them even proposes a merger almost of equals, it is difficult not to believe that this is the real thing and that a great gold mine is being born.

So what in hindsight were some of the warning signs where the lights were at amber at the very least?

Earlier work suggested caution

The early work done on Busang by Westralian and Montague demonstrated gold on the property but the drilling results also suggested inconsistency in the distribution of the gold. In such circumstances further and more extensive drilling could be carried out, and such work can change the view of the deposit's potential. In the case of Bre-X, its own drilling programme on Busang seemed to show that the previous holders of the lease had quit too early. Nonetheless the earlier work should have been remembered when the first doubts began to creep in concerning Busang. It is worth recalling that concern about Bre-X, and what it was up to, had been circulating well before the traumatic events of early 1997.

The search for JV partners

Another telling matter was the search for a joint venture partner. Whilst, as has been said above, the number of large companies chasing Bre-X might have appeared reassuring, a look at the tortuous nature of the negotiations, particularly relating to the right of the prospective joint venturers to drill their own holes to check Bre-X's work, should have given cause for thought. No doubt David Walsh, who primarily conducted these negotiations, would have stuck to the line that such work was unnecessary as Bre-X's drilling and the subsequent assaying was above reproach. The point was that Bre-X did not have the management or financial resources to undertake the development of a mine at Busang, so a big partner was essential, and a big partner would want to do their own comprehensive due diligence. To begin with Bre-X's attitude benefited the shareholders in that the share price kept powering ahead as the company issued increasingly bullish results. The number of chasing companies grew as did their enthusiasm to be part of Busang, but Bre-X stood its ground over the issue of check drilling.

The paperwork was in doubt

At the same time the actual status of Bre-X, with regard to the Busang lease and adjoining ground which Bre-X was also drilling, remained unclear. This was particularly dangerous in relation to the Mines Ministry who handled the various work permissions and the family and associates of the then President Suharto, who was taking a close interest in the giant gold field being uncovered on Kalimantan. The fact was that some of the paperwork relating to the lease was not in order or up-to-date, and this meant that there was a real danger that at any time the Indonesians could have taken Busang away from Bre-X.

Character of the main executives

The two key Bre-X executives, Felderhof and Walsh, might also have provided a clue or two to any sceptical mind. Felderhof, although an important figure in regional geology because of his work on OK Tedi, by all accounts had lived somewhat on the edge financially for a number of years although he was invariably in work. Walsh, the chief promoter within the Bre-X set-up, had also as a stockbroker experienced difficult times, and in Bre-X's early days things became particularly tight. In 1991 Walsh filed for bankruptcy with a mountain of credit card debts and a pending lawsuit from RBC Dominion claiming that he had sold securities that he did not own for his own account some years before when he was working for a subsidiary of the broker. However Bre-X just survived and Walsh was discharged from bankruptcy in April 1993 in time to steer the company towards Indonesia and Busang.

Insider sales

Perhaps the thing that most haunts those who hung on to their Bre-X shares until the bitter end was the fact that just before the Freeport drilling results were announced, with market rumours circulating that all was not well at Busang following de Guzman's death, the shares had rested for a while around the C$15 level. Although this was almost half the peak level the shares had reached (this following a division of the previously heavyweight shares) it still would have provided substantial profits for many of the earlier buyers. Around this time would also have been a good time to ruminate on the selling of Bre-X shares by John Felderhof who raised many millions of dollars. Walsh also was a big seller, but both retained substantial stakes in Bre-X, perhaps because they believed in Busang, but perhaps also because a complete clear-out of their holdings would have been suspicious.

The other fascinating thing about Bre-X was the loyalty that many shareholders displayed even following the Freeport announcement. The death of the project's exploration manager, de Guzman, coupled with a mysterious fire that destroyed all the paper records at Busang just before Freeport started its check drilling, clearly did not dampen the enthusiasm of many. Even some of the brokers following the story believed that de Guzman's death and the fire were coincidences, not evidence of something wrong with the project. The Freeport announcement saw the scales fall from their eyes, but amazingly many others, even as the share price crashed, believed that the problem lay not with Bre-X's work but with Freeport's. This might have flown in the face of logic, Freeport were experienced pros operating the biggest mine in Indonesia, but Bre-X loyalists continued to believe that their geologists and drilling crews really knew Busang, not Freeport, the outsider. They also pointed out that the other mining groups pursuing a Busang joint venture had found gold in the cores they had examined, but these were provided by Bre-X, they were not independently drilled cores.

If ever there was an example of the old maxim of the wish being father to the thought Bre-X was it. It would, however, be unfair not to recognise that holders of Bre-X shares could never have guessed the extent of the scam, its complexity and its audaciousness. The chasing mining giants also provided enormous comfort. As the shares began to weaken in 1997 questions were being asked by some of the US investors and the company was not always particularly cooperative when criticism was implied. Cynics wondered whether Bre-X had something to hide, loyalists would have none of it. The change of practice from declaring hole by hole drill results to declaring updated resource figures was also taken on trust, although it looked strange.

Epilogue

During 2003 a revival in interest in mining shares became very apparent as metal prices strengthened and attention began to focus on China, the great new resources consumer and importer. Interest in the sector also expanded into the more speculative exploration and development shares. Although only time will judge whether a new mining boom was in the making, the background was certainly the most promising for ten years, indeed since the days of Bre-X.

Could Bre-X happen again?

So with securities market regulation much intensified since the time of the Bre-X scandal, could another scam be perpetrated this time round on the scale of Bre-X, or indeed on any scale?

The answer to that must be, at the very least, 'possibly'.

The requirements and procedures for making believable and authentic announcements on mineral finds have been in place in Canada, Australia and indeed all the likely mining markets for many years. However if someone is prepared, for whatever reason, to put his reputation on the line and be less than diligent in verifying exploration results then misleading figures may well get into the public domain. We have seen accountants being duped by such at Enron and WorldCom. Consulting geologists and mining engineers are no less vulnerable, especially if markets are judged hot by unscrupulous or just overexcited promoters.

Investors want to believe

The truth is Bre-X happened because people wanted to believe the story, and they also believed the figures that the company was using had to be correct. Most of the scams in recent times have taken place in a tough regulatory environment when the perpetrators were fully aware they were committing a criminal offence.

And the blame lies where?

Court action against John Felderhof, David Walsh died in 1998, started again in 2000 but was suspended after two months and has not resumed at the time of publication. Others are also involved, and though much has been written on Bre-X over the years, the apportioning of blame, in a legal sense, is probably years away. There has been much speculation as to how much the key executives, particularly Walsh and Felderhof, knew about the scam, although it is generally accepted that de Guzman was operationally at the centre of it. What can be said is that both Walsh and Felderhof benefited materially from the huge rise in the Bre-X share price and both were enormously bullish about the prospects for Busang based on the figures that de Guzman provided. Did they know the figures were false? We may probably never find out, but it still beggars belief that the two executives carried on pulling the wool over the eyes of some of the world's largest mining companies right until the end. Maybe they carried on in the desperate hope that something would turn up in the end. It may also be that at the beginning Walsh and Felderhof believed they were on to something huge at Busang. When they found out that the whole thing was a scam they were in too deep to go back.

The aftermath

Bre-X, of course, was delisted and everyone ended up with worthless paper, and many with huge losses. Felderhof, who in the wake of the disclosures holed up in the Cayman Islands, eventually had all his assets frozen by the authorities there. The mining giants, who so assiduously courted Bre-X, got off lightly and their reputations were not adversely affected, although some like Placer Dome were enormously enthusiastic and furious to lose out to others. No blame was placed on Freeport for bringing the party to an end, all the other mining giants were too embarrassed for that.

The Australian nickel boom

The events of the late 60s and early 70s in Australia did not of themselves constitute a scam. And the Bre-X like performance of Poseidon, the great stock of the era, was based upon a nickel discovery that eventually became a mine, albeit a not very successful one. Nonetheless the Aussie nickel boom was an event that promised far, far more than it finally delivered. In that process a lot of money was made and then lost, and a lot of money was also raised that often went into promotion and other corporate spending rather than into the ground.

'Closeology'

The Aussie boom also introduced a new generation to that old mining concept of *closeology*. The nickel boom started in Western Australia, heart of the country's historic gold mining industry which at that time was on its last legs. The rundown nature of the state's gold mining industry around Kalgoorlie meant that very little land was held for exploration in the first half of the 60s. Once Western Mining had made its nickel discovery at Kambalda, south of Kalgoorlie, activity started to increase. Because of its historic role as a goldminer around Kalgoorlie, Western Mining held a lot of ground in the area, but further north the ground situation was fairly open. When Poseidon made its nickel discovery at Windarra, 150 miles or so north of Kalgoorlie, it was soon joined by a considerable number of hopefuls who clustered around Poseidon's lease. Many of the companies involved had not been listed when they had pegged their ground; when they did list, their closeness to Poseidon guaranteed a successful float. This *closeology* formed the basis of a lot of the corporate strategy of the Aussie boom.

Similarity with the recent internet boom

Many of the excesses of the boom related to or were exacerbated by the practices of the time. When Bre-X struck, the whole regulatory climate had been tightened up enormously and this covered everything from stock exchange practices to geological and financial announcements. Communications had also taken a massive step forward when compared to what was around in the late 60s. Bre-X happened despite the much tightened regulatory environment because it was a scam. The character of the Aussie boom had far more in common with the recent internet boom than with Bre-X. In the Aussie boom investors were for the most part seduced into unrealistic expectations by the prospect of instant riches, a fatal weakness the internet punters also suffered from thirty years later. It is, therefore, easier for investors today to draw obvious lessons from the Aussie boom than from Bre-X.

Just as the frenetic internet boom emerged from the bull market in broad high tech shares which had developed in the second half of the 90s, so the equally frenetic Poseidon-led boom of 1969-70 had emerged from the developing bull market in Australian mining shares which had been born with Western Mining's nickel discovery at Kambalda in 1966. Amazingly, just over a year later in March 1967, the first ore was produced from the discovery orebody, the Fisher shoot. In this pre-Poseidon period there were two other Western Australian nickel discoveries to encourage investor interest, Nepean (Metals Exploration and Freeport) and Scotia (Great Boulder and North Kalgurli). In Queensland, Metals Exploration and our old friend Freeport were also investigating a large laterite nickel deposit at Greenvale.

Although it was eventually Poseidon which took centre stage as the boom took off vertically in 1969, the previous year saw huge rises for many of the bigger Australian miners such as Peko Wallsend and CRA. Indeed a number of these majors, including Western Mining, reached their boom peaks in 1968 as metal prices led by copper and nickel soared. The previous few years had also been very good ones for mining earnings which provided a sound base for interest in the mining sector. As well as Western Mining and the big miners, the other natural resource area where things were hotting up was oil and gas. It is not in our remit to cover oil but the excitement led by Woodside Lakes Entrance and other oil hopefuls in the late 60s was a curtain raiser for the crazy speculation unleashed by Poseidon.

Poseidon

The blow off to this highly profitable bull market in mining shares began in mid 1969. The previous year Poseidon, a company with just 2 million shares in issue, had experienced a short lived surge on the back of some nickel claims it acquired at Bindi Bindi, around 100 miles north of Perth. The shares went from A$0.10 to A$3.45 in a matter of months and then subsided back to A$0.60. New claims at Mount Windarra were acquired, and in early 1969 work started on drilling the prospect. The shares washed above and below the A$1.00 level for a few months. Then in September, as the drilling programme got into full swing and samples began to be delivered to the laboratories of Geomin in Kalgoorlie for assaying, the share price started to move as insiders began to buy.

Insider buying starts

Early in September Poseidon shares traded around the A$0.80 level. By the end of the month the shares had reached A$7.00, with no public announcement having been made. However, internally, Poseidon learnt that the samples being worked on had yielded between 2% and 5% nickel in the core, which had ignited the insider dealing. With grades at Inco's Sudbury, Ontario mine, the world's largest nickel mining operation, below 3% these were good figures.

In early October the company reported that one of the holes at Windarra had assayed 3.17% nickel over 40 feet in massive sulphides. The shares took off and reached A$40 by November, when the next set of drilling results were released. In the early stage there was little London interest in the situation as UK investors continued to follow older favourites like Western Mining, but as September wore on London began to pick up the scent, no doubt encouraged by Poseidon insiders.

New shares issued

Although turnover was very high in the stock, a quarter of the issued capital was traded in just the second half of September, that did not help the financial position of the company which was tight. To address this problem, and to head off what Poseidon director and the company's chief broker, Norman Shierlaw, perceived as a possible attempt to build a control stake in Poseidon, half a million new shares were issued to six new shareholders at between A$5.00 and A$6.00 - including Canadian junior Conwest and, significantly, London's leading mining broker, James Capel. This placing was to be highly controversial as Poseidon's share price soared.

Through October and into November Poseidon's share price pushed on. In the middle of November, after a new drilling report which expanded the possible size of the Windarra orebody but on the basis of a lower than 3% nickel content, the shares hit A$57.50.

Brokers forecast A$250 per share

At the same time the influence of *closeology* was beginning to make itself felt as new listings like Newmetal and Kia Ora, with leases abutting Poseidon, opened at huge premiums to their offer price. Other stocks were also performing strongly on the back of the developing nickel phenomenon and market volumes were running at unprecedented high levels. Brokers both in London and Australia were beginning to try and calculate a value for Poseidon and, as December opened with Poseidon's shares stuck around the A$50 level, two Australian brokers' reports came out suggesting a value of up to A$250 per share over the medium term. In the second week of December Poseidon reached A$94.

As the Christmas month wound on, stock market activity accelerated, new listings continued to pour in barely satisfying the appetite of investors in Australia and the UK. Tips also began to multiply, with both London and Australian newspapers besieged by investors trying to get their favourite stocks into the financial pages. By the third week of December Poseidon had breached A$100 and hit A$121 before falling back.

On the 19th December Poseidon, with exquisite timing, held its AGM in Adelaide. The meeting was packed in marked contrast to the previous year when hardly a shareholder turned up; some shareholders had crossed the globe from London to be present. There was an attempt by some shareholders to get the September placement reversed but they were defeated. Then Poseidon's Chairman announced that on the basis of up-to-date drilling the company had a major mine in the offing with a resource (as we would now have to call it) of 4 million tonnes grading 2.4% nickel. The market was encouraged and the shares finished the trading day at A$130.

On the 23rd December the shares soared, closing at A$175. On Christmas Eve the market was open for only half a day but volume was huge in both Australia and London, and Poseidon closed for the holiday break at A$182. However, the star turn that amazing day was not Poseidon, but one of its associates, North Flinders, which in time became one of Australia's most respected gold miners in a later boom. Flinders had taken 100,000 Poseidon shares in the earlier controversial placing. Just before the AGM, which saw its Poseidon placing confirmed, the shares had stood at A$2.35, when Christmas Eve trading in London closed the shares had reached the sterling equivalent of A$22.

Poseidon finally peaked at A$280, before crashing back to earth

By New Year's Eve Poseidon had pushed on to an amazing A$210. But the boom was near to its end, and ahead of that some of the mining leaders opened 1970 in retreat. For Poseidon the game was not quite over, January proved another good month and intra day Poseidon touched A$280, around £122 in London, ahead of the release of the London broker Panmure Gordon's note on the company putting a value of A$382 on the shares. That proved to be its peak and by the end of the year the shares had sunk as low as A$39. Before that, in mid year, the shares had slumped to A$64, a fall of three quarters, but over the northern summer they actually doubled to A$144 before crashing again to hit the December low.

Whilst a mine was eventually developed at Windarra, poor management saw a number of excellent opportunities to finance the mine on reasonable terms passed over. A number of problems hurt Poseidon, not least of all the fact that its reluctance to enter into a joint venture with a nickel user like Amax of the US meant that the company missed the nickel price boom. It came to production in 1974 in the middle of the mid 70s economic slump when mining investors were almost entirely focused on gold.

The post mortem

Looking back, perhaps, as with all great speculative blow-offs, not enough attention was paid to possible unwelcome facts, one of which was that no later drill result from Windarra matched the figure of 3.17% nickel first reported in early October. Indeed three years earlier Western Mining was regularly pulling 3% results from its Kambalda drilling to the delight of the market. This meant that potential production was being overestimated in the very forward looking forecasts being provided by the broking community. The nickel price was also being overestimated, the record high level reached in 1968 at the height of industrial action at Inco's Sudbury complex was often used as the long term price level; it did not achieve that level again until the late 80s. There was also the issue of mining costs, and few, if any, analysts foresaw the great inflation of the 70s. After the October announcement further results in hindsight were disappointing, a fact that the powerful Sydney broking company, Patrick and Co, realised early in 1970. They sold large amounts of Poseidon stock down to A$200, much of it to London. Ironically by 1975 Patrick had gone bust, forced into liquidation by property investment problems and the collapse of the Mineral Securities group which we will touch on later.

For those interested, a comprehensive history of the nickel boom has been written by Australian journalist, Trevor Sykes, called *The Money Miners* which covers events in the sort of detail which this book cannot go into. Before I conclude the snapshot of the boom with a comment on Mineral Securities I want to touch on three other events to add further flesh to the story of 1969-70.

Tasminex

One of the most unusual price explosions was that of a stock called Tasminex. The company had a lease at Mount Venn in Western Australia which it had begun to drill in late January of 1970 as the great boom began to stutter. It had floated the previous October, like Poseidon with 2 million shares issued, at A$0.25; and by late January it had reached A$3.50. On the 27th of the month its price suddenly jumped to A$18.50. Then sensationally the next day, following the publication of a interview with the company Chairman Bill Singline who said that Tasminex had struck massive sulphides in its drilling, the price in London surged to the equivalent of A$96. Singline also rather rashly was quoted as saying that the find could be bigger than that of Poseidon, which accounted for much of the euphoria.

'Massive sulphides' found

The story which was splashed all over the early editions of the London evening press stated massive sulphides had been found, a classic example of a little knowledge being a dangerous thing. Massive sulphides are to be found in a number of geological settings and essentially are a homogeneous structure of compounds where sulphur is found combined with one or more metals. The discovery of massive sulphides in no way guarantees an economic mineral deposit, although at the height of the Aussie boom the word massive to the untutored eye had a real excitement about it. The high grade section of Poseidon's first reported hole at Windarra had also been in massive sulphides. The London story on Tasminex also reported that the hole had been drilled from an outside latrine on the property which was further inducement for the London papers to give the story prominence.

In essence the Tasminex story was a scam but not deliberate as Bre-X was. In a report prepared for the Tasmanian Attorney-General (Tasminex was incorporated in Tasmania) in 1970 by a local lawyer JW Wilson, the main thrust of the criticisms of the affair was the misleading and grossly overoptimistic statements coming from the company and a large amount of privileged insider trading in the shares. There was no salting of the concentrated samples panned by one of the Tasminex geologists, they had little nickel in them when they were finally assayed. However, unwarranted claims were made about the geological promise of the prospect and fed into a crazed market that would believe almost anything it was told.

Unsurprisingly, Tasminex shares fell back from A$96 and in early March traded at A$7.50.

Surprisingly, Tasminex was one of the few hot stocks of the nickel boom to actually develop a mine, a small tungsten mine in Tasmania which opened in 1978. However by 1985 Tasminex had been de-listed from the Australian Stock Exchange; it had lasted longer than Poseidon which was de-listed in 1976 after appointing a receiver two years after the Windarra mine opened.

Endurance Mining

The boom itself was topped and tailed by two stories that more obviously were scams, and both were officially investigated and labelled as such. The first, Endurance Mining, interestingly was, like Tasminex, a Tasmanian company and a small tin miner who had even managed to pay dividends in the past. It had a tiny number of shares in issue, around 190,000, and in 1968 in its somnolent state traded at close to its par of A$0.50. In pursuit of a listed vehicle to inject mining properties into, a group of primarily mainland investors, including corporate dealers, brokers and geologists, bought out a number of long suffering and willing Endurance shareholders representing 43% of the issued capital for around A$0.73 per share.

The main aim of the new shareholders, who had acquired a public vehicle very cheaply, was to start to generate interest in Endurance through the new projects that would be injected into the company. They also expected to be able to make considerable amounts of money as inside traders of their shares. New capital was raised by way of a funding to provide working capital for Endurance's new activities. To begin with, however, a reconstituted board concentrated on the company's traditional area of interest, tin, and a small Tasmanian tin reserve was acquired from BHP. After gaining control of Endurance the new board had also divided the share capital into A$0.25 par value shares on a 2 for 1 basis and the subsequent capital raising had been done on the basis of 3 for 1 at A$0.10. The original group of new shareholders then had 8 Endurance shares for an overall outlay of just over A$0.16 per share (A$0.73 + 6 x A$0.10).

A JV with Attunga Mining

The events that followed eventually became the subject of an investigation by the Attorney-General of New South Wales. One of Endurance's new shareholders, Paul Murray a corporate dealer, was familiar with a scheelite (tungsten) deposit in New South Wales held by a near insolvent private company called Attunga Mining. Attunga had been drilling its prospect at depth during 1968 and had recorded two holes with interesting results –

- Hole 1: reported in late October, averaged 0.86% tungstic oxide over 412 feet, and
- Hole 2: reported rather later in mid December, averaged 1.44% tungstic ore over 600 feet.

Before the second hole was released Endurance signed a joint venture agreement with Attunga its shares were trading at A$0.80 at the time, having been as high as A$3.00 in August when rumours first started to circulate about a deal with Attunga. Attunga's parlous financial state was not known at that stage.

Speculation about the Attunga prospect drove Endurance's shares higher in December and they hit A$5.00 around Christmas, reaching a peak of A$10.60 at the start of 1969. The excitement over Endurance was further helped by the company's listing on the Sydney Stock Exchange and news that senior miner Peko Wallsend, who already had an operating scheelite mine in Tasmania, was preparing a bid for the Attunga prospect. Peko stepped back but continued to monitor the project and in February Endurance made an all share offer for Attunga, effectively rolling its sound balance sheet into Attunga's weak one. At the same time it announced that reserves at Attunga were now 500,000 tons of 1.4% tungstic oxide.

Ore grades prove disappointing

Interestingly around the same time a geologist from North Broken Hill had visited Attunga and reported back that he thought the reserve figure was around 650,000 tons of 1% tungstic oxide, a little bit more ore but a much lower grade than the company's own figures. NBH stated that the deposit might be economic but it was too small to interest a major, a comment that could well explain the cooling of Peko's interest.

From then on it was all downhill with the major problem a poor result from the third hole at Attunga released in mid February which showed tungstic ore grades of less than 0.1%. Field geologists had also noted a high molybdenum content in Attunga's scheelite ore which could have created treatment problems without potentially costly separation. A substantial increase in Endurance's issued capital as a result of the Attunga takeover and the poor drilling result helped to push the share price down to A$7.50. Doubts were also being expressed internally about the rich second hole, a situation made worse by the fact that communication between Endurance and Attunga was poor.

By August the shares were below A$1.00 as a result of a boardroom battle in June between the Attunga interests and the original new management, after which the latter resigned. Following these resignations there was a flurry of selling which came from both the resigning management and the new Attunga directors. However, it was later discovered that insider selling had started a good bit earlier when doubts about the accuracy of hole 2 began to circulate internally.

The investigation afterwards unearthed that Endurance had sent their geologist to Attunga to check the split core from hole 2 on site and see if he thought that there could be a problem with the assays from the half of the core sent to the laboratory. He reported that reserves were only 220,000 tons averaging 0.35% tungstic oxide, a figure well below both Attunga's earlier bullish calculation and well below even NBH's independent assessment.

A huge scam

In the end it was calculated that insider selling resulted in an aggregate capital gain to the insiders of over A$5 million, and this in less than a year. For those days, over thirty years ago, it was a huge sum which in purchasing power probably exceeded the profit taken by Bre-X insiders as their scam fell apart. Fortunately for the market the Endurance farce happened when investors were still bullish and they were able to move on to other things, and since it was now 1969, that meant Poseidon.

Leopold Minerals

Investors in Leopold Minerals were less lucky because that situation unfolded the other side of the boom, in 1971. In early 1971 Leopold shares stood at A$0.50 having been floated the previous year to exploit some uranium leases at Nullagine in Western Australia. The start of the year had seen the mining market in sharp retreat in the wake of the failure of the mighty Mineral Securities (with whose story I will end this review of the Aussie nickel boom).

Leopold's story is quickly told. Almost as if someone had been preparing the scam, Leopold's shares had doubled in the first three months of 1971 to around A$1.00, despite a continuing fall in the value of Australian mining shares which had accelerated in the final quarter of 1970.

In mid March, out of the blue, the company announced that it had struck 5.22% nickel over 25 feet of drill hole, a result that exceeded anything that Poseidon had reported and reminded some investors of the early days of the boom back in 1966 when Western Mining announced extremely rich assays from its Kambalda discovery. If the boom was by then pretty much over, the Leopold 'discovery' was able to generate three trading days of excitement, pushing the shares up from A$1.00 to a high of A$8.80 before the company's Chairman asked for trading to be suspended. Both the Perth Stock Exchange and the company's brokers, Constable & Co, were concerned and sought more information from Leopold about the rich value of the nickel core. It was at this stage that the shares were suspended.

State and national authorities instigated enquiries into the Leopold situation, and one of the company's directors, Brian Cutler, was eventually arrested, tried and sentenced to 3.5 years in prison for criminal deception. Leopold redrilled the discovery hole, as all the original core had either been pulverised or lost, and the ensuing results showed little or no nickel in the new core. The original results had clearly been tampered with, probably by salting the core. Brian Cutler had made over a quarter of a million dollars trading the shares following the original drilling announcement, and though he denied any wrongdoing, the trial jury found him guilty. Soon after Leopold came the Agnew discovery of Selection Trust and CAST, but though there was considerable interest in the situation, the bounce had gone out of the market and the boom was finally over.

Mineral Securities

Any review of the 1966-70 Australian mining boom cannot conclude without saying something about the nascent mining finance house, Mineral Securities (Minsec) which was formed in 1965, publicly listed in 1967 and declared insolvent in 1971. The company was formed by geologist Ken McMahon with the aim of using its initial capital to invest and trade in mining shares, directing the profits made into long term mining projects. The long term intention was to build a new Australian mining finance house to act as counter weight to the powerful overseas mining operators in Australia like RTZ. Ironically though, McMahon found little local support for his patriotic venture in the early stages, and almost 60% of the initial capital was raised from overseas investors.

Huge trading volumes

Minsec's timing could not have been better. The oil boom was in full flow and Western Mining's discovery was just around the corner. Also the background of strong metal prices and mining earnings, a result of rapid economic growth in the US and the acceleration of US spending on the Vietnam War, perfectly complemented Minsec's strategy. In its first year, 1965-66, Minsec made A$21,000 from share trading. In the year it floated, 1967-68, helped by the consequent increase in capital, the company's share trading profits reached A$1.89 million, and in the year before it collapsed, 1969-70, those trading profits had exploded to A$12.4 million. Although in the course of its short life Minsec accumulated long term control stakes in a number of Australian mining companies it was the scope of its share trading which made it a market giant. Indeed in 1970, its last year before insolvency, the total value of shares traded by Minsec reached A$154 million. This compared with the figure of A$48 million for the same year reported by AMP, by far and away Australia's largest life assurance company. Minsec's trading volumes based on issued capital, borrowings and group deposits were so great that every broker and bank wanted to do business with this Australian phenomenon.

The structure of Minsec divided into long term investments, which gave it control of a number of promising mining projects, and its short term trading investment book, the value of which could seesaw between almost nothing and several millions. For most of the period between 1965 and 1969 the group was heavily exposed to the bull market on its trading book. Also over the period it built up control stakes in a number of companies including Cudgen RZ (mineral sands), Aberfoyle (tin), Invincible Life & General Insurance, Equity Funds of Australia, Petroleum Securities Australia, Pexa Oil and Amad (mineral exploration). But though Minsec's business seemed broadly based, if in hindsight rather speculative, its massive share trading profits in 1969-70 were very narrowly based around Poseidon, although they topped off their rich run in early 1970 by turning a A$1 million profit in just one trade in Tasminex. That was as good as it got, and Poseidon was to be a major element in the group's failure when Minsec, having shrewdly got its trading portfolio down to almost nothing by the end of January 1970, plunged back into the market in June and into Poseidon which rallied over 100% to A$145, having fallen from A$282 to A$64 in less than four months. By December Poseidon had crashed back to A$39 and Minsec had lost around A$3 million from its re-entry into the market.

The build up of long-term investments

Turning to the long term side of Minsec's investment strategy, 1970 also saw the group make three major investments that within a year proved its undoing - Robe River, Kathleen Investments/Queensland Mines and Theiss Holdings. As it rebuilt its trading portfolio Minsec was gearing up massively to expand its long term investment holdings. It participated in the flotation of Robe River, the Western Australian iron ore project with Cleveland Cliffs of the US, a mine with a low grade of ore that was generally considered far less desirable than high grade operations such as Hamersley and Mount Newman. Following the flotation Minsec had between 40% and 50% of Robe River and it was very active in the market both as a trader of Robe shares and as a long term buyer. By the end of 1970 it held around 50% of Robe River which had cost it A$28 million.

The Nabarlek uranium deposit

Whilst this was a very big commitment for Minsec the group was also busy on other fronts, principally buying control of the potentially huge Nabarlek uranium deposit whose discovery was announced in July by Queensland Mines. Queensland Mines in its turn was controlled by Kathleen Investments who also controlled Mary Kathleen, at that time Australia's only operating uranium mine. Queensland Mines also owned the promising uranium prospect at Westmoreland in Queensland state. Nabarlek, however, was in a different class, or so it seemed at the time, and in September Queensland Mines stunned the market by announcing that the Nabarlek deposit contained 55,000 tons of uranium oxide grading 540 lbs per ton. This was a huge uranium discovery by any standards and Queensland shares soared from A$7.20 in August to A$46 in early October. The share price movement was further stimulated by the fact, as in so many cases during the Aussie boom, that the number of issued shares in Queensland Mines was low, around 5 million.

Using top brokers, Patrick Partners, Minsec bought both Queensland and Kathleen shares, the former primarily for trading and the latter for control purposes as Kathleen held just over 50% of Queensland Mines. Unbeknownst to Minsec the September 'indicated reserves' estimate of 55,000 tons was not made on the basis of drill holes but was more an educated guess on the part of

Queensland and Kathleen Chairman, Roy Hudson and senior geologist Emile Rod. Within a month, as Queensland shares peaked at A$46, drill results were received from the laboratory which did not support the reserve figure postulated. These results were kept under wraps for a further year. When they were finally released they indicated a far more modest uranium potential at Nabarlek. But by then the boom was truly over, and the mine eventually developed at Nabarlek by Queensland Mines was a disappointing performer and was closed in 1988.

As for Minsec, it built up its holdings in Kathleen, and in Queensland, at considerable cost and it had to borrow short term to fund its purchases. It also began to buy coalminer Theiss with the aim of injecting its long term energy holdings into a new Patrick supported vehicle called Power Resources of Australia (PRA). In this way Minsec would recoup at least part of the purchase cost of these investments and it would then be in a position to repay the borrowings which had swollen to A$80 million by the end of 1970. These loans were largely collateralised against Minsec's long term investments which for most of its short life had risen year on year. Unfortunately for Minsec with the boom at an end and the fabulous Nabarlek story tarnished by a rising tide of facts, cover for the huge borrowings had evaporated. Also both the market and the lending institutions had begun to worry about some of Minsec's accounting practices, particularly the large profit it had made on its initial Robe River subscription shares. Desperate to bolster its 1969-70 profit figure it washed this holding through a wholly owned subsidiary and tried to book it as a trading profit. Eventually it had to reverse the transaction and a healthy profit turned into a loss. The flotation of PRA got stuck and promises of more permanent capital to alleviate Minsec's heavy short term borrowing position never came to fruition. In February 1971 Minsec was declared insolvent.

The bear market scuppered any rescue plan

Serious attempts were made to construct a rescue plan for Minsec but in a bear market environment the strategy that had worked so well in a bull market was fatally flawed. The expansion of its activities in 1970 could not have been worse timed, but that of course is a hindsight view. At that time the boom had been going since 1966 and the Poseidon blow off had not been recognised as the end of the bull market. Minsec's view was that the growth of the Australian mining industry was set to continue as new mineral discoveries were made, and its strategy of aggressive expansion would eventually make it the country's leading mining group. The size of its borrowings and the fact that some of its key assets, particularly its Nabarlek holdings, were grossly overvalued meant that its demise was very likely even though a lot of people stood to suffer, perhaps fatally, if Minsec did go under. One of the largest associates of Minsec to collapse was Patrick Partners which was severely wounded by its indirect participation in Nabarlek through its house mining trust, Castlereagh Securities, and expired in 1975.

We have concentrated on just a few of the stocks and situations that made the Aussie nickel boom. Those who participated in the excitement may well have their own memories of stocks that they followed. There were many to follow and many good stories that I do not have the space to go into here. Amongst this litany could be included International Mining, Carr Boyd Minerals, Westralian Nickel, Great Boulder/North Kalgurli, VAM, Hampton Areas, Westmoreland Minerals and North Deborah. There were many more and most of the stocks have long since disappeared but a few soldiered on, living to fight another day. More particularly ten years later companies like North Kalgurli and Carr Boyd participated modestly but profitably in the 1979-80 gold boomlet.

Not a global boom

One of the things that makes the Australian mining boom unusual, certainly in today's global market, is the fact that despite the huge gains to be made the boom did not attract worldwide participation, in marked contrast to the recent high tech/internet boom with which it shares a number of often startling similarities. The main participants in terms of portfolio investors were Australian and British. There was some interest from the Continent, particularly Switzerland, and also some Middle Eastern interest. The problem was that exchange controls of some sort or another were fairly widespread. The UK had some flexibility as the Sterling Area was still, just, operative and technically UK investors did not have to purchase investment dollars at a premium to buy Australian securities, as they did if they wanted to buy US shares for example. The authorities did have an informal agreement with UK institutional investors that they would refrain from putting additional money into Australian shares above the level of their holdings in 1969. Although they were able to trade and utilise capital gains on these historic holdings.

The impact of British capital gains tax

Because British participation was so high the market also had to grapple with the consequences of the UK's capital gains tax regime. Here there were two classes of capital gains, short term (made in under a year) and long term (over a year). Short term gains were taxed at the individual's top personal tax rate which in the late 60s reached in certain extraordinary circumstances over 100% and averaged for higher rate payers over 80%. Long term gains, however, were taxed at a much more reasonable rate of 30%. The upshot was that investors often felt compelled to hold on to shares where they had made good profits in the hope that they could realise those capital gains at the lower tax rate after a year. This inevitably meant that liquidity in the market, particularly where the stock was a UK favourite, was poor and share prices were often boosted by UK reluctance to sell. It could, therefore, be said that in many shares a quasi false market existed as the price was partly influenced by this reluctance. If more Australian investors had realised the significance of the UK situation the market might not have developed quite the froth that it did. Time and confidentiality preclude a clear answer, and maybe the dates are not quite right, but could it have been the Poseidon stock of UK holders, freed from punitive tax rates in 1970, that Patrick Partners was selling as Mineral Securities was buying in 1970? Certainly more attention should have been paid to the issue of delayed profit taking by UK investors.

However, even allowing for UK CGT distortions, there is no doubt that the Aussie mining boom was a genuine event as was the internet boom thirty years later. Interestingly the lessons that one could have learned from the Aussie boom could have been applied to the internet boom, with great benefit to those investors prepared to draw the parallels and act accordingly. However, when the global mining team at Paribas tried to draw comparisons between the two booms in their December mining review of 1999 all comparisons in the piece were edited out. The suggestion was that, with plenty of corporate IPO business planned by the firm in the high tech/internet sector in 2000, it would not do to suggest that the high tech boom could have the unhappy ending that the Aussie boom had. Nonetheless the point here is that the broad structure of a stock market boom regularly repeats itself, not only over time in the same sector but also across sectors.

Lessons from the Aussie boom

Few companies survived

One of the main lessons coming out of the Aussie boom was how few of the new exploration companies ultimately survived, largely, of course, because so few of them actually found economic mineral deposits that could be turned into long term mines. Western Mining was one that did find a major new mine, and indeed in the ensuing years has developed other new mines, but it was very much in the minority. Quite a few companies, although mere shadows of what they had been, soldiered on into the 80s but most eventually died.

In hindsight it is easy to see that the nightmare spike on a chart of a company's share price is signalling the final blow off at the end of a market boom. There were plenty of such chart shapes in 1969 as the boom peaked. In the thick of the sort of excitement seen in 1969 investors are prone to believe that any pull back is the prelude to another stomach churning surge in the share price. As happened with Poseidon in mid-1970, a rally often does take place but it soon runs out of steam and the downward drop resumes. It also helps to know how broad based is activity in a share, the mid-1970 Poseidon rally was largely a function of Minsec's return to the market as a short term trader anxious to boost trading profits ahead of its ambitious corporate expansion.

Chart 5.1: Patrick's Speculative Index 1969/71

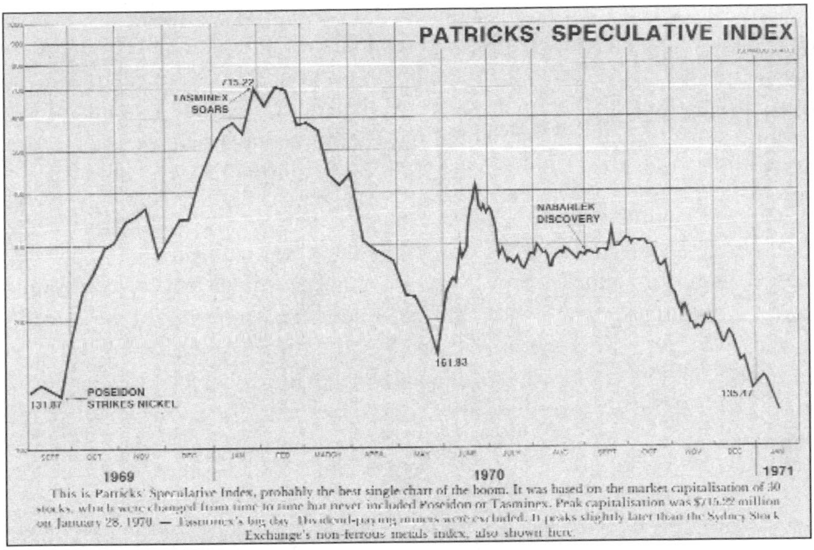

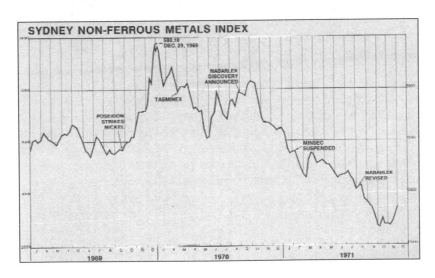

Source: The Money Miners, Trevor Sykes

Chart 5.2: Sydney Non-Ferrous Metals Index 1969/71

Source: The Money Miners, Trevor Sykes

Since the Aussie boom had effectively been going since 1966, the sudden rash of new flotations in 1969, the people involved, and the philosophy of *closeology* apparent in many of the listing documents, can now be seen as the inevitable gathering of the latecomers for the final act of the drama. This was what happened with the Canadian diamond boom in the early 90s, and active but short term participation in the final stages of that boom as the flotation of junior hopefuls gathered momentum would have delivered a stream of trading profits during 1993. Only a very few stocks, most particularly DiaMet, could have been held for long term profits. In that sense DiaMet occupied the same role as Western Mining did in the nickel boom.

Another feature of the boom was the way that as things began to hot up non mining companies began to take stakes in new exploration joint ventures. One example was the participation of Laporte, the UK chemical company. Also a number of small listed industrial companies in Australia decided to abandon their traditional businesses and re-invent themselves as mineral exploration companies. After acquiring some leases they then raised funds on the stock exchange.

This changing of the spots is a feature of runaway stock market booms, and not just in mining, and can be an early signal that the boom may be entering its last and often its most violent leg.

Take profits early

Another lesson that the Australian boom taught was that to take a quick profit might lead to frustration at making too early a departure from a situation, but in the longer term that could well turn out to have been the right thing to do when the particular stock collapsed with the boom. Holders of Poseidon who saw the shares up to, say, A$10 in the third quarter of 1969 and got out might have been feeling awful when the shares were closing on A$300 only a few months later. When the shares were de-listed in 1976 they would have felt a great deal better, and though Poseidon was re-listed two years later as a gold producer it was a literal shadow of its former self. One of the tricks of participation in boom markets is to take profits but stay in the game. The Aussie boom should have been seen as a very well run bus route and the participating shares as the bus fleet - if you miss a bus or get off one, there will always be another one to catch just a few minutes behind.

Another of the old investment dictums - if it's too good to be true it probably isn't - is particularly apt advice for mining booms. If investors had regularly sold on drilling news during the nickel boom and moved on, they would have captured a large slice of the upside and been strategically re-positioned for the next *exciting* situation. As mentioned before, very few small mining companies achieve the elevated status of giant, the Aussie boom threw up Western Mining but nobody else.

The last word

Perhaps one of the most intriguing stories of the Poseidon boom was of the shop girl working in Harrods in London in late 1969 who was run to ground by the UK popular press. She owned 2,000 Poseidon shares bought as a fun punt over a year before on the advice of her boyfriend when the shares stood at around 6d in old money (2.5p today). Her capital gains problems, if she had sold having held the shares for more than a year, would have been confined to paying the standard 30% CGT rate, high but not punitive. History does not relate what happened to her holding, worth around £200,000 then, or about £2 million in today's money, but, perhaps unfairly, one would have to surmise the worst.

That sort of rags to riches opportunity is one of the most compelling aspects of trading the mining share market. It is, therefore, intriguing that over the last year or so the metal that propelled the Aussie boom, nickel, has begun to rise sharply on the back of excellent long term fundamentals. Equally intriguing has been the recent discovery of very high grade nickel by Australian junior Independence in Western Australia. Independence recently acquired a couple of ageing nickel mines and associated exploration land from Western Mining in the Kambalda area where the Aussie boom started in 1966. The results that Independence announced included a very rich drill hole with 10% nickel over 15 metres (50 feet) at the relatively shallow depth of 183 metres. Such results throw up the possibility that much, much more nickel than was outlined in the exploration boom and after in the Kambalda area may still be there to be discovered. In mining lightning often does strike twice in the same place.

Mining projects that refuse to die

Strong mining markets if sustained have a way of encouraging old projects to be dusted down, looked at and if worthy of further promotion they can be repackaged and refinanced. Faced with these kind of investment possibilities, the best thing is probably to run a mile. But if a lot of time has passed since the dusted-down project was last in the news it may be able to be refinanced by investors who do not know the original story.

The example of Tenke Fungurume in the Congo

A fairly recent example of this is the huge copper/cobalt deposit, Tenke Fungurume, in the Congo (DRC). In the 60s it was the prime development project of Charter Consolidated which was then the international mining arm of Anglo American. Eventually due to chronic political problems in then Zaire and a weak copper price Charter dropped the project. It remained dormant until the 90s when, with the fall of President Mobuto, foreign interest in mineral development in the region began to revive. A Canadian company, Tenke Mining, then negotiated the old Tenke Fungurume lease with the new Kabila government in the DRC and started work on a feasibility study of the old deposit. Unfortunately civil war broke out in 1998 and in the following year Tenke stopped work on the project. Its share price which had been as high as C$22 in late 1997 slumped to below C$1.00 in mid 1999 when it suspended work on the project. As this book goes to print, interest in the DRC and in Tenke, spurred by a revival in copper's fortunes, is beginning to rise again!

Southern African offshore diamonds also hold a perennial fascination

Another example of the perennial mining comeback story is the southern African offshore diamond saga. In the early 60s Texan entrepreneur, Sam Collins, backed his judgement that huge quantities of diamonds had washed down the Orange River and accumulated over millennia in the offshore waters of South Africa and Namibia (then South West Africa) and started an ocean diamond mining company, Marine Diamonds (MDC). His earlier efforts led to some spectacular production success, but it was short lived and in the end a combination of patchy, and thus uneconomic, production and operating problems led to the demise of the Sam Collins diamond effort. However, De Beers, who had taken a stake in MDC, believed in the long term possibilities for offshore diamonds and effectively took over the Namibian operation. Over the years De Beers (now called Namdeb in Namibia) has improved the technology of ocean mining, and the combination of this with a strong US dollar diamond price trend and a weak

SA rand/Namibian $ has led to a material expansion in ocean diamond production.

In the late 70s improving prospects for diamonds and some technological advances led to a revival of interest in offshore diamonds. Ivan Prinsep, a very different type of entrepreneur to Sam Collins, being half and half Anglo Russian, entered the scene using very basic hose and pump techniques in an initially successful operation in South African waters. His company, Dawn Diamonds, however ran into trouble and got involved in a messy legal fight with its controlling shareholder, Theron Holdings, after the latter had tried to acquire Trans Hex, another diamond miner. Eventually Theron went bust in 1983 and Dawn Diamonds was broken up. Prinsep bitten by the offshore bug formed and floated another company, Ocean Diamond Mining (ODM), that same year. Others also slowly entered the offshore hunt including Trans Hex, Benco and two Canadian companies, COEC and NAMCO. The late 80s were difficult times for offshore diamonds but ODM kept its head above water and also survived the poor mid 90s diamond market.

With an improvement in the diamond market in 1995 and with investors appetites for the sector whetted by the discoveries in Canada, interest in offshore southern Africa began to rise again. As the millennium dawned NAMCO who had taken offshore technology beyond the hose and pump stage and were using an undersea crawler became the new star of offshore mining. But perhaps the sector is fated, for NAMCO, who had taken over ODM along with its more traditional hose and pump operations, suddenly hit trouble. Its crawler crashed into the sea when it was being winched down to the seabed and was lost. So was the company, and despite desperate efforts to raise rescue capital NAMCO went under. Its operations and assets were purchased by Russian diamond czar Lev Leviev. Currently Leviev, Namdeb and Trans Hex are the main players in offshore mining, but adding together the parts of the offshore waters of both South Africa and Namibia where Orange River-borne diamonds could have been deposited we are talking about thousands of square miles of potential. It would be surprising if another strong mining bull market did not see new players trying to join the offshore hunt; hope as we have shown springs eternal in the cold waters of the south Atlantic.

Other projects that have been through more than one owner and still not made it to production include the Musongati nickel prospect in Burundi, the Petaquilla copper prospect in Panama and the Lady Loretta zinc prospect in Australia. Interestingly a new flotation on AIM, Baseresult, is planned for spring 2004. This will bring the old South Crofty tin mine in Cornwall, which is to be re-opened yet again, back to the London market. There are many more of these dormant projects, picked up, dropped and then picked up again as the metals cycle waxes and wanes. The projects can also change name from time to time which makes them difficult to identify when the time to re-promote them roles round again. The usual reason for this re-promotion is that often the problem that first (or even second) time around scuppered development plans has been dealt with making the project attractive again. This can take the form of

- a **higher metal price** that may push the project back into economic territory,
- it might be that earlier metallurgical problems have been overcome through **technological advance**, or
- that **political restraints** (often a big issue in Africa) have been alleviatedby a change of regime.

Always look closely at the history of any project

If an investor is not familiar with the history of the project being promoted he may well not be able to ascertain easily if he is looking at a well worn mining prospect that has been around undeveloped for a long time. One of the most obvious clues is if the project comes with a substantial resource already identified. Whilst this is not conclusive evidence it does warn any investor that he ought to look closely at the project's provenance before doing anything. Of course in these days of privatisation a resource figure may simply mean that previously there had been work done of a non-commercial nature, perhaps as part of an overseas aid package, and the prospect is being farmed out by the local government for the first time.

However, if further investigation does reveal that the project has been around a long time and defied earlier attempts to develop it commercially, the chances are that a new attempt will also fail. Of course, as alluded to previously in respect of mining shares as trading opportunities, the fact that the project is unlikely to make it to the mine stage is not a reason to ignore the shares as a trading situation as long as you have your eyes fully open. If macro and micro economic conditions are right and the new management intelligent and/or aggressive the shares may perform very well for a while, but profit taking sooner or later is advisable.

The Comeback Kids

And it is not only old projects that get dusted down and re-cycled, mining entrepreneurs/promoters also have a habit of staging comebacks. For obvious legal reasons this book cannot 'name and shame' the promoters who constantly re-invent themselves, usually for their personal benefit and not the benefit of those who provide the capital. Needless to say investors should check out every promoter, as well as every project, they run into, a task made a little easier these days by the internet.

scripophily.net

There is a US run website that is worth looking at from the point of view of historical perspective – www.scripophily.net. Its business is the sale of old style share certificates of companies long since gone, and many of the certificates are almost works of art. The site primarily, but not solely, offers US certificates for sale. One of its largest sections is the one covering mining and gold mining shares and the stock Scriophily has to offer is beautifully laid out and the site provides a large amount of information on the companies whose certificates are offered for sale. Whilst a fascinating site in its own right it also provides a genuinely interesting historical record of an important segment of the mining industry. And who knows, amongst the long dead operations and companies represented by the now defunct share certificates on sale could lurk a potential project, for as the old saying goes the best place to find a new mine is where there used to be an old one.

6. Dealing & Settlement

On the face of it dealing in mining shares should boil down to assessing what service levels an investor is looking for from a broker and how cheaply they can be obtained. Some investors might think that because mining is often seen as a non-core sector it may be difficult and even expensive to invest in.

In fact dealing in mining shares is not particularly difficult, and particularly dealing in UK mining stocks and settling the trades should present no problems. Even in foreign markets I would argue that difficulties are often exaggerated. The US is a market that most London brokers should deal in without argument, although their expenses for so doing might vary quite widely. The other main mining markets – Australia, Canada and South Africa – can be more complicated but not for those who know what they are doing. On-line brokers, offering a dealing service level only, are an option for the large markets and since most brokers automatically register foreign shares, particularly US shares, in their nominees not in the investor's name, it might make sense to find an on-line broker who will deal cheaply in the main mining markets as a long stop for the investor's main conventional broker.

Dealing in a foreign currency

In such a global sector as mining some investors may be worried about dealing in different currencies if they venture outside the UK. This is unnecessary as all stock broking firms should have access to cheap and competitive foreign exchange dealing services. So if an order is given, say, in a Canadian mining share in the Toronto market it should be straightforward to convert the consideration into sterling for crediting or debiting the client's account. A good broker will be able to mitigate a fair proportion of the inevitable transaction costs by obtaining competitive rates, in some contrast to the investor's experience as a tourist where he can be skinned alive by the foreign exchange bureaux.

Some investors might like to open a foreign currency account if they trade frequently overseas, and most brokers should be able to do this without difficulty. However it is not really necessary for the average investor and there would almost certainly be administrative costs in running such an account

Dealing in the UK

The actual mechanics of dealing in the big FTSE100 UK mining shares and the middle range UK or foreign AIM-listed mining stocks, and settling the trades, should represent no problem.

Own name, nominee and CREST accounts

One issue is whether the investor wants personal registration so that he can be in direct contact with the company or whether he is prepared to accept registration in his broker's nominee name. Part of the decision relates to how the investor keeps in touch with his investment, a subject we will come on to a little later. However, many private investors in the UK these days no longer have their shares registered in their own names but have been persuaded to use their broker's nominee service, or some have personal CREST (the London Stock Exchange settlement system) membership which is sponsored by their broker.

Personal CREST membership means that you are registered with each UK company you own shares in, and receive all corporate communications, dividends etc. directly, but the account is an electronic one without certificates or the need for transfer forms. You can also hold some foreign shares through CREST but these will be held in the name of the broker who sponsors your CREST membership and not directly in your name.

Investors directed towards FTSE100 stocks

As a broad investment principle UK brokers, hampered by compliance and regulatory issues, increasingly try to direct their clients into stocks in the FTSE100, and are often reluctant to recommend going for smaller stocks, or foreign stocks outside the main markets of the US, Japan and Europe. Because of this they may well try to direct clients interested in mining into the four big easy-to-deal-in mining stocks in the FTSE100 rather than a foreign mining stock.

If you know what you want to do, stick to your guns and deal in the stock of your choice. So if you want to buy a South African gold share or a Canadian copper share, for example, and you want pure exposure, don't be persuaded into a diversified like Anglo American or Rio Tinto just to please your broker.

Dealing on AIM or the domestic market

There is, however, an issue to be faced when dealing in mining shares listed on AIM, for some of them remain incorporated in their country of origin and have retained a listing, often the primary one, in their home market.

These shares are usually Australian, although there are a few Canadian stocks now on AIM. It is quite possible that a broker with an order in an AIM listed Australian mining company will try and transact it in London which will be cheaper, and certainly easier, for him if not for the client. The problem for the investor is that very probably the London market, if the stock is an Australian one which because of the time difference means that the Australian market is closed, will offer to deal on a wider spread than would be the case in Australia and in a smaller volume also. In this situation it usually pays to ignore the London market and have the order placed in the Australian market for execution the following day. The price and volume are likely to be better than would have been achieved in London. Of course because of unexpected news or market movements it might be that waiting will lead to a less satisfactory outcome, but in my experience that is a rare occurrence, and the reverse may even be the case. The other downside of buying AIM rather than foreign register stock is that UK stamp duty is charged on UK register purchases.

There is one anomaly between AIM and the Canadian market that is worth bearing in mind, particularly where the Canadian company is placing stock with UK investors. If a Canadian company places Canadian register stock, under Canadian market rules it is usual for there to be a hold period where the buying investor is not allowed to sell his stock, and the period can vary between a few weeks and a year. The stock so placed will carry a legend to this effect and will not be accepted for good delivery in the Canadian market until the hold period is over. There is no such limitation in the UK market where UK register stock is involved, although investors as part of the placing agreement may pledge not to sell their shares for an agreed period. This is, however, in the way of an informal arrangement and is not part of UK market regulations. Therefore if a Canadian company uses its AIM quotation to place stock outside Canada there is no formal hold period attached to the placing. Some UK and Continental investors refuse to participate in placings where there is a formal hold period, so an AIM listing may well make it easier for a Canadian company to raise money in the UK and Europe if it places UK register stock.

Dealing in non-UK markets

Australia

Australia is also noted for its paperless settlement system; when you deal there is no certificate to receive or send in and no transfer form to sign. UK brokers try and steer their clients towards nominee registration so that the client no longer has any paper to deal with (save for filing the contract note), and the broker's settlement department takes over sole responsibility for settling the bargain. In Australia companies sponsor registration of their shareholders with their registrars. When a shareholder deals he receives a statement and a shareholder number and if he sells, or buys more stock in the company, he merely informs his broker of his account details and on settlement a book entry changing the shareholder register is made by the registrar. No paper has to be signed or sent by the shareholder. The system is simple to understand, efficient and allows the shareholder to remain registered directly with the company.

Perhaps because they have little Australian business some London brokers find the simplicity of the Chess approach (the Australian paperless settlement system) slightly off putting and have been known to try and complicate the process.

South Africa

The South African market also has a paperless, or dematerialised as they call it, system (STRATE) but it is more complicated than the Australian system and investors dealing in South African stocks may because of this choose to hold their stocks in their broker's nominees. This unfortunately will result in paying additional overseas annual holding charges, as indeed does using the broker's nominees for US and other foreign stocks. Ironically two major South African gold shares, AngloGold and Durban Deep, have Australian listings due to acquisitions and therefore can be traded in Australia and settled using the Chess system.

The problem with South Africa is that under the new dematerialised system personal registration is still possible and certificates can still be issued, but before you deal the certificates must be dematerialised by submitting them to the Johannesburg stock exchange for the holding to be recorded electronically. Once that is done (it should take two or three days) the stock can then be sold. If the certificate is coming from the UK then several days need to be added to the dematerialisation process. In the new STRATE system South African investors now register with Central Securities Depository Participants (CSDPs) either in that CSDP's nominee name or in their own name, depending on which CSDP they are using. Unfortunately the system at the moment is complicated for foreign shareholders and they are probably better off using their own broker's nominees.

There are a couple of ways round this for UK investors. In the past most South African mining companies set up London registers for use by UK and other foreign shareholders. This meant that investors could deal in the London market, with the trades generally taking place between foreign brokers and investors in sterling. The trade was then settled in London with no need for stock to travel to Johannesburg, although if there was a price difference between London and Johannesburg it was (and still is) open to the broker to deliver London stock to Johannesburg. In due course dealing in London became more expensive for large investors due to stamp duty and commission rates and they began to use Johannesburg or ADRs (American depository receipts) in New York. Although many South Africans retain London registers, many market makers and traders no longer accept London register trades, largely as a result of the shrinking number of such trades. As a consequence dealers have to unwind the trade in Johannesburg, and the time needed to deliver London stock to Johannesburg to be dematerialised and then delivered to the Johannesburg market is around two weeks against the three days settlement time allowed in the STRATE system. If this is the case most brokers will insist the shares are dematerialised before they will place an order in the market.

Having said that, a few brokers in London will still deal in certificated stock before the shares have been dematerialised for delivery to the Johannesburg market. They get round the delivery time problem by borrowing stock in South Africa to fulfil the three days settlement requirement; in due course the stock from London is delivered in Johannesburg and dematerialised and the borrowed stock is returned. The expenses of doing the trade this way are rolled into the price that the investor in London receives if he is selling. Buying is not quite such a problem but investors may find that their brokers and/or the market makers will dictate how the stock is delivered and therefore the manner in which its ownership is registered.

The effective restrictions on SA dealing in terms of available options is in some contrast to the situation for UK investors thirty years ago when the London broking community had few problems in dealing in SA mining shares. It is particularly ironic that in the post apartheid era dealing in South African shares in London has become something that many brokers are reluctant to encourage although some of the big investment banks have SA subsideries. In the 70s every London broker of substance had both advisory and dealing competence in South African shares. It is the same story in Australian shares, although there are still a good number of Australian brokers with London offices which makes it slightly easier for London brokers without agents on the ground in Australia to place orders, as they can use these offices to transact client business. Although, as mentioned above, price and size may be less satisfactory this way.

North America

Dealing in the US and Canadian markets should pose few problems. These days virtually all dealing for UK private investors in these markets is done by their broker through that broker's agent (either a US broker in New York or a Canadian broker in Toronto) in the local market where price and size are more competitive. A few UK private investors have opened dealing accounts with the London office of a US broker; such an arrangement is more than likely to use an on-line account. It is also open to an investor to approach a North America broker to deal through the local office. The main reason for this is that US broker commissions for private clients are lower than UK rates. Although both the US and Canadian markets deal in registered stock, which means that an investor could have stock registered in his name, stock is usually registered in a nominee name and held to the dealing broker's account which, of course, incurs a charge.

It is possible to buy many of the non North American mining stocks in the US in the form of ADRs as mentioned above, and many larger institutional investors do so, but it is much less used by private investors. In effect ADRs are bundled receipts representing registered stock already in existence and issued in receipt form by a US custodian. One of the snags is that a private investor will effectively suffer two management charges as a result of the ADRs firstly being held to the account of his broker and secondly because his broker will normally pass on the US custodian charge to him.

Miscellaneous dealing vehicles

In the main this book is aimed at investors who are interested in the mining sector and would deal conventionally in mining shares to gain exposure to the sector. However it is worth mentioning in passing that an investor can gear up his investment strategy by using traded options, warrants, spread betting or contracts for difference (CFDs) for example.

One should remember though that in the UK these kinds of trading vehicles are usually available only for the leading miners. In the South African market, again it is the leaders where options etc. can be used, as is also the case in Australia. North America, particularly the US, provides a much wider choice of mining stocks (many of them non US stocks) where unconventional, leveraged trading, particularly traded options, is possible.

Don't forget that many mining stocks are highly geared investments already

However, if an investor is tempted to leverage his mining market strategy he ought not to forget that this can be done within the conventional share market by buying high beta stocks. So if you fancy the copper price you don't have to buy a Rio Tinto CFD, with its open ended liability exposure, to massage your performance – our old friends the Zambian copper twins ZCI and ZCCM, and their straight ordinary shares will do the job just as well, and your risk is confined to the original purchase consideration and the country of operation.

The role of the stockbroker

I have made a number of general comments in other parts of the book about stockbrokers. Since an investor is bound to use the services of a stockbroker somewhere along the transaction path, a few dedicated comments are appropriate here.

Does the broker have mining experience?

If an investor already has a personal broker he will know whether that broker has any mining sector expertise, or whether there is anyone in the firm who knows anything about the sector. If the answer is no, then the investor is on his own unless he thinks it worthwhile to find a more knowledgeable broker to act for him. He, of course, has to work out whether his interest in mining shares is likely over the whole economic cycle to be substantial and persistent, thus making the switching of brokers worthwhile. He could simply take just his mining business to another broker, but it would probably need to be substantial for this to be sensible.

Stockbrokers as a source of information

Earlier we observed a developing trend among brokers to try and direct clients into large marketable stocks and away from smaller and thus possibly more speculative companies. This does mean that brokers, for compliance and regulatory reasons, may be reluctant to offer advice in an unfamiliar area like mining. But as we shall see in the next section there are other sources of information for investors looking at the sector, and these are perhaps more reliable, fuller and, what's more, available on tap. Of course some investors value the support and participation of their broker in what they do, and do look to him or her to alert them to events affecting their portfolio. In a fast moving sector like mining such support is obviously helpful in keeping the investor in touch. However if the broker does not have any expertise in the mining area and cannot, therefore, help in this way, it is not the end of the world as the investor can these days do the research himself.

The importance of dealing expertise

However, an investor's minimum requirement must be that his broker be able to instruct the firm's dealers correctly so that any dealings in mining shares are carried out efficiently and in the appropriate market with regard to dealing size, settlement costs and holding expenses. Previously we have looked at the issue of dealing and settlement in the mining sector in some detail, and believe that any competent broking firm should be able to transact business in foreign markets without a major problem. If they cannot, or say they cannot, then a prudent investor will obviously need to look for another broker to carry out mining orders.

7. Information Sources

Above we have deliberately, in talking about dealing, laid some stress on the options available to a shareholder in how his ownership is registered. The reason for this relates to the importance we lay on having access to timely information in a sector where things can change very quickly. Broadly an investor/shareholder has four main sources of information that he can use –

1. press and specialist press,
2. the company itself,
3. the internet, and
4. his stockbroker.

Media

In the past the mining sector was well served in the UK by newspapers and investment magazines. There were also a number of specialist mining publications some of which survive to this day. However, coverage of mining in the financial pages of UK daily and Sunday newspapers today is very much reduced, and the contraction in the space for mining stories and comment in the Financial Times over the years is typical of the trend.

FT

Thirty years ago the *FT* had two regular mining columns - the Lodestar comment piece on Mondays written by Leslie Parker, the highly respected mining journalist, and a Saturday sector review piece written by Ken Marston. During the week there was also a daily mining news column covering a wide range of mining company issues including financial results, exploration news and other corporate activity. In addition there was also a commodities review on Saturday. Eventually the Monday column, on Leslie Parker's retirement in 1978, was dropped and this was followed by the dropping of the Saturday review in 1987 following the retirement of Ken Marston. The special news column was also dropped in 1987 and mining news was either dispersed around the relevant company news pages or found in a new page that covered all commodity news including London and New York commodity prices.

In due course commodities were reduced to half a page and then recently this was reduced further to the bottom corner of a page, and the full metal price service, which included overnight New York metal prices, was also dropped at the same time. Mining company news stories are now confined to the UK or overseas company pages and are much reduced in number.

Last year the FT had no review or comment on Rio Tinto's interim results!

Stories, particularly relating to foreign mining companies, are prone to be replaced in the FT's final UK edition which is often the one distributed in London and the Home Counties. Other UK newspapers are even less interested in mining, and comment here is usually confined to the big three UK FTSE100 mining companies. Another measure of the fall in the status of the mining sector is in the sharp reduction in mining companies seeking a listing in the FT's prices page. In the 70s and 80s around 180 companies had an FT quote, today there are 47 mining companies listed on the main FT prices page and 30 or so others bundled together in the FT's list of AIM companies.

Other magazines

A number of UK magazines covering finance/saving and stock market activities, including the *Investors Chronicle* and *Shares*, do review mining shares from time to time, but coverage is sporadic and fairly basic. Amongst the specialist mining press in the UK there is the *Mining Journal, Metal Bulletin* and *World Gold* which provide a comprehensive view of the metals and mining industry and there are also specialist mining publications in mining countries like Canada and Australia - the *Northern Miner* in Canada is one of the most widely read. Others include *Resource World, Canadian Miner* and *The Prospector* from Canada and Australia's *Paydirt* and *Gold Mining Journal*. Overseas publications like the Northern Miner are relatively easy to subscribe to, but they will always reach UK readers a few days after publication in their home country. Although increasingly publications can be obtained on-line which gets round this problem.

Company investor relations

If a shareholder is registered in his own name then the company will communicate directly, although the flow of information is likely to be confined to annual reports and published results, the latter often arriving some weeks after their public release.

Companies are obliged to publish a substantial stream of news these days, partly as a result of stock exchange requirements regarding price sensitive information, but this news does not have to be communicated directly to shareholders, only released to the relevant stock exchange.

In the UK a shareholder could access this information through UK-Wire (www.uk-wire.com), which is the premier source of UK company announcements, and has a page dedicated to mining stocks.

Company websites

Most companies have websites and news of this nature and more besides should be found on the company website. All of the big mining companies have extensive websites as do many of the smaller companies. The problem is that keeping track of this tide of information can be hugely time consuming, although a system of news alerts can be put in place to sieve at least some of this news flow.

Mining company websites in general have been designed by specialist organisations whose expertise lies in design rather than the activities of the client company. Therefore corporate websites tend to cover the same broad categories as each other and a mining company website, although it will carry information specific to it and its industry, will not look much different to that of other public companies seeking to communicate with their shareholders.

The essential information that a potential investor will be after about the company's operations and its information releases are most likely to be found on pages with titles like

- *Operations*
- *Projects*
- *Press releases*
- *Investor information*
- *Results and news*

The title of these information pages does differ from site to site so a little experimentation will probably be necessary. There is usually a *contacts page* which can have names of the corporate officers and group addresses with phone/fax and e-mail contact details. The site may also have either a dedicated section or a site within a site where copies of the *annual reports* and *interim announcements* can be downloaded. The process of downloading and then printing can be time consuming, but then that is a general comment on using the internet as an information source.

Annual reports and WILink

An alternative to downloading company reports from the internet is to get them delivered free by post through WILink, which operates an annual reports distribution service.

An alternative to downloading company reports from the internet is to get them delivered free by post through WILink, which operates an annual reports distribution service. They can be ordered by phone or fax through the FT which carries the relevant contact numbers at the bottom of the UK share prices page.

They can also be ordered online at: www.harriman-house.com/annualreports

A list of mining companies whose annual reports can be ordered through WILink is given in the Appendix.

Internet

On the internet there are a number of free-to-use mining news sites, Mineweb and Minesite are two of the better known ones, and gold bugs are very well catered for also. Using these kinds of information sources does mean that a lot of sifting of the news is done for investors, and the expert interpretation of stories can also be helpful.

The internet is a very powerful information tool and it makes it fairly straightforward to follow developing mining stories, and it probably helps in normal times to gauge the accuracy and significance of items of information. The role of the internet during boom times may be rather different and it will be interesting to see how the bulletin boards attached to sites like Mineweb are used by visitors to the site. Whilst punters in the Australian boom used to pester journalists with comment and opinion, they had to hope that the journalist would find something interesting in what they said and publish it. On the internet, websites are very keen to encourage interactivity over the news stories that they run, and in a mining boom like the Australian nickel boom there would be ample scope for spicing up news stories.

In the following table, listed are number of the available mining and metals information sites on the internet. Two things must be noted however. Firstly the list is not meant to be comprehensive and there are certainly far more sites available than we have listed here. Secondly some of the sites are free to view and browse, others are wholly subscription services and others are part free and part subscription. This situation is a fluid one and so we have not specifically marked the particular status of the sites on the list. What we will say is that at the time of writing three of the most informative and interesting sites

- *Mineweb,*
- *Gold Eagle and*
- *Kitco*

were still free.

Table 7.1 - Mining related web sites

Site name	Service
www.321gold.com	Gold, financial news
www.a1-guide-to-goldinvestments.com	Gold and gold shares trading and news
www.canadianminingnews.com	As site name
www.freebuck.com	General financial news and gold
www.goldcolony.com	Metal and mining company news
www.gold-eagle.com	Gold and precious metal news and comment
www.goldenbar.com	Gold and financial sector comment
www.goldensextant.com	Gold, financial sector comment and opinion
www.goldseek.com	Gold, financial news and comment
www.howestree.com	General financial news with mining bias
www.investmentrarities.com	Precious metals trading and comment
www.jsmineset.com	Gold news and opinion
www.kitco.com	Gold and precious metal news and prices
www.lemetropolecafe.com	Gold and gold share comment and opinion
www.minebox.com	Australian based mining news
www.mineralstox.com	Precious/base metal and mining news
www.minersmanual.com	Mining information with precious metals slant
www.minesite.com	General mining news and comment
www.mineweb.com	Full mining news for all markets
www.mininglife.com	General mining news and reference
www.miningstocks.com	Gold and technology shares news and opinion
www.sharelynx.com	Precious metals news and comment
www.silver-investor.com	Silver news and comment
www.silverseek.com	Silver and financial news and comment
www.thebulliondesk.com	Precious metals news and comment
www.usagold.com	Gold metal/coins trading and comment

Stockbrokers

We considered the general role of the stockbroker a little earlier. However in the context of the provision of information the last source of information would be an investor's own stockbroker.

I mentioned earlier that the mining sector no longer commands the interest of the average stockbroker be they servicing institutional investors or private clients. This, of course, was not always so and the Aussie boom and the following South African gold share boom were two times when London stockbrokers had a reasonably good grasp of the mining sector, and with industrial equities out of favour they were only too happy to advise their clients on mining shares. That situation no longer holds sway and private client stockbrokers in particular prefer to play it safe when offering investment advice. A few private client stockbroking firms have recently acquired mining research expertise, but the bigger investment banks have in many cases continued to cut back in this area..

A reasonably comprehensive list of brokers interested in mining can be found at *minesite.com* under mining advisors, brokers with mining interests. It is, however, important to realise that many smaller brokers are only interested in mining as a source of fees from listing and funding work, and few provide resources for research and client servicing. It is therefore more than likely that individual investors will have a better idea than their stockbrokers where to go for mining sector information, and will also probably be better able to interpret and act on what they uncover.

Three examples of UK private client orientated brokers who research the mining sector are Numis Securities, Seymour Pierce and Evolution Beeson Gregory. It has to be remembered though that smaller brokers who have research departments, and coverage of specialist sectors like mining, probably have institutional/corporate ambitions and therefore have not put mining research efforts in place primarily to support their private investment business. In these cases private clients of these firms will still have to direct any enquiries on the mining sector to their designated broker, and hope that he or she has a good relationship with the research department. It is also not certain that ordinary private clients would be able to receive the mining research product 'legally'; as these days FSA rules direct that professional research can only be distributed to competent investors – institutional and qualifying experienced private investors as defined. Clearly dealing through a broking firm that does have some specialist mining experience is better than using a firm with absolutely no expertise, but do not expect your business to be welcomed as it would have been 35 years ago at the height of the ubiquitous Aussie boom.

8. Ten Key Points to Grasp

I want to distil what we have learnt about the mining sector into ten points to keep in mind whenever we think about investing in the mining sector. Some of the base principles are also applicable to other stock market sectors.

1. Stripped down to bare essentials, mining shares are often like the proverbial tin of sardines – for trading but never for eating – so **always take profits**.

2. The sector is **irretrievably cyclical** – for example the Zambian copper twins (ZCI and ZCCM) historically experience bull market rises of between 10 and 20 times and in bear markets lose more than 90% of their value.

3. Many mining companies are formed but **only a handful survive for any length of time** to earn profits and pay dividends, and only once in a blue moon does one of these become a giant.

4. A **flow of information** and a good understanding of its importance or otherwise is essential.

5. Before you place a mining sector order be sure you are absolutely clear what should happen in terms of **dealing** because your broker may well not know.

6. Always check the **provenance of 'exciting' mining stories** and/or excitable mining promoters to make sure that you're not being sold a 'retread'.

7. Always be aware of the underlying **macroeconomic situation** as it affects metal demand and prices when you are thinking of investing in the mining share sector.

8. Mining bull markets often develop very slowly but **spike very quickly** and the ensuing bear market retreat can be very fast.

9. Mining shares often **bottom out well before the metals cycle turns up**.

10. **Never fall in love with a mining share**, it will invariably jilt you in the end.

Many of the above points may seem obvious to readers, indeed some of them may even appear rather mundane. That may well be, but the points are listed as they are in my view absolutely essential if potential investors are going to participate profitably in the mining share sector.

I cannot reiterate enough that the mining share sector is endemically cyclical, and these cycles are usually unpredictable in terms of how long they last and the extent of price movements in both directions. The theme for investors then must be one of setting price targets and of taking profits. Anyone coming new to the game and thinking, as many of us did in our youth when playing the Aussie nickel boom, that they have stumbled upon a money making machine with an infinite life would be repeating mistakes made in all past stock market booms when the new paradigm argument was put forward to support continued participation in the action.

In the main, mining shares really are like the proverbial can of sardines. If you don't grasp that, the sector will provide you with nothing but tears. But if you do grasp that, you will have opened up the prospect of being able to make money in the stock market even when all but the mining sector is in ragged and painful retreat.

Conclusion

At the end of this trip through the mining sector it is now time to try and draw some, hopefully, useful conclusions from what has been written. In particular we have sought to be persuasive on whether mining, especially gold mining, deserves a core position in any portfolio, a position which broadly it does not enjoy today.

Mining no longer a core sector

Although the FTSE100 in the UK includes the three largest mining companies in the world the sector has lost the acclaim that it enjoyed thirty years ago, when in rapid succession the Australian nickel boom and the South African gold boom captured the imagination of private and institutional investors, and saved the bacon of UK brokers at a time when other markets were almost moribund. In the ensuing years other sectors have pushed mining into the background, and though FTSE100 tracker funds have to have an exposure to what is quite large mining representation in the index, one senses limited enthusiasm in the funds themselves. Even in mining countries like Australia and Canada, investors no longer see mining as a key investment area, instead concentrating their long term growth expectations on sectors like technology, telecommunications and biotech/pharmaceuticals.

This book has set out to explain both the rewards and the pitfalls of investing in mining shares and in doing that has also tried to promote the idea of mining as a core sector once again. Our main thesis has been that gold in particular has a negative correlation to the movement of ordinary industrial equities, and because of that gold shares can usefully improve the performance of a general portfolio when equity markets are in retreat.

Cyclicality is an important characteristic of mining stocks

I have mixed history with contemporary events to draw conclusions about the all important issue of securing the profits that investors make in mining, an issue not exclusive to mining. The problem is that mining is highly cyclical and when it is running strongly investors have a tendency to forget that when the sector reverses, capital gains can melt away quickly, sometimes alarmingly so, which explains why we often refer, in terms of comparison, to the recent and infamous internet boom. This cyclicality is so well established that, unless the investor has stumbled upon the once in a lifetime mining junior heading for immortality and a seat at the mining giants' table, he ignores it at his peril.

One of the problems facing the smaller investor is that he often sees the mining sector as providing the sort of volatility that can make him rich quickly, and he is not wrong in so thinking. The snag here is that many investors are looking for the multiple times share price rise that turns a modest sum of money into something altogether more serious, a perfectly acceptable 40% profit would not be enough. To elaborate, if an investor puts in, say, £2,000 into a mining share then such a 40% rise would lead to an increase in his capital to £2,800, satisfactory, but unlikely to change his life. If he puts in £20,000 a similar 40% profit would see his capital rise to a nice £28,000.

One doesn't have to rely on ten-baggers to get rich

However if we were in the middle of a mining boom and the investor was able to reap a 40% profit every two months and re-invest, then after two years the £2,000 investor would find his capital had grown to a very acceptable £112,000. To achieve this he would have had to be lucky enough to find 12 situations where quick profits could be made, but in a boom that is not an impossibility. Of course if he had started with £20,000, the consequence of taking 40% profits would be rather more dramatic, and after two years his capital would have grown to £1.1 million. What we think this demonstrates is that if one is active when the market is right then it is not necessary to stumble across a multiple '*bagger*' like Poseidon to make money. Unfortunately greed has been the downfall of many investors in the mining sector, although we appreciate that the advice, that at one and the same time an investor in mining should be both aggressive and careful, may be difficult to square.

A portfolio of large or small stocks?

Following on, in terms of stock picking one of the bigger issues covered has been whether smaller investors should go for the handful of global mining giants with their spread of interests, or instead concentrate on identifying promising situations in the medium sized mining and smaller exploration companies categories where the beta is much higher. There is an issue of management here amongst the more speculative smaller stocks which we addressed at some length, but the balanced approach would lead to a core of large stocks with a group of carefully chosen and closely watched smaller situations to provide the performance. However those who have confidence that they have grasped the sector's fundamentals and foibles will probably want to chance their luck on following the smaller companies, where the outperformance will undoubtedly be found in a mining bull market.

It's a global industry, but still with national problems

We have also put the mining sector's global image under the microscope in order to assess the relative attractions of mining markets from a geopolitical viewpoint. Whilst all the main markets which have strong mining sectors have equally sound trading and settlement procedures these days, each of them has problems on a macro level. South Africa has the black empowerment issue to tackle, Canada has a strong environmental lobby and Australia has the problem of native title. Some like the UK are more expensive to trade in than their peer markets.

We have also sought to give readers an idea of the fun that the mining sector can provide investors. This acts as something of a counterweight to the serious need for mining investors to be well informed because, in some contrast to other sectors, mining is seen as a Cinderella sector by the mainstream media and is widely ignored by them these days.

The metals cycle

Importantly though, investors must not lose sight of the fact that the mining sector has its own macro driver - metals. The mining share cycle is driven by the metals cycle, a cycle which itself is influenced by a mix of metal price and sales volume. But on occasions mining can throw up a situation where the discovery of a new mineral province leads to sustained stock market activity despite a poor outlook for the metal/mineral involved - the discovery of diamonds in Canada in the mid 90s was an example of this. This means that in a mining downturn not all the sector needs to be in the same doldrums as the metals market. It also needs to be appreciated that mining shares may become strong buys long before the metals cycle turns up, because the sector's sometimes extreme volatility can lead to substantial overshoot on the downside (as well as on the upside of course).

The issue of what metal to follow obviously has a direct impact on stock choice and we have spent some time looking at a wide range of metals and assessing their key characteristics. The mining sector is driven by gold, but copper, nickel and platinum are also important and attract strong investor interest. Whilst it can also be argued that minor metals have potential, much greater care has to be exercised in assessing the investment merits of an occasional high flyer like tantalum as opposed to a major long term growth metal such as nickel.

We also live in an increasingly regulated securities environment so the old method of seeking illumination on investment issues by tapping insider knowledge is no longer the wisest and safest route to take. Nonetheless an early steer on a metal need not necessarily be illegal and may often be nothing more than a perceptive observation by someone knowledgeable about the sector. The huge late 90s boom in mobile phones provided a window for tantalum miners and explorers, and some investors had early warning of the link which they were able to profit from.

Information sources and the decline of stockbroking expertise

On the more prosaic subject of where sector information is to be found and how an investor values mining situations, we can provide a clear lead on the former but unfortunately only a tentative one on the latter. One thing that is clear in the observation of information sources is that the broking community is of limited help these days. There are a few specialists scattered around, although in London they are still shrinking in total despite the rising number of mining companies listing in the City. These specialists are also discouraged from talking to private investors, and some of the larger investment banks do not encourage them to speak to the smaller institutions either. The average private client adviser in the UK then knows very little about mining and therefore does not encourage client interest in the sector. Fortunately the expansion of the internet has led to the creation of a large body of constantly updated information, and the mining sector is well served in this area which materially mitigates the limited help an investor can expect from his broker.

Learning the lessons of history

We have taken some time in these pages to outline what are arguably the two greatest mining market events of the last thirty or so years - the Australian mining boom and the Bre-X scam. These two episodes are entertaining yarns in their own right, but they also have lessons for those interested in participating aggressively in the mining sector in the future. Stock market history is scattered around with other booms and scams, some quite recent, others far away in time. What we are absolutely clear about is that new mining booms are more than probable in the future, and learning the lessons of Bre-X or the Aussie boom will be enormously helpful in maximising profits when those booms emerge.

The last glass of champagne

Finally, we return to the subject of the mining sector as fun. The world of securities is a highly regulated place these days and the pressure of the compliance regime found in most brokers tends to drain the spirits of the industry's practitioners. The investor, however, is not similarly constrained, and, within reason, can pursue a developing mining boom with hedonistic abandon.

When the mining sector begins to run it can be an awesome sight and the excitement generated can be every bit as seductive and heady as that which enveloped markets during the internet boom. Many of the promoters are larger than life and even though they can exude great charm, they should come with storm warnings prominently displayed. However their participation only adds to the fun.

Of course, as we have warned, parties do end and midnight does strike. It is best to be gone before that, leaving the last glass of champagne to someone else, returning to one's mining core to enjoy a few warm memories and await the next call to action.

APPENDICES

UK listed mining companies

See the following tables

Name	EPIC	Sub-Sector	Listing	Capital (£m)	Volatility	Beta	Price high (£)	Price high date	Price low (£)	Price low date	Prelim. results	Interims ann.	Float date	Website
African Diamonds PLC	AFD	Other mineral extractors & mines	AIM	26	7.46	-0.8	0.735	6/2/04	0.0675	23/9/03	17/12/03		14/7/03	www.afdiamonds.com
African Eagle Resources PLC	AFE	Gold mining	AIM	16.6	5.11	0.05	0.2775	9/2/04	0.0625	27/6/03	30/9/03	25/6/03		www.africaneagle.co.uk
African Gold PLC	AFG	Gold mining	AIM	25.2	5.79	0.03	0.1475	11/2/04	0.0062	22/4/03	6/8/03	22/12/03	29/9/95	www.africangoldplc.com
Anglesey Mining PLC	AYM	Other mineral extractors & mines	Full	4.9	4.24	-0.05	0.0463	10/2/04	0.0137	5/3/03	27/6/03	23/12/03	6/6/88	www.angleseymining.co.uk
Anglo American PLC	AAL	Other mineral extractors & mines	Full	20308.3	2.35	1.14	14.2	2/3/04	8.435	12/3/03	25/2/04	8/8/03	24/5/99	www.angloamerican.co.uk
Anglo Pacific Group PLC	APF	Mining finance	Full	58.2	2.12	0.12	0.69	26/2/04	0.2975	9/4/03	11/4/03	12/9/03	30/12/96	
Angus & Ross PLC	AGU	Other mineral extractors & mines	AIM	5.1	5.66	0.28	0.14	18/2/04	0.0525	15/5/03	18/7/03	24/11/03	28/8/01	www.angusandross.com
Antofagasta PLC	ANTO	Other mineral extractors & mines	Full	2318.7	1.68	0.15	12.58	20/2/04	5.66	26/3/03	11/3/03	2/9/03	5/7/82	www.antofagasta.co.uk
Aquarius Platinum	AQP	Other mineral extractors & mines	Full		2.5	0.34	3.9175	28/1/04	2.085	30/4/03				
Archipelago Resources PLC	AR.	Gold mining	AIM	17.8	1.7	-0.06	0.405	15/1/04	0.275	9/9/03			9/9/03	
Arcon International Resources PLC	AIN	Other mineral extractors & mines	Full	64.4	3.66	0.09	0.0435	6/1/04	0.0188	9/6/03	30/4/03	22/9/03	3/4/95	www.arcon.ie
Avocet Mining PLC	AVM	Gold mining	AIM	63.3	3.3	0.08	0.785	14/1/04	0.25	17/4/03	23/7/03	26/11/03	26/7/02	www.avocet.co.uk
Bema Gold Corporation	BAU	Gold mining	AIM		3.82	-0.23	2.46	1/12/03	1.455	6/10/03				
BHP Billiton PLC	BLT	Other mineral extractors & mines	Full	12488.8	2.62	0.96	5.2625	2/3/04	2.955	12/3/03	28/8/03	19/2/04	28/7/97	www.bhpbilliton.com
Bisichi Mining PLC	BISI	Mining finance	Full	9.6	1.85	0.08	0.92	4/3/04	0.32	5/3/03	6/3/03	29/9/03	14/3/48	www.bisichi.co.uk
Brazilian Diamonds Ltd	BDY	Other mineral extractors & mines	AIM		3.72	0.36	0.37	8/12/03	0.255	18/12/03				
Bullion Resources PLC	BLO	Gold mining	AIM	2.4	5.33	0.21	0.22	10/3/03	0.04	12/2/04	20/8/03	30/9/03	10/6/02	www.bullionresources.net
Caledon Resources PLC	CDN	Other mineral extractors & mines	AIM	21.9	6.98	0.12	0.1625	4/12/03	0.01	20/3/03	30/1/04	30/4/03	7/12/00	www.caledonresources.com
Cambrian Mining PLC	CBM	Other mineral extractors & mines	AIM	16.4	3.42	0.26	0.66	17/2/04	0.385	4/9/03	17/11/03		4/8/03	www.cambrianmining.com

Name	EPIC	Sub-Sector	Listing	Capital (£m)	Volatility	Beta	Price high (£)	Price high date	Price low (£)	Price low date	Prelim. results	Interims ann.	Float date	Website
Cambridge Mineral Resources PLC	CMR	Other mineral extractors & mines	AIM	20	4.19	0.32	0.1662	16/2/04	0.09	1/7/03	5/6/03	30/9/03	26/7/00	www.cambmin.co.uk
Celtic Resources Holdings PLC	CER	Gold mining	AIM	176.5	7.82	-0.14	5.315	24/2/04	1.2	17/4/03	23/6/03	15/9/03	14/10/02	www.celticresources.com
Centamin Egypt	CEY	Gold mining	AIM	2.54		-0.04	0.1637	14/11/03	0.0763	23/4/03				
Central African Mining & Exploration Company PLC	CFM	Other mineral extractors & mines	AIM	48.7	5.19	-0.2	0.1275	5/2/04	0.0187	13/5/03	22/9/03	31/12/03	9/10/02	www.camec-plc.com
Cluff Mining PLC	CLU	Other mineral extractors & mines	AIM	21.7	2.4	0.11	1.6	19/3/03	0.825	2/3/04	2/4/03	29/9/03	5/5/00	www.cluff-mining.com
Conroy Diamonds & Gold PLC	CCG	Gold mining	AIM	3.2	5.51	0.36	0.095	10/9/03	0.0425	31/3/03	14/11/03	16/2/04	31/5/00	www.conroydiamondsandgold.com
Consolidated Minerals	CNM	Other mineral extractors & mines	AIM			-0.22	0.555	2/3/04	0.39	31/12/03				
Eurasia Mining PLC	EUA	Other mineral extractors & mines	AIM	6.4	2.44	0.3	0.0862	26/1/04	0.0475	14/4/03	29/4/03	30/7/03	2/10/96	www.eurasia-mining.plc.uk
Eureka Mining PLC	EKA	Other mineral extractors & mines	AIM	22.2	4.85	-0.21	1.37	25/2/04	1.17	21/1/04			11/12/03	
European Diamonds PLC	EPD	Other mineral extractors & mines	AIM	17.3	1.17	0.02	0.92	16/6/03	0.535	16/5/03	18/11/03	31/3/03	11/12/00	www.europeandiamondsplc.com
Firestone Diamonds PLC	FDI	Other mineral extractors & mines	AIM	18.1	2.58	0.19	0.505	21/11/03	0.28	3/4/03	5/12/03	31/3/03	14/8/98	www.firestonediamonds.com
First Quantum Minerals LD	FQM	Other mineral extractors & mines	AIM		3.68	0	6.975	22/1/04	2.05	4/4/03				
Galahad Gold PLC	GLF	Mining finance	AIM	103.3	2.41	0.01	0.2675	23/1/04	0.0625	1/4/03	10/2/04	13/9/03	22/1/01	www.galahadcapital.com
GMA Resources PLC	GMA	Gold mining	AIM	33.3	3.04	-0.01	0.3275	29/9/03	0.1375	8/7/03		24/9/03	14/5/03	
Gold Bullion Securities	GBS	Gold mining	Full		2.67	0	42.7	12/1/04	39.3	3/3/04				
Gold Mines of Sardinia PLC	GMN	Gold mining	AIM	4.1	0.97	0.23	0.115	5/9/03	0.0125	3/3/04				
Greenwich Resources PLC	GRWA	Gold mining	Full	8.3	5.99	0.16	0.0337	10/2/04	0.0137	2/6/03	16/1/04	27/6/03	29/8/85	www.greenwichresourcesplc.com
Griffin Mining	GFM	Other mineral extractors & mines	AIM		3.43	0.19	0.3025	18/2/04	0.1	10/4/03				

233

Name	EPIC	Sub-Sector	Listing	Capital (£m)	Volatility	Beta	Price high (£)	Price high date	Price low (£)	Price low date	Prelim. results	Interims ann.	Float date	Website
Hereward Ventures PLC	HEV	Gold mining	AIM	8.3	3.73	0.26	0.0763	17/2/04	0.0388	24/3/03	16/9/03	8/12/03	12/2/01	www.hereward.com
Hidefield PLC	HIF	Other mineral extractors & mines	AIM	10.4	5.45	0.34	0.0975	20/2/04	0.0213	28/4/03	28/3/03	26/6/03	7/12/00	
Highland Gold Mining Ltd	HGM	Gold mining	AIM	320.6	2.05	-0.07	3.05	9/1/04	1.83	7/8/03	29/4/03	24/9/03	17/12/02	
Jubilee Platinum PLC	JLP	Other mineral extractors & mines	AIM	15.2	2.56	0.09	0.335	9/2/04	0.165	7/10/03	4/11/03	28/3/03	31/7/02	www.jubileeplatinum.com
Kenmare Resources PLC	KMR	Other mineral extractors & mines	Full	53.9	3.54	0.24	0.2	16/9/03	0.09	12/5/03	30/4/03	12/9/03	17/11/94	www.kenmareresources.com
Lonmin PLC	LMI	Other mineral extractors & mines	Full	1707.8	2.07	0.44	12.45	2/3/04	6.615	28/4/03	26/11/03	29/5/03	22/9/61	www.lonmin.com
Mano River Resources Inc	MANA	Other mineral extractors & mines	AIM		4.46	0.18	0.1675	1/3/04	0.0262	8/8/03				
Marakand Minerals Ltd	MKD	Other mineral extractors & mines	AIM	60.6	3.31	0.04	0.66	26/2/04	0.37	9/12/03			4/12/03	
Minco PLC	MIO	Other mineral extractors & mines	AIM	18.4	4.93	0.02	0.3525	9/2/04	0.035	17/4/03	22/7/03	13/1/04	29/1/01	www.minco.ie
Monterrico Metals PLC	MNA	Other mineral extractors & mines	AIM	48.5	2.55	0.09	2.675	12/2/04	0.745	24/4/03	20/6/03	26/9/03	21/6/02	www.monterrico.co.uk
Murchison United	MUU	Other mineral extractors & mines	AIM		8.16	0.36	0.0187	28/5/03	0.0075	25/6/03				
Ocean Resources Capital Holdings PLC	OCE	Other mineral extractors & mines	AIM	25.1	2.59	0.02	0.65	8/7/03	0.275	12/11/03		30/9/03	28/2/03	
Ormonde Mining PLC	ORM	Other mineral extractors & mines	Full	8.1	5.72	-0.03	0.0799	2/3/04	0.03	29/7/03	30/6/03	23/10/03	20/2/96	www.ormondemining.com
Ovoca Resources PLC	OVG	Other mineral extractors & mines	Full	3.4	5.59	-0.08	0.09	4/3/04	0.055	5/8/03	15/9/03	30/12/03		
Oxus Gold PLC	OXS	Gold mining	AIM	146.1	4.84	0.19	0.9175	9/12/03	0.1025	15/4/03	23/9/03	25/2/04	4/7/01	www.oxusgold.co.uk
Palladex PLC	PLX	Gold mining	AIM	17.1	4.03	0.14	0.305	9/2/04	0.245	4/2/04			2/2/04	www.palladex.co.uk
Palmaris Capital PLC	PMS	Mining finance	AIM	16.6	4.12	0.14	0.1525	17/2/04	0.065	23/5/03	5/11/03	27/3/03	15/11/01	www.palmariscapital.com
Patagonia Gold PLC	PGD	Gold mining	AIM	37	3.39	0.19	0.1875	13/1/04	0.09	10/6/03	19/12/03	30/6/03	5/3/03	www.hpdexploration.com
Peter Hambro Mining PLC	POG	Gold mining	AIM	332.8	2.53	0.1	5.225	27/2/04	1.46	6/3/03	10/3/03	22/9/03	29/4/02	www.peterhambro.com

Name	EPIC	Sub-Sector	Listing	Capital (£m)	Volatility	Beta	Price high (£)	Price high date	Price low (£)	Price low date	Prelim. results	Interims ann.	Float date	Website
Petra Diamonds	PDL	Other mineral extractors & mines	AIM		4.59	0.56	0.665	20/2/04	0.175	25/3/03				
Portman PLC	POR	Other mineral extractors & mines	AIM		2.2	0.11	0.65	5/11/03	0.34	5/3/03				
Randgold Resources Ltd	RRS	Gold mining	Full		3.08	-0.02	18.5	14/5/03	9.55	16/7/03				
Reefton Mining NL	RTM	Other mineral	AIM		2.1	-0.12	0.0313	12/3/03	0.02	2/7/03				
Rio Tinto PLC	RIO	Other mineral extractors & mines	Full	15295.3	1.95	0.86	15.74	5/1/04	11.29	24/4/03	2/2/04	31/7/03	1/11/73	www.riotinto.com
Southernera	SRE	Other mineral extractors & mines	AIM		1.92	0.15	2.9	10/9/03	2.075	3/3/04				
St Barbara Mines Ltd	SBM	Gold mining	AIM		4.58	0.1	0.0425	4/11/03	0.015	15/5/03				
Tertiary Minerals PLC	TYM	Other mineral extractors & mines	AIM	7.3	4.85	0.14	0.205	23/2/04	0.08	28/10/03	5/12/03	20/5/03	18/11/99	www.tertiaryminerals.com
Thistle Mining	TMG	Other mineral extractors & mines	AIM		4.59	0	0.325	5/3/03	0.1175	4/2/04				
Tiger Resource Finance PLC	TIR	Mining finance	AIM	5.4	4.19	0.11	0.023	4/3/04	0.0088	29/7/03	14/3/03	5/8/03	22/1/01	www.tiger-rf.com
Trans-Siberian Gold PLC	TSG	Gold mining	AIM	33.1	2.25	0.15	1.595	26/1/04	1.155	4/3/04		20/11/03	25/11/03	www.trans-siberiangold.com
UK Coal PLC	JKC	Other mineral extractors & mines	Full	198.4	2.7	0.19	1.395	16/2/04	0.61	12/3/03	6/3/03	10/9/03	7/6/93	www.ukcoal.com
Vedanta Resources PLC	VED	Other mineral extractors & mines	Full	975.3	1.85	0.37	3.83	7/1/04	3.26	27/1/04				
Water Hall Group PLC	WTH	Other mineral extractors & mines	AIM	2.3	5.53	0.15	0.05	29/7/03	0.025	14/4/03	30/6/03	10/9/03	5/7/01	
Xstrata PLC	XTA	Other mineral extractors & mines	Full	4625.8	2.58	1.06	7.62	2/3/04	3.188	25/3/03	24/2/04	17/9/03	25/3/02	www.xstrata.com
Yamana Gold Inc	YAU	Gold mining	AIM		3.58	0.52	1.64	1/12/03	1.14	17/12/03				
ZincOx Resources PLC	ZOX	Other mineral extractors & mines	AIM	20.8	2.61	0.22	0.925	1/3/04	0.39	16/4/03	18/6/03	30/9/03	10/12/01	www.zincox.com

Source: Sharescope, Hemscott

WILink Annual Reports

Annual reports for the companies listed below can be ordered for free through the WILlink service.

African Diamonds plc
African Gold plc
Ashanti Goldfields Co. Ltd
Ashton Mining of Canada Inc.
Bisichi Mining PLC
Cambrian Mining plc
Canadian Royalties Inc
Cosalt PLC
Eurasia Mining plc
Euro Zinc Mining Corporation
Firestone Diamonds plc
Gold Fields Ltd
Gossan Resources Limited
Graphit Kropfmuehl AG
Griffin Mining Limited
Hereward Ventures plc
Highland Gold Mining Ltd
Lonmin Plc
MINCO plc
Monterrico Metals plc
Murchison United NL
OxusGold plc
Palmaris Capital Plc
SouthernEra Resources Limited
UK Coal PLC
Umicore
Vallourec
Voestalpine AG
Xstrata PLC
ZincOx Resources PLC

Glossary

The terms used below in the glossary and their description may differ slightly from other, particularly professional, interpretations. The difference is deliberate and often is a result of wanting to avoid jargon or opaqueness.

Arbitrage	The purchase of a security in one market and its often simultaneous sale in another to exploit a price difference between the two markets
Assay	To test/analyse an ore or mineral to determine the amount and composition of contained metals
Base metals	The more common chemically active metals such as copper, lead, zinc, tin and nickel
Beta	The volatility (high - greater, low - lesser) of a share relative to the market or its sector
Bonanza gold	The term used to describe extremely rich gold mineralisation
Bulk minerals	Minerals and metals mined in huge quantities such as iron ore, coal and bauxite which usually have a relatively low unit value
Bullion	Gold or silver bars
By-product metal	The residual, i.e not prime, metals mined alongside the 'main' metal in a multi-metal deposit
Carat	The unit of weight for gemstones - one carat weighs 200 mgs. Also the word describing the measurement of the purity of gold in a gold item, thus 24 carat is pure gold and 9 carat is 36% gold
Certified gold	Gold metal purchased for investment where the holder is given a certificate outlining the gold held to his name, such gold is not specifically identifiable
Claim	An area legally licenced to an entity to be explored for minerals
Closcology	The concept in exploration that leads to the acquisition of mineral leases close to a major new minerals discovery
Core samples	Samples of rock/ore produced by diamond drilling
Costs	Operating - mining and treatment Central - administration and selling Financial - interest payments and depreciation
Derivatives	Futures and options contracts to sell metals at a future date for an agreed price
Diamond	Industrial - low value stones used primarily in abrasives or cutting tools due to hardness Gem - used in jewellery due to high quality (clarity and colour) and value

Dollar premium	The percentage cost, above the official sterling exchange rate, of investment currency for overseas asset purchases by UK residents before the abandonment of UK exchange controls in 1979
Drift mining	The technique whereby a decline roadway is sunk into an underground orebody allowing mechanical extraction of the ore
Forward metal price	The price of a metal sold forward for delivery at a future date
Gearing	The application of increased resources (usually borrowings) to enhance the return on a project
Gold bugs	Investors and commentators with a, usually, lifetime belief in the key importance of gold as a reserve/financial asset
Gold reserves	The central banks' holdings of gold as monetary metal in their foreign currency and gold reserves
Grade	The percentage amount of metal in an ore sample or drill core
Hedging	Primarily refers to the process of fixing a sale price for gold, and occasionally other metals, to protect against untoward price movements
Industrial minerals	Minerals such as sulphur, beach sands (zirconium) and borax which are used in industrial processes like chemical manufacturing
Kimberlite pipe	An orebody shaped like a flute or pipe which can contain diamonds
Laterite ore	Ore occurring in the form of soil residue containing secondary oxides of metal, often associated with nickel
Mineral deposit	Economic - a deposit whose grade, cost and financing structure indicates that it could be developed profitably Uneconomic - a deposit that currently cannot be developed profitably
Monetary metal	Gold and silver used as money
Native title	The claim by indigenous Australians that certain areas have been used by them historically
Open - cast, cut or pit	A mine where the orebody is shallow enough to be mined without sinking a shaft or drive to get at the ore
Ore	Naturally occurring material containing extractable metals
Physical delivery	The actual delivery of 'live' metal to consumers
Placing	Usually the sale of stock to a limited number of professional investors who may well not be current shareholders of the placing company
Prospectivity	The level of expectation of success or otherwise in the exploration for and development of mineral deposits

Reserves	Measured economic ore forming the basis for a mining plan
Resources	Mineralised part of an orebody which requires more drilling to convert it to mineable reserves
Royalties	A financial impost on the value of mine turnover or profits collected by central/local government or by private mine royalty owners
Salting	The (illegal) process by which 'foreign' metal is added to ore samples or drill core to enhance its value when it is assayed
Spot metal price	The daily 'real time' price of a metal as determined by the relevant metal trading market
Strike length	The distance and direction along which drilling results have established mineralisation
Suphide ore	Ore where sulphur is combined with one or more metals
Surface sample	A sample taken from a potentially mineralised area by hand for analysing as to whether follow up drilling should be undertaken
Use it or lose it	The concept in South Africa of requiring mining companies holding long leases on undeveloped mineral areas to either develop them or surrender them for issuance to other more willing groups

Bibliography

Bernstein, Peter L; *The Power of Gold*: John Wiley 2000

Casey, Gavin and Mayman, Ted; *The Mile that Midas Touched*; Seal Books 1976

Cassidy, John; *dot.con*; Allen Lane, Penguin Press 2002

Financial Times; *Mining News*; 1971-2003

Green, Timothy; *The Prospect for Gold*; Rosendale Press 1987

Johnson, Paul; *Gold Fields*; Weidenfeld & Nicholson 1987

Kernot, Charles; *Mining Equities: Evaluation and Trading*; Woodhead Publishing 1991

Lassonde, Pierre; The Gold Book; Penguin Books 1990

Lips, Ferdinand; *Gold Wars*; Foundation for the Advancement of Monetary Education 2001

Regan, James; *The Gold Explorer's Handbook*; Rosendale Press 1997

Sutton, Antony C; *The War on Gold*; Valiant Publishers 1977

Sykes, Trevor; *The Money Miners*; Wildcat Press 1978

The Australian; *The A to Z of Mining and Oil Companies*; Ibis Imprints 1969

Uren, Malcolm; *Glint of Gold*; Angus & Robertson 1980

Wells, Jennifer; *Bre-X*; Orion Business Books 1998

Western Financial Intelligence; *Who's Who in the Nickel Search*; Lipscombe & Associates 1970

Williams, Roger; *King of Sea Diamonds*;WJ Flesch 1996

As well as the Financial Times (above) where the author has an almost compete record of the mining news published in the newspaper since 1971, the following publications have been important additional source material:

Gold. Various Annual Surveys. Consolidated Gold Fields, Gold Fields Mineral Services, London.

Northern Miner, Toronto.

Financial Mail, Johannesburg.

Mining Annual Review, Mining Journal, London.

Mining Journal, London.

Mining Year Book, Walter R Skinner, London.

The Gold Book, L Messel, Panmure Gordon, Phillips & Drew, Kitcat & Aitken, Lafferty & Partners, and Paribas, London.

All titles are available from the Global Investor bookshop:
www.global-investor.com/books

Index